CONSUMING ETHNICITY
AND NATIONALISM

ConsumAsiaN Book Series
edited by
Brian Moeran and Lise Skov
The Curzon Press and The University of Hawai'i Press

Women, Media and Consumption in Japan
Edited by Lise Skov and Brian Moeran
Published 1995

A Japanese Advertising Agency
An Anthropology of Media and Markets
Brian Moeran
Published 1996

Contemporary Japan and Popular Culture
Edited by John Whittier Treat
Published 1996

Packaged Japaneseness
Weddings, Business and Brides
Ofra Goldstein-Gidoni
Published 1997

Australia and Asia
Cultural Transactions
Edited by Maryanne Dever
Published 1997

Asian Department Stores
Edited by Kerrie L. MacPherson
Published 1998

Consuming Ethnicity and Nationalism
Edited by Kosaku Yoshino
Published 1999

CONSUMING ETHNICITY AND NATIONALISM

Asian Experiences

Edited by
Kosaku Yoshino

UNIVERSITY OF HAWAI'I PRESS
HONOLULU

Editorial matter © 1999 Kosaku Yoshino

Published in North America by
University of Hawai'i Press
2840 Kolowalu Street
Honolulu, Hawai'i 96822

First published in the United Kingdom
by Curzon Press
15 The Quadrant, Richmond
Surrey, TW9 1BP
England

Printed in Great Britain

The responsibility for the opinions expressed and for the accuracy of the
statements in this book rests with the individual contributors.

Library of Congress Cataloguing-in-Publication Data

Consuming ethnicity and nationalism : Asian experiences / edited by
Kosaku Yoshino.
p.   cm. – (ConsumAsiaN book series)
Includes bibliographical references.
ISBN 0–8248–2247–1 (cloth : alk. paper). – ISBN 0–8248–2248–X
(paper : alk. paper)
1. Nationalism.   2. Nationalism—Asia.   3. Ethnicity.
4. Ethnicity—Asia.   I. Yoshino, Kosaku, 1951–   .   II. Series.
JC311.C6455   1999
320.54′095–dc21   99-22772
CIP

CONTENTS

NOTES ON CONTRIBUTORS

Dru C. Gladney is Dean of Academics at the Asia-Pacific Center in Honolulu, and Professor of Asian Studies and Anthropology at the University of Hawai'i at Manoa. His books include *Muslim Chinese: Ethnic Nationalism in the People's Republic* (Harvard University Press, 2nd edition, 1996); *Ethnic Identity: The Making of a Muslim Minority Nationality* (Harcourt-Brace, 1998); *Making Majorities: Constituting the Nation in Japan, Korea, China, Malaysia, Fiji, Turkey and the U.S.* (editor, Stanford University Press, 1998).

Shih-chung Hsieh received his Ph.D. from the University of Washington, Seattle in 1989. He is a Professor of Anthropology at the National Taiwan University. His interests include ethnicity, ethnohistory, interpretive anthropology, ethnography of northern Southeast Asia, Taiwan's aborigines and the Tai-Lue, a Thai-speaking ground in Yunnan, China. He has published nearly sixty academic pieces in Chinese and English on these themes.

Koichi Iwabuchi is a doctorate candidate in the Faculty of Humanities and Social Sciences, the University of Western Sydney, Australia. His thesis concerns transnational popular culture in Asia and Japanese cultural presence in the region. His main publications include 'Complicit exoticism: Japan and its other' (*Continuum*, 1994), 'Purposeless globalisation or idealess Japanisation?: Japanese cultural industries in Asia' (*Culture and Policy*, 1996), and 'Pure impurity: Japan's genius for hybridism' (*Communal and Plural*, forthcoming). He previously worked for the Nippon Television Network (NTV) in Tokyo as a journalist and producer.

Steven Kemper is Professor of Anthropology at Bates College. He took a Ph.D. at the University of Chicago in anthropology, carrying out fieldwork on the Buddhist monkhood. Since then he has worked on issues focused on historical anthropology, in the case of astrology, marriage practices, the updating of the Sri Lankan chronicle tradition, and the advertising business. His publications include: *The Presence of the Past: Chronicles, Politics, and Culture in Sinhala Life* (Cornell University Press, 1991). His ethnographic interests have spread from South to Southeast Asia.

Laurel Kendall is Curator in Charge of Asian Ethnographic Collections at the American Museum of Natural History and teaches in the Department of Anthropology at Columbia University. She is the author of *Shamans, Housewives and Other Restless Spirits: Women in Korean Ritual Life* (University of Hawaii Press, 1985), *The Life and Hard Times of a Korean Shaman: of Tales and the Telling of Tales* (University of Hawaii Press, 1988), and *Getting Married in Korea: of Gender, Morality, and Modernity* (University of California Press, 1996) as well as numerous articles on gender, shamanism, and healing. She is co-editor of several books including *Asian Visions of Authority: Religion and the Modern States of East and Southeast Asia* (University of Hawaii Press, 1995). Her recent work examines ritual as both a lens on social transformation and a locus of argument about modernity. She is currently writing a book about changes in the Korean shaman world over the last twenty years. Kendall received a Ph.D. in anthropology, with distinction, from Columbia University in 1979.

Shamsul A.B. is Professor of Social Anthropology at Universiti Kebangsaan Malaysia (UKM), Bangi. He writes extensively in Malay and English on politics and culture, with an empirical focus on Southeast Asia, in particular Malaysia. His best-known book is *From British to Bumiputera Rule* (Singapore: Institute of Southeast Asian Studies, 1986) nominated for the coveted Harry Benda Prize, Association of Asian Studies USA. Currently, he is working on a book based on his decade long research on 'Competing Nations-of-Intent: Identity and Nation Formation in Malaysia'. At present, he is the Dean of the Faculty of Social Science and Humanities at UKM.

Christine R. Yano is an Assistant Professor of Anthropology at University of Hawai'i at Manoa. She is currently at work on a book, *Tears of Longing: Nostalgia and the Nation in Japanese Popular Song*, as well as a project on Japanese songs of World War II.

Kosaku Yoshino is an Associate Professor of Sociology at the University of Tokyo. He took a Ph.D. at the London School of Economics and Political Science. He is the author of *Cultural Nationalism in Contemporary Japan: A Sociological Enquiry* (Routledge, 1992) and *A Sociology of Cultural Nationalism* (in Japanese, Nagoya University Press, 1997).

PREFACE

There have been two formative moments in the conception of this book. The first was a meeting with a Malaysian anthropologist, Shamsul A.B., at a conference dinner table in Oxford in July 1993. At the Association of Social Anthropologists' Decennial Conference, I gave a paper on discourses on the distinctiveness of Japanese culture and behaviour – a subject that had long been regarded as considerably important by students of Japan. Such discourses were so prevalent in Japan that there was even a specific name for the phenomenon, namely, *nihonjinron*. Previously, studies of *nihonjinron* had centred on ideological 'production' by elites. My argument was that the relationship of discourses on Japanese uniqueness to nationalism can better be understood by paying attention to how such discourses are 'reproduced' and 'consumed' in the marketplace. In the early 1990s, there was little scholarly work in countries other than Japan on phenomena comparable to *nihonjinron*. In addition, studies of discourses on national distinctiveness were on the whole still limited to 'high culture' and tended to overlook aspects of everyday behavioural culture. At the dinner, Shamsul told me the amazing story that in Malaysia anthropology was so popular that his department had an average annual enrollment of nearly one thousand students. He explained to me that anthropological ideas of cultural differences (as well as similarities) of ethnic groups were popular because of everyday applications among various sections of the multi-ethnic society. I am not suggesting simplistically that anthropology in Malaysia is all about discourses on cultural differences, but his remark suggested that this was at least one way in which anthropology was 'consumed' in the multi-ethnic society of Malaysia.

I began to consider the possibility of a comparative study of how discourses on cultural differences are 'consumed' by members of society. Studies of discourses on national distinctiveness and, for that matter, of nationalism were confined to the *production* of such discourses by elites. I felt that a new comparative approach would make a useful contribution to sociological studies of nationalism. The early 1990s was a time when the influence of Said's *Orientalism* was most conspicuous among students of cultural studies, including literary scholars. They produced increasing numbers of literary critiques of intellectuals' representation of national identity without really investigating the *social* dimensions: who 'consumes' the representations and for what purposes? I hoped that an approach could be developed that combined a comparative perspective with a sociological one.

In November of the same year, as I was cultivating my ideas for a project, I received a letter from Brian Moeran, one of the ConsumAsiaN series editors. This was the second significant moment which led to the planning of the present volume. He asked me if I might be interested in editing a volume for the series. At first, I hesitated somewhat because I was originally going to write a monograph on my own and because it did not originally occur to me to limit the book's scope to Asia. But this seemed a good opportunity to start my project. It also appeared more practical to start with Asian cases. In addition, I was intrigued by the prospects of including various aspects of culture such as popular and media culture which I may not have included otherwise. I decided to join the series.

It did not take long to realise that the notion of Asia itself is an extremely difficult one to define. I travelled in Asia and Australia looking for interesting topics for the book as well as prospective authors. While there, I tried to find convincing definitions of 'Asia'. This turned out to be a futile attempt because trying to define Asia means participating in the Asian values debate. What is Asia? Where do countries like Australia and New Zealand fit in? What is the significance of lumping various geographical and cultural areas together into 'Asia' or 'Asia-Pacific'? These questions still puzzle me. Asia is certainly a convenient word to denote a region which is neither Europe, America nor Africa. But it is more than a residual category. Asia is a social construct pregnant with specific social, political and economic meanings.

If one of the joys of a collaborative book project is meeting its authors, one of the hardships is meeting deadlines. While working on a project, the subject of study is always changing. In this case, the economic conditions of Asia since the time of the conception of the project have changed dramatically. Asia had a booming economy throughout the early to mid 1990s but in 1997 began to show signs of economic recession. It is expected that this economic crisis in Asia (including Japan) will influence cultural rhetoric in the region. 'Asian values', for example, have been predicated upon the industrial success of many Asian countries. The *nihonjinron* have had a similar background. With problems in Asian economies, the directions of cultural discourses will undoubtedly change. But it is too early to make any scholarly predictions and comments as to how recent events might affect the various themes outlined in the chapters of this book. The effects of the economic crisis will surely become an increasingly important research topic in future. Furthermore, how the social construction and reconstruction of 'Asia' will reflect the economic downturn is extremely interesting in itself.

I would like to take this opportunity to thank Anthony D. Smith, my former teacher at the LSE, for introducing me to studies of nationalism, John Hutchinson, one of the most perceptive scholars of nationalism, for always being a source of intellectual inspiration, and to John Clammer and Patrick Pillai for their friendly support. I am also grateful to two anonymous readers of the manuscript for their encouragement and critical comments, to Matthew Crosby and John Bowler for their valuable help in editing some of the chapters, and to Reiko Nagashima, Els Claeys and Ibarra Mateo for proofreading the texts. I would also like to thank Brian Moeran and Lise Skov, the Series Editors for their continued patience and encouragement, although we did not always agree on all matters. They carefully read the manuscripts and offered useful comments. Finally, I would like to express my sincere thanks to the contributors. As the editor of this book, it has been my pleasure to continue our long-distance correspondence and meet occasionally for discussions about the project. A book of this sort is a creative work of many hands indeed.

Kosaku Yoshino
Tokyo

INTRODUCTION

Kosaku Yoshino

We are living in an age when, although the gradual disappearance of nationalism is sometimes debated, nationalism in fact continues to be a central feature of the world. The remarkable growth in studies of nationalism as well as globalism and other forms of collective identity over the past decade reflects these seemingly contradictory tendencies. Some scholars such as Anthony Smith (1995) emphasize the persistent power of nation and nationalism, while on the other side of the spectrum increasing numbers of writers suggest the prospects of a 'post-national' world. Whether or not nationalism will wither in the wake of globalization and the creation of supra-national entities apparently in conflict with nationalism is an issue that will continue to be debated for many years to come. However, rather than concern ourselves with such an either-or question, it is more constructive to focus our attention on the arenas where nationalism is being produced and reproduced in ways that have yet to be studied in depth.

The word 'nationalism' is used in many different ways depending on the context. For our purposes, nationalism may broadly be defined as the sentiment among a people that they constitute a community with distinctive characteristics as well as the project of maintaining and enhancing that distinctiveness within an autonomous state. While in reality the two are often closely linked, we may distinguish cultural nationalism and political nationalism for their different aims. Whereas political nationalism seeks to achieve a representative state for its community and to secure citizenship rights for its members, cultural nationalism is the regeneration of the national community by creating, preserving or strengthening a people's cultural identity when it is felt to be lacking, inadequate or threatened. Most, if not all, chapters in this volume examine various aspects of cultural nationalism.

1

The study of nationalism had long been regarded as the domain of political science. In the early 1980s, when I began my own study of nationalism, the subject of culture and nationalism was still a relatively unexplored area (Yoshino 1992). The increase in the literature on this topic over the last decade shows something of the increasing recognition of the importance of culture in what was once regarded as the realm of political ideology. There is no doubt that the creation and dissemination of nationalist ideology is an important feature of nationalism, especially in its early stage. But nationalism is not only production and one-sided transmission of ideology from above, but also an on-going consumption (and therefore reproduction) of culture in which various sections of the population participate.

This collection of essays shows, with reference to various Asian cases, the importance of a perspective that takes consumption into account in understanding the formation and promotion of nationalism. Although all the contributors to this volume share such an interest, their various usages of 'consumption' reflect the elasticity of the term as found among anthropologists and sociologists in general. I do not wish to enter into any detailed discussion of consumption here.[1] Let us define consumption broadly as 'the meaningful use people make of the objects that are associated with them' (Carrier 1996:128). In this definition, the nature of consumption is wide-ranging in that 'the use can be mental or material', 'the objects can be things, ideas or relationships', and 'the association can range from ownership to contemplation' (Carrier 1996:128).

The important point about this definition is that consumption does not only refer to the process of exchanging money for real objects but also to the experience of receiving meanings as well as tangible objects. This approach is increasingly evident in recent theories of consumption. Campbell (1995:110) writes that consumption, viewed in this light, means 'the interaction of individuals with all sources of information or images, whether via the mass media, computerised data systems . . . or directly through their own senses when viewing artefacts in museums and art galleries, listening to music at concerts, or even simply "enjoying the sights" as a tourist' (Campbell 1995:110). Indeed, tourism is an excellent example of consumption. Here, the essence of consumption is to be found not in the actual purchase of goods but 'the imaginative pleasure-seeking to which the product image lends itself, real consumption being largely a resultant of this mentalistic hedonism' (p.118). Setting aside the question of the pleasure-seeking element, not necessarily present in all forms of

2

consumption, chapters in this volume focus on the symbolic aspects of consumption rather than its material (instrumental) aspects.[2]

The relationship between consumption and nationalism is as complex and varied as it is fascinating. This is reflected in the variety of theoretical themes and empirical topics covered in this volume. In Chapter 1, we find that the workings of contemporary nationalism in Japan can usefully be examined by paying attention to the marketplace in which the ideas of Japanese cultural distinctiveness – generally referred to as the *nihonjinron* – are 'reproduced' and 'consumed'. This demonstrates the limitations of conventional theories of nationalism in light of the contemporary Japanese case. The importance of the consumption approach is highlighted in contrast to the more traditional theorizing which has tended to focus on the process of ideological manipulation whereby elites 'produce' national identity and impose it on the masses through state-sponsored education. Chapter 1 stresses the ways in which ideas of cultural differences are used by various social groups in order to make sense of the problems of everyday life. What may be called a 'sociology-of-everyday-life' approach to nationalism, advanced in this chapter, is further discussed in Chapter 2.

In Chapter 2, Steven Kemper looks at state-run lotteries for development projects in Sri Lanka and examines how it generates nationalism in the everyday world of ordinary people. In contrast to previous studies of nationalism that stressed ideological imposition of high culture from the top, Kemper looks at how national identity is created in the everyday-life of ordinary people. Kemper points out that what is remarkable about lotteries is that they blur the boundary between a political act and consumption behaviour as well as require betters to keep their eyes fixed on the prize. Ordinary people exposed to advertisements for the lottery and so also to the state agenda are thus induced to think nationally. In the words of Kemper, 'a lottery ticket puts the nation in the hands of ordinary people' (p.44).

Approaches to national identity may vary depending on the national contexts. The Japanese approach to national identity, discussed in Chapter 1, is highly 'holistic' in the sense of assuming and emphasizing the existence of common cultural patterns among 'the Japanese' as a whole. It may be said that the holistic approach is characteristic of 'ethno-national states' such as Japan (where the vast majority of the population is seen as belonging to the same ethnic group). By contrast, expressions of national identity in multi-ethnic states tend to be more 'institutional' and 'objectifying'. This is understandable given the explicit heterogeneity of their population and the absence of holistic ethno-national culture supposedly embraced by most of its citizens. In multi-ethnic states, national identity is more likely to be expressed in terms of objectified cultural items such as practices and customs, artefacts and rituals, rather than ethno-national sentiment based on a common cultural ethos. Sometimes, objectified cultural items, symbolizing the otherness of ethnic minorities, are used to enhance and stabilize majority 'national' identity. Chapters 3 and 4 show how nationalism of a majority and dominant group is constructed through consuming ethnicity of minority groups. In other cases, the very ethno-cultural diversity of minorities within a multi-ethnic nation is transformed into an important source of larger collective 'national' identity (see, esp. Chapters 3 and 6). Through processes such as these, the consumption of ethnicity becomes part and parcel of the formation of nationalism.[3]

In Chapter 3, Dru Gladney utilizes rich ethnographic materials to argue that the definition and representation of the 'minority' as colourful, exotic, erotic and 'primitive' serves to homogenize the undefined majority group, the Han, as a modern, united people in China. Gladney notes that the commodification of minority-other is a 'symbolic capital' used for the nationalization and modernization project of the Chinese nation-state. The pleasure-seeking role of consumption in the construction of the nation is illustrated here with vivid descriptions of visual art portraying ethnic minorities.

Chapter 3 suggests some connections with tourism. Tourism, as a quintessentially modern form of consumption is discussed at length in Chapter 4 in relation to ethnic tourism and ethnic theme parks in Taiwan. By using his fieldwork notes on the Taiwan Aboriginal Cultural Park and the Formosan Aboriginal Culture Village, Shih-chung Hsieh demonstrates how the tourist institutions help to construct images of indigenous ethnic groups among tourists who are members of the Taiwanese/Chinese dominant ethnic group. In Chapter 5, Laurel Kendall examines the museum, a social artefact closely connected to tourism that has increasingly attracted scholarly attention. By comparing and contrasting the National Folklore Museum in Seoul and the Yunnan Museum of Nationalities in China, Kendall looks into many fascinating aspects of how these two very different museums package the stories of 'us' and 'them', both the internal and external, for public consumption.

In his study of ethnic theme parks in Taiwan, Hsieh pays particular attention to the role of anthropologists. Anthropologists help both the state and the tourist industry to establish the sites for ethnic tourism by providing anthropological knowledge of the cultures of indigenous ethnic groups. In the present socio-economic environment, humanistic disciplines such as anthropology are increasingly expected to present themselves as socially 'useful' and viable (Chapter 4). The role of anthropology in nation-formation and nationalism is further explored in Chapter 6 in the context of Malaysia. Looking at the relationship between multiethnicity and nationalism, Shamsul A.B. examines the consumption of ideas of cultural differences in the multi-ethnic setting of Malaysia and provides an insightful analysis of how the anthropological ideas of Malayness, Chineseness and Indianness are consumed by people working in various sectors of the economy and in government offices. Looking at the broader context of the nation-formation and the development of anthropology in Malaysia, Shamsul explains why and how anthropological knowledge has become an important 'consumer item' in the multi-ethnic social settings. The chapters on Malaysia and Taiwan indicate an environment where social sciences and nation-building are often closely linked.

The subject of the final two chapters is pop culture, specifically with a focus on music. Anthropologists continue to study the role of music in shaping and maintaining identity in a rapidly changing world. In Chapter 7, Christine Yano depicts how the notion of the homeland is embodied in *enka*, a very 'national' form of popular song in Japan. Scholars of music increasingly find themselves with the task of understanding social worlds penetrated by media industries, both national and transnational. Koichi Iwabuchi pursues this topic in Chapter 8, investigating Japan's culture industries' infiltration into the Asian market. Interestingly, what Japan exports to Asia is not the 'authentic' national culture of Japan but rather the 'very Japanese' habit of indigenizing and domesticating Western culture. It is this hybridization which captures the attention of Asian audience and cultural industries. This final chapter addresses a number of issues that lead us to challenge the essentialized notion of 'national culture'.

There are a number of theoretical themes which are suggested in various chapters of this volume and which may profitably be pursued in further studies. One such area is the relationship between state and market in the formation and promotion of nationalism. A remark of Zigmund Bauman is especially pertinent here. He writes that 'as the interest of the state in culture faded (meaning that the relevance of culture to the reproduction of political power diminished), culture was coming within the orbit of another power', that is, the market (1992:17). But does the market replace the state in forming nationalism? Throughout most of this volume, we not only see that nationalism is generated in the marketplace but are also reminded that the state is not just another agent but remains a key player in the marketplace. The case of a national lottery is a very good example of the state's active use of the market mechanism to promote nationalism (Chapter 2). The crucial question in this regard is: what are the intricate relationships between the state and various market-based agencies of cultural production and reproduction such as advertising agencies, travel agencies, the media and consultancy?

Here we might also note the flourishing of contemporary culture industries, which are attracting attention as a social site for the production and reproduction of ethnic/national cultures and identities. While culture industries are still, in part, state-led, they increasingly work in and through mechanisms of the market, where the new middle classes are key players. Many theorists maintain that it is these sections of the population who seek the experience of cultural differences and novelty (e.g. Featherstone 1991). As such, they are prominent producers, reproducers and consumers of ethnic, national and other identities in the marketplace. This raises some important questions. For example, an enquiry should be made into the types of the new middle classes, since they may not be so homogeneous as they are portrayed in literature in terms of cultural assets, organizational positions and economic statuses. Also, how do we compare the middle classes within Asia itself and between Asia and other regions such as Europe and America? The formation of the new middle classes in Asia is closely linked with the economic prosperity which the region has enjoyed until fairly recently (see, e.g. *The New Rich in Asia* by Robinson and Goodman, 1996). These developments suggest opportunities for yet further research of the market in the formation of ethnicity and nationalism in Asia.

For the time being, we will leave these questions unanswered. The empirical discussions in the following chapters will provide, if not solutions, at least useful hints to the formulation of theoretical orientations towards examining the role of the state and market, the new middle classes, and many other extremely important features of ethnicity and nationalism.

Notes

1 For various sociological approaches to consumption, see Campbell (1995).
2 Apart from economic and materialist perspectives on consumption, the

development of studies of consumption as cultural phenomenon was profoundly influenced by critical theory, postmodernism and cultural studies. In particular, the association of postmodern society with consumer society, initiated largely by theories of post modernity, has subsequently filtered into the thinking of many other writers (e.g. Baudrillard 1988). It has now become commonplace to say that contemporary society is a consumer society with consumption being understood as symbolic and cultural activity rather than an instrumental and material activity.

3 The use of ethnicity can be extended beyond a mere synonym for a minority to any sense of difference based on culture and descent. In this sense, ambiguities surround the boundaries between 'ethnic' and 'national' sentiment.

References

Baudrillard, Jean 1988 *Jean Baudrillard: selected writings*, ed. Mark Poster, Oxford: Polity Press.

Campbell, Colin 1995 'The sociology of consumption', pp. 96–126 in Daniel Miller (ed.) *Acknowledging Consumption: a review of new studies*, London and New York: Routledge, 1995.

Carrier, James G. 1996 'Consumption', pp. 128–9 in Alan Barnard and Jonathan Spencer (eds.) *Encyclopedia of Social and Cultural Anthropology*, London and New York: Routledge.

Featherstone, Mike 1991 *Consumer Culture and Postmodernism*, London: Sage.

Hobsbawm, Eric 1990 *Nations and Nationalism since 1780*, Cambridge: Cambridge University Press.

Robinson, Richard and David S.G. Goodman (eds.) 1996 *The New Rich in Asia: mobile phones, McDonald's and middle-class revolution*, London and New York: Routledge.

Smith, Anthony D. 1995 *Nations and Nationalism in a Global Era*, Oxford: Polity Press.

Yoshino, Kosaku 1992 *Cultural Nationalism in Contemporary Japan: a sociological enquiry*, London and New York: Routledge. (paperback edn. 1995).

1

RETHINKING THEORIES OF NATIONALISM

Japan's Nationalism in a Marketplace Perspective[1]

Kosaku Yoshino

Theories of nationalism have tended to confine themselves to the process of ideological manipulation whereby elites 'invent' national identity and impose it on the masses through state-sponsored education. I argue that the workings of nationalism in contemporary Japan can fruitfully be examined by paying attention to the cultural 'marketplace' in which ideas of national distinctiveness are 'produced', 'reproduced', 'distributed' and 'consumed'. Special attention is drawn to the hitherto neglected role of 'cultural intermediaries' in the promotion of cultural nationalism. This chapter aims to examine nationalism in contemporary Japan and its implications for theories of nationalism. It should be made clear at the outset that this chapter does not attempt to furnish an inclusive account of Japan's nationalism. Nationalism works differently for different groups and diverse processes are at work in forming the phenomenon of nationalism. This chapter focuses on one of such processes.

Theories of nationalism have long been limited in their scope to the classic cases of 'old nationalism' or the more recent cases of 'neo-nationalism' in minority regions. In either case, they have dealt with what I call 'primary nationalism' – that is, original nationalism as concerned with creating national identity – without paying adequate attention to the subsequent maintenance and re-enhancement of national identity in established nations ('secondary nationalism').[2] Japan from the 1970s onward has experienced 'secondary nationalism', which has developed in close association with the vast amount of publications by 'thinking elites' on Japanese distinctiveness.[3] The genre of such literature is commonly referred to as the *nihonjinron*. The aim of this chapter is a re-examination of conventional theories of nationalism in the light of the type of cultural nationalism associated with the *nihonjinron*. In doing so, I will problematize what may be called the 'productivist' and 'statist' bias of conventional theories of nationalism.

Nationalism is a dual phenomenon consisting of the formal, state-supervised process and the informal, market-oriented process. Nationalism also comprises a dual process by which national identity is 'produced' and 'consumed'. None the less, most theories of nationalism have confined themselves to the process of ideological manipulation by which elites 'produce' national myth and ideology and by which the state inculcates such myth and ideology into the masses through state-controlled formal education. The 'productivist' bias is also reflected in one popular explanation of the phenomenon of the *nihonjinron* (discourses on Japanese uniqueness). It is widely believed that the *nihonjinron* constitute a nationalist ideology which cultural and political elites 'produced' to manipulate nationalism among the Japanese by attributing Japan's economic success and apparent social stability to its supposedly unique cultural virtues. I will argue that such a conventional view of nationalism that simplistically assumes ideological manipulation 'from above' is inappropriate or, at least, insufficient as a perspective on cultural nationalism in contemporary Japan. Instead, I will show the importance of inquiry into a 'market' process whereby ideas of cultural differences are 'produced', 'reproduced' and 'consumed' in order to shed light on the nature of 'secondary nationalism' in contemporary society.

'Productivist' and 'Statist' Orientations in Theories of Nationalism

The 'productivist' and 'statist' orientations in theories of nationalism derive from preoccupation with 'primary' nationalism where national identity tends to be imposed 'from above' and inculcated through formal processes via the state educational system and official ceremonies. The salient features of what I have called 'primary' and 'secondary' nationalism will therefore be compared here. It should be noted that terms such as 'primary' and 'secondary' are not presented here in a temporal sense. It would be grossly simplistic to suppose that nationalism has become domesticated and routinized in contemporary societies and that the age of oppressive nationalism is gone. 'Primary' features of nationalism often persist and recur in established nations, as will be discussed later in the context of the Japanese case.[4] None the less, I will argue that failure to grasp the characteristic workings of 'secondary nationalism' results in failure to recognize a number of relevant issues of nationalism in contemporary society.

In order to highlight the 'productivist' and 'statist' orientations in conventional theories of nationalism, I will draw attention to the two closely related yet separate aspects of the phenomenon of nationalism: elites' formulation of ideas of national distinctiveness (or the ideology of national identity) and diffusion of such ideas (or ideology) in society.

Scholars of nationalism are divided over the question of whether the emergence of nationalism derives from the very make-up of modern industrial society or whether it is rooted in a long, continuous historical process antedating the modern era (see Yoshino 1992:68–86; Hutchinson 1994a:1–38). Regardless of their position, 'modernists' and 'historicists' share the productivist view that nationalist *elites* have given rise to national identity. This is in general an accurate description of primary nationalism, where, indeed, nationalist elites, especially 'historians' or myth makers, play a key role. It is a prevalent mode of thinking among nationalists that a nation is genuine when it has ancestral 'history' and culture. A sense of having a common and distinctive ancestral 'history' and culture not only provides a feeling of communal uniqueness but unites past and present generations. For this reason, nationalist elites explore, articulate or invent a nation's ancestral myth and 'historical' culture.

Anthony Smith is one of the most articulate scholars to have theorized the formation of nation and nationalism from a historicist point of view. He argues that modern nations were reconstructed from the earlier ethnic identities and communities (which he calls *ethnie*).[5] In analysing the historical depth of nations, Smith (1986:15) lays special emphasis on myths and remarks that one has to look for the special qualities and durability of *ethnie* in 'the nature (forms and content) of their myths and symbols, their historical memories and central values . . . [in] the mechanisms of their diffusion (or lack of it) through a given population, and their transmission to future generations . . .'. In contrast to Smith's historicist concern with *ethnic origins* of nations, modernists interpret the emergence of nationalism as the product of modernity, as Gellner (1964:164) puts it: 'Nationalism is not the awakening of nations to self-consciousness: it invents nations where they do not exist'. Nevertheless, modernists are no different from historicists in that they, too, depend for a fundamental source of national identity on historical memory, traditions and even ancestral myths. *The Invention of Tradition* by Hobsbawm and Ranger (and other contributors) (1983) is a particularly good example of this approach. As modernists, they ignore pre-existing ethnic ties and their impact on the formation of nation, but it is intriguing that they, too, are preoccupied with the process whereby elites invent traditions in order to establish a sense of continuity with 'the past'.

In contrast to primary nationalism, historical memory and ancestral myth no longer constitute a predominant concern in secondary nationalism, or at least in its contemporary Japanese version, where a sense of belonging to a 'historical nation' is already taken for granted. Of course, the 'rewriting' of history continues to occur, but the nation's origin *per se* becomes less relevant as a chief source of conscious national identity. Rather, a nation's contemporary 'social culture' becomes a source of greater importance with which to reaffirm a sense of difference for its members. Writers on Japanese uniqueness in the 1970s and 1980s were, as it were, 'popular sociologists' who formulated ideas concerning the peculiarities of the Japanese patterns of behaviour and thought in contrast to the Western patterns, as will be discussed later.

Such a difference in types of ideas of national distinctiveness is reflected in the difference in the ways in which and the channels through which these ideas are diffused in primary and secondary nationalism. In primary nationalism, ancestral 'myth' – articulated or invented by elites – is taught rather unilaterally to 'ordinary' people through the medium of formal education because the masses cannot obtain 'historical knowledge' without the guidance of elites. This may be why *mobilization* is assumed in much of the existing literature. It is widely assumed in classical theories of nationalism that elites *mobilize* the ordinary sections of the population by 'giving' them their ideas of the identity of the nation. By contrast, the realm of contemporary social culture, an important source of national identity in secondary nationalism, is part of the experience of ordinary people. The role of thinking elites here is not to inculcate unknown knowledge but to provide ordinary people with perspectives from which to think more systematically about their own society and behaviour. Elites' mobilization of ordinary people is less likely to occur in Japan's secondary nationalism. This should not be taken as suggesting simplistically that the masses are not affected by elites' ideas. Rather, in contemporary Japan, where the use of obviously nationalistic ideas and symbols cannot have a wide appeal (for reasons discussed later), one has to look at the intricate (and quite often unintended) workings of ideas which may result in the recreation and enhancement of nationalism.

11

This leads us to another salient, and closely related, feature of conventional theories of nationalism: the view of state-controlled, formal education as the main agent in disseminating national culture. The role of formal education in spreading national culture is not merely a question of theory of nationalism but is widely assumed in modern sociology in general, which tends to identify society as conterminous with the boundaries of the nation-state. The emergence of nation-states (i.e. 'national societies') led to an increasing emphasis on indoctrination in formal education. The inculcation of national (societal) values by means of the school is regarded as an essential feature of modern societies. Generally, there are two aspects of formal education: cultural transmission and social control. These are closely related to each other since social control (and, therefore, social solidarity) presupposes the transmission of a society's culture. Based on this distinction, we will focus on two of the representative versions of the theory of nationalism: namely, the political-scientific theory of Elie Kedourie and the sociological and anthropological theory of Ernest Gellner. Kedourie's theory deals with the aspect of social control and Gellner's with the aspect of transmission of national culture as homogenized by the state. Kedourie and Gellner advanced their theories from very differing standpoints, but they both emphasize the role of the state and state-sponsored educational system in disseminating national identity.

The view that gives primary attention to formal education is explicitly formulated by Elie Kedourie (1960), who equates the German, organic version of nationalism with nationalism *tout court*. His ideas of the prominent role of the school in nationalism derive largely from Fichte's notion of national self-realisation through absorption of the individual's will in that of the organic state. As an admirer of the French Revolution, Fichte valued the role of the state and school as a political instrument for injecting national spirit. The goal of national education, Fichte stated, was to mould the people's will in order to create an organic state. Commenting on Fichte's conception, Kedourie maintains that the state and formal education have a central place in nationalist theory. Interestingly, this idea itself becomes part and parcel of his own theory of nationalism, as Kedourie (1960:83-4) remarks that the purpose of education is 'to bend the will of the young to the will of the nation' and that 'schools are the instruments of state policy'.

Ernest Gellner's theory is more subtle and closely associated with assumptions of other social theories – in particular, modernization theory. Gellner argues that the erosion of traditional social structures of kinship and community, caused by industrialization, necessitate a shared culture in creating and maintaining social cohesion. Furthermore, since the new type of social integration in industrial society has to meet the needs of a highly specialized division of labour, it requires a unified, central culture. This, he argues, is created and strengthened by the state-sponsored education system. In Gellner's own words: 'the economy needs both the new type of central culture and the central state; the culture needs the state; and the state probably needs the homogeneous cultural branding of its flock' (1983:140). Because he attributes the mutual relationship of a modern culture and the state to the requirements of a modern economy, it is understandable that Perry Anderson (1992:207) should refer to Gellner's theory as 'single-minded economic functionalism'.

As perspectives on primary nationalism, classic theories of nationalism certainly have valid points to make. The 'productivist' and 'statist' theoretical orientations help explain the creation and development of primary nationalism in Japan from the end of the nineteenth century to 1945. Even in contemporary Japan, 'primary' features persist. It is therefore necessary to consider these points in the context of Japan's nationalism before pointing out the limitations of classic theories of nationalism.

The State and Formal Education in Japan's Primary and Secondary Nationalism

Primary nationalism, as it developed in Japan, was the domain of nationalist elites and the state. After the overthrow of the Tokugawa regime in 1868, Meiji elites 'invented' the tradition of the emperor system upon the foundations of familism and State Shinto and used this tradition as a means of creating and enhancing national identity and solidarity. *The Imperial Rescript on Education* of 1890 emphasized the 'historical' vision of the unbroken imperial lineage from time immemorial and projected the *Volk* view of nation by stating that the emperor presided as the head of the main family, from which all Japanese families subsequently branched out. The state was the main agent in creating nation and nationalism, exerting firm control over moral education in schools. The Ministry of Education instructed elementary school authorities that familism and State Shinto, expounded in *The Imperial Rescript*, should be the basis of moral education. Textbooks were compiled directly by the Ministry after 1903, and the reading of *The Imperial Rescript* became a semi-religious ritual in school that was used as a means of indoctrinating national myths and ideology into people until 1945. The pre-war and wartime Japanese experience epitomizes the role of the state's ideological manipulation in the formation and enhancement of national identity.

Following Japan's defeat in 1945, Japanese society experienced democratization and the elimination of nationalistic elements and ideas under the guidance of the Occupation. Reforms included separation of religion and state, adoption of a new constitution, change of the constitutional position of the emperor, a new educational system, elimination of the feudalistic *ie* (household/family) system, land reform, and so on. Criticisms of feudalistic social legacies as well as state-initiated nationalism came from among Japanese thinkers themselves. Two opposing sentiments have existed side by side throughout the postwar period until recently. On the one hand, particular caution has been exercised to prevent a revival of those symbols and practices reminiscent of pre-war and wartime ultra-nationalism such as the display of the 'Rising Sun' flag and singing of the *Kimigayo* anthem at school ceremonies, introduction of elements of national pride into school curriculum, and so on. On the other hand, there has always been an argument that it is necessary to restore a sense of national pride and patriotism. The development of nationalism from 1945 forward may best be seen in terms of the Occupation-imposed and self-imposed restraints on nationalism and reactions against these restraints. Education is one main arena in which the clash between the two opposing sentiments has been evident and where the state has had a prominent place in the debate.

The Ministry of Education's guidelines on the content and goals of the school curriculum, which are reviewed approximately every ten years, are indicative of the state's stance and intentions towards nationalism. The guidelines, which were put into effect in 1992, revealed an ever stronger emphasis on nationalism, reflecting conservatives' demand for the removal of Occupation-imposed elements in the education system and a return to traditional values and morals. The state also controls the content of the curriculum by way of the system for authorizing textbooks. The state's interest in nationalism is also shown in its selection of historical figures in the primary school curriculum on history, which includes 42 figures including admiral Tōgō Heihachirō, whose exploits in the Russo-Japanese War (1904–1905) were used to promote militarism in textbooks during the Second World War. Furthermore, the state now requires the *Hinomaru* flag to be displayed and the *Kimigayo* anthem to be sung at school ceremonies as a way of restoring national pride which was long suppressed in the post-war period. The previous guidelines only stated that it is 'desirable' to use these symbols at school ceremonies and left it to the discretion of school and the board of education of each administrative region, but the revision made this practice mandatory to the extent that teachers who refuse to comply will be subjected to punishment. (The textbook debate has continued to undergo significant developments in recent years, but that issue falls outside the scope of this chapter.)

These examples show the persistent power of the state, but I find it difficult to assess whether the role of the state has increased. It may be that the state is only responding to changes in the public's perceptions of national identity and pride, which are, in turn, strongly congruent with other factors such as the activity of 'thinking elites' who 'produce' ideas of Japanese uniqueness as well as the sentiment and activities of other social groups who 'consume' such ideas of thinking elites. Furthermore, it is questionable whether the state can effectively enhance national sentiment compared to the influence exercised by other social groups such as intellectuals, media people, business elites, and so on. It should be borne in mind that the state's programme to enhance nationalism often makes some groups more active in their opposition to it. Robert Bocock's point regarding Britain's royal rituals is pertinent here. He says that rituals 'may also make some groups feel less part of the national group in that they are made conscious of the fact that they do not share some of the values which seem to lie behind the group's ritual' (1974:98). Indeed, there have always been significant numbers of people whose opposition to nationalistic values has been reinforced precisely because of the existence of these 'nationalistic' rituals such as the display of the 'national' flag and singing of the 'national' anthem at school ceremonies, the 'National Foundation Day', Cabinet Ministers' visits to the Yasukuni Shrine[6] and so on. 'Nationalistic' rituals are nothing but a reminder of their opposition to nationalism. Precisely because state-initiated nationalism centres around obviously nationalistic ideas and symbols, it often fails to elicit voluntary and active support from large sections of the population. Strictly classic and statist views of nationalism may overlook a number of important issues of nationalism in contemporary Japan.

In the following discussion, I will draw attention to the 'non-statist' type of nationalism that has developed in close association with the *nihonjinron*. I will show that, even in an analysis of this kind of cultural nationalism, scholars are constrained by the 'productivist' assumption,

15

thereby failing to recognize the characteristic ways in which nationalism is promoted in contemporary society.

The *Nihonjinron* and Cultural Nationalism in Contemporary Japan

Japan's 'secondary nationalism' as examined here is the type of cultural nationalism that has developed in close association with the *nihonjinron* (discourses on the distinctiveness of Japanese society and culture). It will be shown that this type of nationalism has been generated to a considerable extent through an informal, market-oriented process – informal in the sense of the relative absence of the state. Focusing on the ways in which the *nihonjinron* have promoted nationalism in contemporary Japan, I will point out the limitations of the classical theories of nationalism and propose an alternative approach to 'secondary nationalism' in contemporary society.

The 'producers' of the *nihonjinron* included 'thinking elites' of diverse occupations, ranging from intellectuals, critics and journalists to diplomats and even business elites. The *nihonjinron* appeared in great quantity in popular editions of books and occasional essays in newspapers and general interest magazines.[7] Publications on Japanese uniqueness reached their peak in the 1970s but continued into the 1980s and 90s. This study is concerned with the 1980s and 90s because it is in these decades that the *nihonjinron* diffused to wider sections of the population and their effects became strongly felt. There is such a vast array of *nihonjinron* literature that a detailed discussion of their content is beyond the scope of this chapter.[8] For the present purpose, it will suffice to summarize briefly the four main themes prominent in the *nihonjinron*. First, Japanese society is characterized by group-orientation, 'interpersonalism' *(kanjinshugi),* vertical stratification (intra-company solidarity) and dependence (other-directedness) in contrast to Western society which is represented as individualistic, horizontal (class-based solidarity) and valuing independence (self-autonomy) (e.g. Nakane 1967, 1970; Hamaguchi 1982; Doi 1971). Second, the Japanese patterns of interpersonal communication are characterized by a lack of emphasis on logical and linguistic presentation in contrast to the Western patterns which are supposed to encourage logical and linguistic confrontation. In other words, essential communication among the Japanese is supposed to be performed empathetically without the use of explicit spoken words and logical presentation (e.g. Matsumoto 1984). Third, Japanese society is characterized as being homogeneous and uni-racial in contrast to the heterogeneous and multi-racial society of the West.[9] Fourth, the *nihonjinron* closely associates the cultural and 'racial' distinctiveness of the Japanese, thereby promoting the perception that the Japanese mode of thinking and behaving is so unique that one has to be born a Japanese to understand it.

Considering the profound impact of the *nihonjinron* on perceptions of Japanese identity, criticisms and interpretations of this phenomenon naturally arose in the 1980s. One such controversy dealt with the *nihonjinron*'s relationship to nationalism.[10] What is particularly important in the context of the present study is that the 'productivist' assumptions associated with classic nationalism have often been applied to this contemporary Japanese case. It is thus widely believed that the *nihonjinron* constitute a cultural nationalist ideology which elites have created to manipulate the masses in the direction of nationalism. Some regarded the *nihonjinron* as a culturalistic attempt to attribute Japan's economic success to the unique virtues of Japanese society and national character such as group loyalty, consensus, paternalistic management and vertical social organization based on a dependent mentality (e.g. Mouer and Sugimoto 1980:7). Others saw the *nihonjinron* as having promoted the view that 'Japanese society has avoided most of the evils that have accompanied industrialization elsewhere (crime, drugs, social division, family breakdown) thanks to the operation of these peculiar virtues, and that to the extent these problems do exist they are due to failure to preserve Japanese ways against foreign influences' (Crawcour 1980:186). The *nihonjinron* are thus considered to have fostered the perception that Japan's economic success and social stability represent a cultural victory of the Japanese.

Ideological manipulation may have occurred between certain sections of the population, as critics claim. Certain sections of the political, economic and cultural elite may have consciously propagated an ideology which stressed a sense of cultural pride and victory, to which certain types of readers – especially business elites, according to my findings – were attracted (Yoshino 1992:chs. 7 and 8).[11] Even if deliberate ideological manipulation happened, this explains only a segment of the whole picture. Cultural nationalism in contemporary nationalism cannot adequately be explained in terms of ideological manipulation alone. I will show the importance of inquiry into a 'market' process by which ideas of Japanese distinctiveness are 'reproduced' and 'consumed' in contemporary Japan.

As I stated earlier, 'producers' of the *nihonjinron* were 'popular sociologists' who formulated 'theories' of Japan's *social* culture. The

17

role of 'popular sociologists' was to provide ordinary people with perspectives from which to think more systematically about their own behaviour and society rather than 'giving' them knowledge about what they do not know. One should also recognize the point that ordinary Japanese – ordinary in the sense of not being professional thinkers – did not normally concern themselves with such *abstract* themes as the crisis of cultural identity threatened by Westernization and explanations of Japan's industrial strengths in cultural terms, as many critics claim. It is one thing to explain why thinking elites 'produced' ideas of Japanese distinctiveness and quite another to explain why the more ordinary sections of the population 'consumed' such ideas. Other social groups, when responding to the ideas of thinking elites, concerned themselves with the ideas in so far as they were related to their immediate surroundings. Ordinary people 'consumed' the *nihonjinron* out of their *practical* concerns to understand and solve concrete problems in their own immediate surroundings. Analysis of formation of nationalism should, therefore, focus on small groups or groups on which ordinary people's immediate, practical life depends. We are reminded here of a number of sociologists and political scientists who have pointed out, albeit in differing contexts, that the immediate group to which one belongs exerts a major influence on shaping one's orientation towards the political and social system – whether it is Nazism, communism or democracy (Verba 1961; Mannheim 1951; Almond 1952; Shils and Janowitz 1948). One's commitment to one's immediate surroundings often has significant effects on the larger political and social system by leading one to behave in such a manner as to support the system.

It is therefore necessary here to inquire into the types of practical concerns among the ordinary members of the Japanese population that led them to behave in a such way as to support cultural nationalism. (Among 'ordinary' members, we are specifically concerned here with the fairly well-educated middle-class sections of the population.[12]) Two types of practical concerns were prevalent among those who actively responded to the *nihonjinron*: cross-cultural and organizational. The *nihonjinron* attracted their readers by providing them with ideas on cultural differences considered useful for cross-cultural contacts. Because Japan's social characteristics are frequently discussed in the *nihonjinron* in the context of the company and its management and business practices, it is not surprising that those who had organizational concerns at the workplace were the typical consumers of the *nihonjinron*. These concerns are especially relevant to business elites, who, indeed, were typical consumers of the *nihonjinron*.[13]

Cross-cultural Manuals and the Role of Cultural Intermediaries

If we are interested in the process whereby intellectuals' ideas of Japanese society and culture have been consumed by, and dispersed among, the fairly well-educated sections of the Japanese population, we must pay attention to the role of reproducers and distributors who convert such ideas into a form that can be consumed by ordinary people. Based on the distinction which Edward Shils (1972:22) made between 'productive intellectuals' (who produce intellectual works) and 'reproductive intellectuals' (who engage in the interpretation and transmission of intellectual works), we may draw attention to the type of people who, as 'reproductive intellectuals', interpreted academics' theories of Japanese society and culture and reinterpreted them to suit more practical concerns or reproduced them in a form that could be consumed by 'ordinary' people. Eisenstadt (1972:18) also made a similar point that 'reproductive' intellectuals – 'secondary intellectuals' in his own words – 'serve as channels of institutionalization, and even as possible creators of new types of symbols of cultural orientations, of traditions, and of collective and cultural identity' through their activities in teaching, communications, entertainment and so on. Eisenstadt also noted that we have few systematic studies of the different types of secondary intellectuals. This point made more than two decades ago still applies to the contemporary sociology of knowledge and political sociology, not to mention studies of nationalism, where analysts' focus is usually on 'productive intellectuals'.

Bourdieu (1984:370) pursues this question even further and draws special attention to a type of new petite bourgeoisie, which he calls 'new intellectuals', who stand between 'classic' intellectuals and the masses. 'New intellectuals' are increasingly playing an important role not merely as eager audience but as transmitters and intermediaries for the popularization of intellectuals' ideas in contemporary society. Following Bourdieu, Featherstone (1991:43, 90–94) takes special note of the expanding group of 'cultural intermediaries', who are engaged in providing symbolic goods and services such as marketing, advertising and public relations personnel, television producers and presenters, social workers and counsellors. What is particularly noteworthy in the contemporary Japanese context is that business elites may be regarded as an epitome of such 'new intellectuals' acting as 'cultural intermediaries'. Business elites were not merely keen consumers of the *nihonjinron* but also played an important role as 'reproductive intellectuals' or 'cultural intermediaries', popularizing academics' theories of Japanese society and dispersing them to wider sections of the population. In fact, businessmen's popularizations were an important channel through which academics' *nihonjinron* were diffused to a wider readership. To provide one illustration, I found that, contrary to the assumption of many Japanologists that Nakane Chie's book (1967) had been widely read, not many of the school teachers I interviewed had actually read the book. (I had assumed that, as a well-educated group, school teachers would be interested in ideas of culture and society.) This is probably because insights provided in Nakane's book are not intrinsic to occupational concerns of educators. By contrast, large numbers of businessmen, who I had assumed to be preoccupied with mundane, money matters, had in fact read the book, since Nakane's analysis of Japanese society focused on company organization and industrial relations and, as such, was directly relevant to 'company men'. However, even the school teachers, who had not read the book, had often heard of it and even knew its main arguments because Nakane's theory was often quoted and referred to in business elites' writings, lectures and talks on television (Yoshino 1992:ch. 7). Business elites were popularizers of the academics' *nihonjinron*.

What deserves our special attention here is the type of literature – which may be called 'cross-cultural manuals' – written and edited by the staff of major Japanese companies. These comprise handbooks, English conversation materials and glossaries which deal in one way or another with the distinctiveness of Japanese behaviour and society manifested in business and management practices, company employees' everyday lifestyle, 'unique' Japanese customs and expressions, and so forth. These manuals were published by major Japanese companies. A dual-language handbook, *Nippon: The Land and Its People*, written by the personnel development office of the Nippon Steel Corporation (1984) is an epitome of such a manual. It covers a wide range of subjects on Japanese society, culture and national character. This handbook is essentially a businessmen's interpretation of the academics' *nihonjinron*, in view of the fact that its reference materials cover the vast extent of the *nihonjinron* including books by Nakane and Doi.

In these cross-cultural manuals, theories of cultural differences, provided in the *nihonjinron*, are popularized in such a way that their consumers may apply such theories to the practical context of cross-cultural interactions in which the Japanese are expected to explain things Japanese to non-Japanese. Perhaps best illustrative of this point

20

is the following excerpt from an English conversation manual *Talking about Japan* written by the staff of Nippon Steel Human Resources Development Co.Ltd. (1987). This manual is designed for someone interested in studying practical English as well as explaining the peculiarities of Japanese behaviour in English. Here, the four main propositions of the *nihonjinron*, discussed earlier, are neatly summarized and presented in the form of English dialogues:

> *Mr. Jones* (an American): . . . I don't think I could ever learn to make the subtle distinctions you need in Japanese.
>
> *Mr. Suzuki* (a Japanese businessman): It's so tied in with the whole culture. It's difficult to master for someone who grew up in another country. Also, most Japanese tend to avoid doing anything that sets them off from others. They worry about what others think and change their behavior accordingly.
>
> *Mr. J*: That's probably one of the reasons why people talk about Japanese groupism.
>
> *Mr. S*: It's a factor. It's also why Japanese are poor at asserting themselves. We tend to speak and act only after considering the other person's feelings and point of view.
>
> *Mr. J*: You can't say that for most Westerners. In America, we try to teach our children to be independent, take individual responsibility . . . We also try to train them to think logically, and learn how to express their thoughts and opinions.
>
> *Mr. S*: Yes, I know . . . Foreigners often criticize us Japanese for not giving clear-cut yes or no answers. This is probably connected to our being basically a homogeneous society and our traditional tendency to try to avoid conflicts . . .
>
> (Nippon Steel Human Resources Development
> Co.Ltd. 1987:405)

It can be seen that this type of conversation manual, for which cassette tapes and compact discs are also available, tends to narrowly channel one's expression of ideas of Japanese society. Since language learners often parrot model sentences and absorb them uncritically, these manuals subtly determine one's perceptions of Japanese society.

Many of these manuals published by companies were originally intended for, and distributed to, their employees and students (or prospective employees) (e.g. Mitsubishi Corp. 1983; Taiyō Kōbe Bank 1988). It is noteworthy that the personnel department is often in charge of such publications. This suggests that major Japanese companies play a direct role in socializing businessmen and students to be aware of the distinctiveness of Japanese society and behaviour. It may be argued that, whereas school textbooks are a chief means of ideological transmission in state-initiated primary nationalism, cross-cultural manuals such as the one illustrated above are one important tool of reproduction of national identity in secondary cultural nationalism. Moreover, whereas school textbooks are a means of childhood socialization, these manuals play a role in the process of adult socialization by helping to reconstruct and reinforce Japanese identity. This case may be presented not only as a challenge to the classic theory of nationalism but also to modern sociology in general which tends to neglect adult socialization in favour of childhood socialization.[14] We are reminded here of the insights of Norbert Elias (1978, 1982) in *The Civilizing Process,* in which he analysed manuals and manner books used by medieval court elites in order to acquire appropriate manners and etiquette as a means of surviving in court power struggles. We may say that cross-cultural manuals are intended to be used in the 'civilizing process' by which elites acquire proper manners and behaviour as 'internationalized persons' in the increasingly global world.

One important point is that many of the 'cultural intermediaries' who reproduced the *nihonjinron* in the form of cross-cultural manuals claim to have the aim of improving intercultural communication between the Japanese and non-Japanese. They also claim to wish to promote the emergence of large numbers of internationally-minded Japanese with the ability to communicate well in English and knowledge about cultural differences. Their 'good intentions' are declared in the editorial comments of many cross-cultural manuals. For example, the General Manager of the Corporate Communications Office of Mitsubishi Corporation (1983:6) says that their manual is intended to 'help smooth the way for better international communication'. Also, the General Manager of the Personnel Development Division of the Nippon Steel Corporation (1984:11) says that their handbook has been published 'in the hope of making some further contribution to mutual understanding between the people of Japan and the people of other countries'. The status of a *kokusaijin* (international person), desired by increasing numbers of the well-educated Japanese, is considered to be achieved by acquiring the ability to use practical English as well as knowledge of cultural differences. A condition for the status of a *kokusaijin* may therefore by measured by one's ability to express Japanese culture in English. This is well illustrated in the following paragraph:

Like many Japanese companies, Nippon Steel has been internationalizing its business operations very rapidly the past few years, with the result that the employees are now coming into increasingly frequent contact with foreigners . . . At such times, the conversation often turns to subjects about Japan, and our employees are often asked about Japanese culture and other aspects of their country . . . [T]he employee often does not know enough about the subject, and even when he does know the answer, he is often incapable of expressing it well in a foreign language.

(Nippon Steel Corporation 1984:7)

These remarks may merely represent their rhetorical self-justification. But, regardless of the authenticity of their declared intentions, we may say that an interest in improving intercultural understanding can have an ironic tendency to result in cultural nationalism. This is due mainly to the underlying assumption widely held among elites that intercultural communication is made difficult by the peculiarities of Japanese patterns of behaviour and thought. When dealing with non-Japanese, conscious recognition of Japanese peculiarities is considered the first step towards better intercultural understanding. Ethnicity is often understood as 'the process by which "*their*" difference is used to enhance the sense of "us" for the purposes of organization or identification' (Wallman 1973:3, italics added). In the *nihonjinron*, however, it is not 'their' differences but '*our*' differences that are actively used for the enhancement of 'our' national identity. Such a particularistic perception of Japanese identity may largely be explained historically. Elites in Japan have long perceived Japan as being on the 'periphery' in relation to the 'central' civilizations (first that of China, then of the West, and recently of the USA), thereby in response constructing Japan's identity through emphasis of the differences of its 'particularistic' culture from the 'central' and 'universal' civilizations. This type of thinking may be referred to as 'ethnoperipherism' (as opposed to ethnocentrism).[15]

An attempt to improve intercultural communication, accompanied by an excessive emphasis on Japanese peculiarities, can ironically have the unintended consequence of strengthening cultural nationalism. In fact, the large increase in the *nihonjinron* and its popularized version, cross-cultural manuals, had the effect of emphasizing Japanese 'differences' to the extent of neglecting the commonality between Japanese and non-Japanese. Here, we find that an activity designed to

23

improve intercultural communication has had the ironic consequence of sensitizing the Japanese excessively to their distinctiveness, real or imaginary, and thereby creating another obstacle to social interaction between the Japanese and non-Japanese. Foreign residents often find themselves alienated in Japanese society because of the belief held among Japanese people that non-Japanese cannot truly understand Japanese people.[16]

Concluding Remarks: The State and the Cultural Marketplace

In this chapter I have stressed the importance of the perspective of the cultural 'marketplace' where ideas of national distinctiveness are 'produced', 'reproduced', 'distributed' and 'consumed'. My criticism has been directed, first, towards the conventional theoretical pre-occupation with state-initiated, primary nationalism and its 'producti-vist' and 'statist' bias, and, secondly, towards the 'productivist' theoretical orientation prevalent even in an analysis of informal, secondary nationalism.

The 'marketplace' perspective has proven particularly useful for the analysis of contemporary Japan where people's participation in cultural nationalism is no longer explicitly supervised by the state. It is questionable, however, whether, as Bauman (1992:17) argues, the area of culture, which has been 'freed from direct supervision by the state', is 'now reduced to things of no concern to political powers'. It is certainly not my aim to argue that the market has replaced the state. Nor am I suggesting that there was no room for market-oriented nationalism in pre-war Japan. State-initiated nationalism and market-oriented nationalism are often complementary. Even today, the state's interest in cultural nationalism via formal education is evident, as was discussed earlier. One should not neglect the interrelationships, either, between the state and agencies of cultural production and reproduction such as television, the press and advertising agencies.

None the less, precisely because state-initiated nationalism in Japan centres around obviously nationalistic ideas and symbols, it is unable to elicit voluntary and positive support from significant sections of the population who do not wish to see a revival of the 'narrow-minded' nationalism of the prewar type. On the other hand, informal, market-oriented cultural nationalism in contemporary Japan has been promoted due to the unintended consequences of attempts to 'internationalize' and to improve international understanding through an emphasis on cultural differences. Unlike nationalism, 'internationalization' is a catchword that appeals favourably to many sections of contemporary Japanese society. Ironically, nationalism – in the sense of raising national consciousness, cultivating national identity, and stressing Japan's culture and tradition – is promoted in the name of the internationalization of Japan.

I have drawn attention to the hitherto neglected role of 'cultural intermediaries' in the cultural 'marketplace' in promoting cultural nationalism. The classic analysis of cultural nationalism has tended to be confined to the political process of ideological manipulation and mobilisation whereby elites produce nationalist myth and ideology and impose them on obedient subjects of the state. By shifting the focus, the workings of nationalism, especially secondary nationalism, can usefully be examined by paying attention to the 'market' process in which 'producers', 'cultural intermediaries' and 'consumers' of national identity interact. We have seen the relevance of cross-cultural manuals to Japanese business elites working in increasingly global settings, but cross-cultural concerns are not restricted to business elites only. They can be expected to be shared by anyone interested in international contacts such as tourists, exchange students, overseas volunteers, and cross-cultural counsellors and social workers, for whom a variety of cross-cultural manuals written by various types of cultural intermediaries and reproductive intellectuals are available.

Notes

1 Portions of my arguments in this chapter have appeared in preliminary forms in 'Cultural nationalism in contemporary Japan: the role of the state and the role of the market', *Papers of the British Association for Korean Studies* 6 (1996) and 'Cultural nationalism and "internationalization" in contemporary Japan' in W.A. Van Horne (ed.) *Global Convulsions* (N.Y.: State University of New York Press, 1997). A Japanese version of this chapter was presented in my *Bunka Nashonarizumu no Shakaigaku* (A Sociology of Cultural Nationalism), (Nagoya: Nagoya University Press, 1997). My first use of an expressly 'consumption'-oriented approach to ethnicity and nationalism appeared in 'Shōhi shakai ni okeru esunisitii to nashonarizumu: Nihon to Igirisu no "bunka-sangyō" o chūshin ni' (Ethnicity and nationalism in consumer society: with special reference to 'culture industries' in Japan and Britain), pp. 20–35 in *Shakaigaku Hyōron* (Japanese Sociological Review) 44(4).
2 'Secondary nationalism' in already established nations is gradually becoming a subject of inquiry. Billig's *Banal Nationalism* (1995) is one attempt to study this phenomenon.
3 I have coined the term 'thinking elites' to refer to the type of people who engaged in the discourse on Japanese uniqueness. Since they include elites

of diverse occupations, including not just academics and journalists but also diplomats and business elites, who are not devoted to creative intellectual pursuits, it would be inappropriate to call them intellectuals. 'Thinking elites' seems a more appropriate term in that they are a small group which has had a great deal of influence on the rest of the society by virtue of thinking (and writing) about a particular subject, in this case Japanese uniqueness.

4 I owe this qualification to John Hutchinson (1994b:8–9).

5 Here, Smith (1988) has in mind the first nations of Europe and several other nations such as Russia, Japan, Egypt, Turkey, Burma, Iran and Ethiopia.

6 Yasukuni Shrine is dedicated to the spirits of the war-dead in Japan's past wars. It was established in the Meiji era to venerate those who died in the cause of Japan's imperial rule. Following Japan's defeat in 1945, government support of the shrine was prohibited. Since then, there has been controversy as to government's renewed support for the shrine.

7 Befu (1987:54–67) characterizes the *nihonjinron* as 'mass consumption goods' rather than academics works.

8 For a detailed discussion of the content of the *nihonjinron*, see e.g. Mouer and Sugimoto (1986), Befu (1987), Dale (1986) and Aoki (1990).

9 The notion of Japan as a *tan'itsu minzoku* (uni-racial/ethnic nation) is attracting strong criticism as part of the now dominant trend towards demythologization of a homogeneous Japan. A critique of the *tan'itsu minzoku* myth is being stimulated by the increasing number of foreign migrant workers in Japan as well as the development of scholarly interests in ethnicity and nationalism.

10 See Yoshino (1992:ch. 9) for other interpretations of the *nihonjinron* phenomenon. Some saw the *nihonjinron* as an attempt to explore and reconstruct national identity threatened by Westernization (e.g. Befu, 1984). Others regarded the *nihonjinron* as an ideological instrument of class domination by which the dominant class manipulates the subordinate class by propagating a popular ideology of the uniquely homogeneous and harmonious culture of Japan (e.g. Kawamura, 1982).

11 We have no means of knowing whether deliberate ideological manipulation has actually happened and, if so, to what extent. It is nearly impossible to know the true intentions of the thinking elites who wrote on Japanese uniqueness more than a decade ago.

12 I conducted field research in a fairly large provincial city in central Japan with a population of several hundred thousand people. The main part of the research, which consisted mainly of intensive interviews with 35 educators (school teachers and principals) and 36 businessmen ('company men'), was conducted between October 1986 and September 1988. My research strategy was to concentrate on educators and businessmen, considering that both groups have a profound influence on Japanese society. For the methods and findings of this research, see Yoshino (1992: chs. 6–10).

13 Of the two groups I studied, a significantly larger proportion of businessmen (75.5 per cent) than educators (28.6 per cent) actively responded to the *nihonjinron*.

14 For a cogent criticism of preoccupation with childhood socialization in sociological theory, see Tsurumi (1970:391–409).

15 I do not wish to suggest that 'ethnoperipherism' is unique to the Japan's intellectual culture. I am presenting this concept as a general analytical tool.
16 It would be unfair if we did not point out that Japanese perceptions of national identity are also undergoing significant changes. See Yoshino (1994).

References

Almond, G. 1952 *The Appeals of Communism*, Princeton. NJ: Princeton University Press.
Anderson, Perry 1992 'Science, politics, enchantment' in J. Hall and I. Jarvie (eds.) *Transition to Modernity*, Cambridge: Cambridge University Press.
Aoki, Tamotsu 1990 '*Nihonbunkaron' no Henyō: Sengo no bunka to aidentitii* (The transformation of 'Theories of Japanese Culture': culture and identity in post-war Japan), Tokyo: Chūōkōronsha.
Bauman, Zigmund 1992 *Intimations of Postmodernity,* London and New York: Routledge.
Befu, Harumi 1984 'Civilization and culture: Japan in search of identity', pp. 59–75 in T. Umesao, H. Befu and J. Kreiner (eds.) *Japanese Civilization in the Modern World*, a special issue of *Senri Ethnological Studies* (16).
—— 1987 *Ideorogii toshite no Nihonbunkaron* (The Theory of Japanese Culture as an Ideology). Tokyo: Shisō no Kagakusha.
Billig, Michael 1995 *Banal Nationalism*, London: Sage.
Bocock, Robert 1974 *Ritual in Industrial Society: a sociological analysis of ritualism in modern England*, London: Allen & Unwin.
Bourdieu, Pierre 1984 *Distinction*, London: Routledge.
Crawcour, Sydney 1980 'Alternative models of Japanese society: an overview', pp. 184–8 in R. Mouer and Y. Sugimoto (eds.) *Japanese Society: reappraisals and new directions, Social Analysis* (5/6).
Dale, Peter 1986 *The Myth of Japanese Uniqueness,* London: Routledge.
Doi, Takeo 1971 *Amae no Kōzō* (Structure of Dependence), Tokyo: Kōbundo, translated as *The Anatomy of Dependence* by J. Bester, Tokyo: Kodansha International, 1973.
Eisenstadt, S.N. 1972 'Intellectuals and Tradition', pp. 1–19 in *Dædalus* (Spring).
Elias, Norbert 1978 *The Civilizing Process*, vol.1: *the history of manners*, Oxford: Basil Blackwell.
—— 1982 *The Civilizing Process*, vol.2: *state formation and civilization*, Oxford: Basil Blackwell.
Featherstone, Mike 1991 *Consumer Culture and Postmodernism*, London: Sage.
Gellner, Ernest 1964 *Thought and Change*, London: Weidenfeld and Nicolson.
—— 1983 *Nations and Nationalism*, Oxford: Basil Blackwell.
Hamaguchi, Eshun 1982 *Kanjinshugi no Shakai Nihon* (Japan: the inter-personalistic society). Tokyo: Tōyō Keizai Shinpōsha.
Hutchinson, John 1994a *Modern Nationalism*, London: Fontana Press.
—— 1994b 'Back from the dead?: the rediscovery of cultural nationalism', pp. 4–9 in *The ASEN Bulletin* (8).

Hobsbawm, Eric 1990 *Nations and Nationalism since 1780*, Cambridge: Cambridge University Press.

Hobsbawm, Eric and Terence Ranger 1983 *The Invention of Tradition*, Cambridge: Cambridge University Press.

Kawamura, Nozomu 1982 *Nihonbunkaron no Shūhen* (Some Arguments on Theories of Japanese Culture), Tokyo: Ningen no Kagakusha.

Kedourie, Elie 1960 *Nationalism*, London: Hutchinson.

Mannheim, Karl 1951 *Freedom, Power and Democratic Planning*, London: Routledge & Kegan Paul.

Matsumoto, Michihiro 1984 *Haragei*, Tokyo: Kōdansha.

Mitsubishi Corp. 1983 *Japanese Business Glossary/Nihonjingo*. Tokyo: Kōdansha.

Mouer, Ross and Yoshio Sugimoto (eds.) 1980 *Japanese Society: reappraisals and new directions, Social Analysis* (5/6).

Mouer, Ross and Yoshio Sugimoto 1986 *Images of Japanese Society*, London: Kegan Paul International.

Nakane, Chie 1967 *Tate Shakai no Ningen Kankei: tan'itsu shakai no riron* (Human Relations in Vertical Society: a theory of a unitary society), Tokyo: Kōdansha.

—— 1970 *Japanese Society.* Berkeley and Los Angeles: University of California Press.

Nippon Steel Corp., Personnel Development Office 1984 *Nippon: the land and its people,* 2nd edn. Tokyo: Gakuseisha.

Nippon Steel Human Resources Development Co.Ltd. 1987 *Talking About Japan/Nihon o kataru,* Tokyo: ALC.

Shils, Edward 1972 'Intellectuals, tradition, and the traditions of intellectuals: some preliminary considerations', pp. 21–33 in *Dædalus* (Spring).

Shils, Edward and M. Janowitz 1948 'Cohesion and disintegration in the Wehrmacht', pp. 280–315 in *Public Opinion Quarterly* 12.

Smith, Anthony D. 1986 *The Ethnic Origins of Nations,* Oxford: Basil Blackwell.

—— 1988 'The myth of the 'modern' nation' and the myths of nations', pp. 1–26 in *Ethnic and Racial Studies* 11(1).

—— 1991 *National Identity,* Harmondsworth: Penguin.

Taiyō Kōbe Bank 1988 *The 'Nippon'jin/The Scrutable Japanese,* Tokyo: Gakuseisha.

Tsurumi, Kazuko 1970 *Social Change and the Individual: Japan before and after defeat in World War II,* Princeton, N.J.: Princeton University Press.

Verba, Sidney 1961 *Small Groups and Political Behavior: a study of leadership,* Princeton, NJ: Princeton University Press.

Wallman, Sandra 1979 'Introduction: the scope for ethnicity' pp. 1–14 in Wallman (ed.) *Ethnicity at Work,* London: Macmillan.

Yoshino, Kosaku 1992 *Cultural Nationalism in Contemporary Japan: a sociological enquiry,* London and New York: Routledge. (pbk edn. 1995)

—— 1994 'The changing discourse on race, ethnicity and nationalism in Japan', pp. 10–13 in *The ASEN Bulletin* (8).

—— 1997 *Bunka Nashonarizumu no Shakaigaku* (A Sociology of Cultural Nationalism), Nagoya: Nagoya University Press.

2

THE NATION CONSUMED

Buying and Believing in Sri Lanka[1]

Steven Kemper

In the days when the study of nationalism stressed ideology, it talked about the role that engaged intellectuals played in creating national solidarity. On these accounts Marat, Abbé Raynal, and Abbé Sieyès propagated a set of values that provided French people with a basis for a common identity (see, e.g. Kohn 1955:9–41). By contrast Benedict Anderson's study of the rise of the nation looks to the function that print journalism served in making the nation imaginable (Anderson 1983). For my purposes, the more promising part of Anderson's argument is not so much the shift of attention from ideology to the medium by which ideology was diffused as his focus on the interaction between that medium and its consumers. The regularity of newspapers, Anderson suggests, their demotic character, and their segmented, yet totalized representation of the world brought readers into a single time and place, turning readers into a 'league of anonymous equals'. Voilà, the nation!

These approaches to the rise of national identity share two problems. Both overstate how quickly a 'single time and place' was created, and both make ordinary people passive beneficiaries of this transformation. These problems derive from the cataclysmic character of the Revolution itself, which gives the emergence of the French nation a certainty, a generality that has overwhelmed both popular discourse and scholarship on nationalism. As it turned out, a century passed before many people living within the boundaries of France thought of themselves as French (Weber 1976). Eugen Weber cites the case of a school inspector in Lozère who was incensed to learn in 1864 that at one school he visited not a single child could answer such questions as 'Are you English or Russian?' or 'What country is the department of Lozère in?' Every year, reported Bodley shortly before 1914, 'there are recruits who had never heard of the Franco-German war of 1870'. At that same period, 'only one man in four could explain why July 14 was a national holiday' (Weber 1976). Even in a nation-state with a beginning as momentous as the Revolution, people came to occupy a common time and space only when a sense of national identity came to be recapitulated in their own experience.

Anderson is clearly onto something in emphasizing the regularity, synchronicity, and demotic character of newspapers, but he does not give readers of those newspapers much of a role in the nationalist project. Part of the problem is that virtually all studies of nationalism concentrate on what the center does to the periphery. To this extent, Anderson's argument parallels Gellner's – both treat nationalism as a set of ripples spreading concentrically from a stone dropped in a pond. 'Nationalism' Gellner says, 'is the general imposition of a high culture on society, where previously low cultures had taken up the lives of the majority. . . . It means the generalized diffusion of a school-mediated, academy-supervised idiom, codified by the requirements of reasonably precise bureaucratic and technological communication' (Gellner 1983:57). As in Anderson's case, the burden falls on the medium of communication, with negligible attention paid to the process by which individuals on whom that high culture was imposed adapted, misunderstood, and resisted that culture.

I think the study of nationalism should follow the lead of Peter Sahlins's work on the process by which the border between France and Spain came to be constructed. Sahlins presents a case in which the emergence of national identity was a process whose conditions were negotiated by ordinary actors. 'The historical appearance of territory – the territorialization of sovereignty – was matched and shaped by a territorialization of the village communities, and it was the dialectic of local and national interests that produced the boundaries of national territory. In the same way, national identity – as French people or Spaniards – appeared on the periphery before it was imposed there by the center. It appeared less as a result of state intentions than from the local process of adopting and appropriating the nation without abandoning local interests' (Sahlins 1989:8–9). Local society both opposed the state on some occasions and exploited it on others, drawing the nation into the village only when circumstances warranted.

Whatever virtue there may be in treating the rise of a sense of national identity as a cumulative, reciprocal process, that perspective faces new problems in making sense of what is going on nowadays in Third World settings. The circumstances are different – these are most often nations-states that achieved independence at a historical moment

30

when a global system of political and economic practices was firmly in place. As the postcolonial period has developed, media have proliferated, reducing print to one technology among many. What to make of the emergence of national identity in circumstances in which the insistent presence of media seems to create a 'league of anonymous equals' in an instant? How can there be a place for human agency in a world where technology exercises such power?

National Identity in the Third World

Nations must always be imagined communities, and the process is always gradual and negotiated, but new circumstances shape exactly how Third World nations are being made believable. The most powerful development, to follow Appadurai, is a global shift in the way the imagination itself functions:

> The image, the imagined, the imaginary – these are all terms which direct us to something critical and new in global cultural processes; *the imagination as a social practice.* No longer mere fantasy (opium for the masses whose real work is elsewhere), no longer simple escape (from a world defined principally by more concrete purposes and structures), no longer elite pastime (thus not relevant to the lives of ordinary people), and no longer mere contemplation (irrelevant to new forms of desire and subjectivity), the imagination has become an organized field of social practices, a form of work (both in the sense of labor and a culturally organized practice) and a form of negotiation between sites of agency ('individuals') and globally defined fields of possibility. It is this unleashing of the imagination which links the play of pastiche (in some settings) to the terror and coercion of states and their competitors. The imagination is now central to all forms of agency, is itself a social fact, and is the key component of the new global order.
>
> (Appadurai 1990:5)

The institutionalization of the imagination as an 'organized field of social practices' rests on several historical processes, principally the explosion of new forms of communication – of which television is the most portentous – and the markedly increased movement of persons and things around the world, creating diasporas, hybridization, and extraordinary changes in the character of nations. Together these forces have created a global cultural economy, organized around a few professions that now exert powerful effects at unheard-of distances – the movie, television, and music industries, transnational corporations, press and broadcast services, development agencies, nongovernmental organizations, and the advertising business. If there are differences between the emergence of national identities in the West and the transformation that is occurring in Africa and Asia now, those differences derive from the distinctive ways that the imagination is institutionalized in these professions.

These agents of belief expose individuals to forms of subjectivity and desire that have referents that lack any particular geographical or historical location. Yet in the midst of these global flows of subjectivity, nationalism swims against the current. In the case of consumption, identity has little to do with history and territory; in the case of nationalism, it has everything to do with both. When James Clifford asks what can it mean at the end of the twentieth century to speak of a 'native land', I want to refer him to Serbs, Sinhalas, Macedonians, and Malays for an answer (1988:275). The hybridity and flux of many human lives is a point well and frequently made; it is a point that now informs the study of transnationalism, diasporic communities, and the world system, not to mention the shift to more sophisticated ways of writing ethnography, to return to Clifford's primary concern. But emphasizing the 'generalized condition of homelessness' is clearly as partial as an anthropology that reduces cultures to their essences and ties them to a territory. Surely the predicament of culture nowadays is the simultaneous deterritorialization of some human communities and the bloody territorialization of others, the fragmentation and dispersion of some cultural practices along with the reification of others. The imagination as a social practice is complicit in each of these processes.

The second circumstance that shapes the rise of national feeling in Third World settings is the role that the state plays in its own construction. In Hamza Alavi's Marxist vocabulary: 'The apparatus of the state . . . assumes a new and relatively autonomous *economic* role, which is not paralleled in the classical bourgeois state. The state in the post-colonial society directly appropriates a very large part of the economic surplus and deploys it in bureaucratically directed economic activity in the name of promoting economic development' (1972:59–81, italics in original). What Alavi neglects and what increasingly characterizes Third World cases is the state's celebration of its role in that cause. Sri Lankan advertising agencies receive more than half of their revenues from the national government. Raymond Williams calls advertising the 'official art' of capitalism.[2] In postcolonial societies, advertising has become the 'official art' of government.

Where studies of nationalism characteristically neglect the people in the provinces, they also neglect forms of agency that operate in a supranational context. One of the defining features of the moment is that Third World nations find themselves in a world not only of other nations but a world where rich nations seek to direct the development of poor nations. This influence takes several forms, the most pertinent of which is development practice, which has played a formative role in managing the Third World, inventing the peasantry, and imposing discipline and rationality on its peoples (see Escobar 1988:428–43). These changes have largely occurred since World War II, when development began to bring together an extraordinary cast of actors – a cosmopolitan group of scholars (centered not surprisingly in institutions located in donor nations), a transnational cadre of development professionals, and a local network of government officials, contractors, advertising agencies, and development workers. In this transnational context, Alavi's postcolonial state still plays a central role, but that centrality increasingly depends on its capacity to shape, challenge, and appropriate the forces of development.

Consider the example of a nongovernmental organization that wants to encourage the use of birth-control devices in a 'developing' country. The need to convince the local government to support the project goes without saying, but before it can go forward, the project will also need a working understanding with a regional supplier of condoms and the services of both a local advertising agency and a market-research group, as well as a system of distribution that can regularly put birth-control in the hands of householders. The apparatus of development must bring into alignment a wide variety of interests long before discovering whether local people will yield to the project's vision of what is natural, moral, and rational. Under these conditions the sovereignty of nations is tested in unusual ways.

A third circumstance ties together the first two. It has become an anthropological commonplace to say that totems are good to think, and it is equally clear that goods are good to think. In the emergence of national identity in Third World countries, goods are put to new purposes. They allow people to think the nation. There are precedents. When the citizens of Paris took apart the Bastille after the Revolution, an enterprising contractor was allowed to sell bits and pieces of the rubble to interested citizens – probably a practice that brought feelings of liberty, equality, and fraternity into the lives of French people as vividly as Marat's tracts (Schama 1989:408–19). Some of the material objects that circulate through Third World economies today go even further in blurring the distinction between consumption and citizenship. A building stone from the Bastille was a political artifact, not a consumer product; I can think of several South Asian examples that are both. The example I will draw on is the Sri Lankan lottery, a practice that probably does not leap to mind when one hears talk of constructing the nation. Lottery gambling in its Sri Lankan form has been shaped by Western technology and social thinking, development practice, petty capitalism, the transnational flow of domestics and chauffeurs to the Persian Gulf, and television and print advertising. For my purposes, lottery gambling is an exercise in making the nation believable.

One problem in understanding the role of consumption in Third World countries derives from having to conceptualize how global currents of ideas and things meet 'indigenous trajectories of desire and fear' (Appadurai 1990:3). Remember that the birth control project cannot promote the use of condoms without hiring a local advertising agency. The trick is to avoid reducing the intercultural encounter 'to a kind of physics on one side or a teleology on the other', for the global economy is not simply a force field of materiality and local societies are not passive objects, lacking material interests, and prone to cultural corruption (Sahlins 1988:1–51). When a practice as alien as birth control or lottery gambling enters a new context, the practice must be negotiated by vendors, bureaucrats, and advertising executives as well as consumers, as it enters into a contest with local economic interests.

Development and Desire

On my last stay in Sri Lanka in 1991, I ate in a Tamil restaurant located close to several advertising agencies where I had gotten to know people. One day as I was eating a *paper dosai*, I looked up from my meal and saw a decal on a water cooler in front of me. It stood just below five life-size lithographs of Śiva, Krishna, Sri Venkateswara, Lord Buddha, and Jesus Christ. The decal had a familiar ring, here couched in local terms: 'We honor *Visa* cards – a Visa for the People from the Bankers to the Nation'. A wonderful confusion of figures – Visa cards, 'visas', 'the people', 'the nation', as well as five images of older sources of power and identity. I asked myself just what the advertisement wanted consumers to believe makes Sri Lanka a nation? The Bank of Ceylon's providing 'the people' with Visa cards, the capitalist device par excellence for transcending local identities and jurisdictions? How many people in one of the world's twenty poorest nations could own a Visa card anyway? How many would ever travel on a visa? Could I charge a meal that cost less than 70 cents on a credit card while 12,000 miles from home? Was everything everywhere?[3]

The more I thought about the contradictions of Sri Lankan life – as a business that has been dominated until very recently by British firms and commercial interests, banking has no obvious connection to nationalism – the more I realized that consumption had direct implications for national identity and citizenship. A number of studies have argued that the rise of nationalist movements all over the world was closely tied to capitalist interests. Could it have been otherwise? But the economic interests that motivated nationalist movements were seldomly acknowledged openly; indeed, creating an emotional space for love of country and national solidarity required suppressing talk about the new advantages local notables stood to gain from independence.[4] The decal in the Tamil restaurant did quite the opposite, celebrating the unity of domains usually kept separate-the market and the forum, the private place of the consumer and the public arena of the citizen, exchange and persuasion. 'A Visa for the People from the Bankers to the Nation'?

To the extent that postcolonial societies are undergoing a rapid transformation that is equally economic and political, perhaps it is not surprising that advertising copy makes something of that linkage. Capitalist interest has a stake in the political success of the nation, just as the nation depends on the economic expansion that capitalism promises. If an advertising agency positions a particular bank by associating a financial product with the interests of the nation, the idea was bound to occur to someone. Surely it was bound to occur to an advertising firm in the service of an institution such as the Bank of Ceylon established by the national government. All the same, what is surprising is the believability that this association has acquired in the same context where the *jatika cintanaya* (the local mode of thought or way of life) is seen to be threatened by capitalism, the more so by transnational practices such as credit cards.

The key figure in suppressing the contradiction between encouraging economic growth and protecting the local way of life is the idea of development, for it implies both rising standards of living and continuity with the past.[5] Advertising as such follows a rhetorical strategy that fits neatly with the logic of development. Both begin from the assumption of the incompleteness and unsatisfactoriness of things, the universalized character of pleasure and pain, and both offer a remedy. Development offers a remedy that satisfies interests at various levels, and its links to these multiple interests give development practices great power. It serves the collective needs of governments, donor countries, nongovernmental organizations, and both transnational and local businesses, while it also speaks to individual aspirations for a better life. The discourse of development persuades because it is self-evidently sensible and because it offers a prospect that furnishes government a moral trajectory in a world where the invocation of religious values or cultural tradition has practical problems. What recommends development as a trope on the personal level is the parallel between the nation's envisioned development and the individual's. Come, the ads say, let us develop together.

For most economically ascendant nation-states – South Korea, Singapore, Hong Kong, Malaysia, Thailand, Indonesia, India, and Sri Lanka, to name just some of the Asian cases – economic growth and political development alike have become explicit public goals. In the Sri Lankan example, government treats development as the natural context for invoking the national purpose:

> Development is the subject of, as well as the context for, political speeches transformed into news headlines and disseminated nationwide through the press, radio, and television. Development also produces national- and international-level conferences and meetings, as well as extensive local media coverage of these events. The media are further saturated by development advertisements, development journals and special publications of the various ministries, and countless documentary and feature productions on radio and television. (Notable in this regard are the new, single-episode television dramas spun around specific state development projects). Development discourse pervades the pedestrian consciousness in the guise of noisy Development Lottery ticket booths and vivid posters advertising upcoming development celebrations. Today, the genre of development celebrations includes opening ceremonies, rituals, exhibitions, carnivals and concerts. As a senior cabinet minister acknowledged in a newspaper interview, celebrating development – in modes sacred or secular – has become an indispensable tradition in Sri Lanka.
>
> (Tennekoon 1988:295).

The lotteries that enter the pedestrian consciousness by way of sidewalk loudspeakers are government enterprises. That a government which regularly promises to protect the local way of life also offers its citizens a vehicle to gamble constitutes the kind of irony that politics often provides. Gambling – in the local case, wagering at casinos or at 'bucket' shops where bettors wager on horse races broadcast from England – cannot be advertised on state-controlled television at all, and for many Sri Lankans both casino gambling and 'bucket shop' gambling constitute disreputable practices that need to be suppressed by government.[6] But lottery advertisements as well as lottery drawings appear regularly on television because lotteries – in the West as much as Sri Lanka – constitute a form of wagering privileged for its socially beneficial consequences, consequences that outweigh the negative influence on the local way of life (not to say, on individuals who cannot afford to lose their rupees). Lotteries pay for development.

'National' Lotteries

Sri Lankans wager on five lotteries, the *Sevana* lottery, the *Sanvardhana* (Development) Lottery, the *Mahapola* Lottery, the National Lottery, and Lotto, which, despite its vaguely Sinhala sound, is the same game played in Norway, Germany, France, Spain, Ghana, Jamaica, Hong Kong, Indonesia, Canada, and the United States. Participation in lotteries links Sri Lankans to a practice that has prospered as much in the West as in Sri Lanka. As of 1989, lotteries were played in seventy-nine countries, where players gambled some $154 million each day. New York established the first American state lottery in 1967, but several European lotteries are substantially older. Spain had organized a lottery in 1763, Portugal in 1783, and Austria in 1787 (*Sunday Times*, 2 October 1989). Lotto claims to derive from a game played in Italy in the sixteenth century, but nowadays it has become a distinctly transnational lottery, and it is advertised as such. Sri Lankan television introduces spots for Lotto by showing a bouncing ball that moves across the screen from New York to London to Bombay to Colombo.

Despite its self-conscious foreign-ness, Lotto is controlled by the National Lotteries Board, which also runs its own lottery, taking the profits from both games for development projects. Three new lotteries were introduced during J. R. Jayewardene's tenure, and each was linked directly to a development project and more diffusely to the ethos of Jayewardene's probusiness, accelerated development administration. *Sevana* was started in 1977 and dedicated to supplying funds to build a million new houses; the *Mahapola* Lottery appeared in 1980 and contributes profits to a scholarship fund for needy university students, and the Development Lottery began in 1983, its profits being used in various ways through the President's Fund. Each has been immensely successful, especially the Development Lottery, which owes its popularity to the size of its jackpots. Although the jackpot initially was Rs. 100,000, the prize then rose to Rs. 500,000 and more recently to Rs. 1,000,000. Development Lottery drawings are staged for television – if a bettor's ticket fails to produce a winner on the Friday spinning of the 'Wheel of Fortune' (*Wasana Chakra*), she can tune in again for another chance in a 'Saturday Fortune' game decided by a ball-mixing machine that chooses five winning numbers marked on ping-pong balls.[7]

This all sounds very familiar until one hears how risk-taking for profit is locally constructed. The *Mahapola* Lotteries Board stresses the good done by a game that had supported 16,000 scholarships by 1988, but it also says that placing a bet on the *Mahapola* Lottery is itself motivated by Buddhist virtue:

> Since the Mahapola Lottery was launched in 1980, millions have bought tickets out of [a] sense of charity, though it is also true that the human instinct to 'gamble' or the desire to win a prize was not totally absent . . . . The majority of those who buy these tickets once a year are conscious of the cause. They are mainly parents, teachers, or brothers and sisters of those waiting to enter the portals of higher education . . . . Almost every year the concept of Dana [charity] was extended beyond the initial commitment to 'give' when buying a Mahapola Lottery ticket. Prize winners every year accepted the money but gave back at least a modest sum to the scholarship fund.
>
> (Gunewardena 1988)

To refigure wagering as an act of charity requires considerable imaginative power, but the point is not the naturalizing of an alien and dangerous practice because some practices cannot be altogether naturalized. The pertinent point is the oscillation of discourse between opposed registers, the self-interested wager and the selfless act of charity, the calculus of individual benefit and the familial character of the bettors. In a world where university admission has been tied to ethnic and regional quotas, the *Mahapola* Lottery has another virtue by default. As the advertising supplement adds, 'another unique feature of the Mahapola scheme is that it is not a parochial or partisan exercise open to abuse. There are no political, religious, caste, or class considerations in the award of scholarships'. That assertion is motivated by the recent history of university admissions policies, which have been marked by partisan considerations. In this regard, the *Mahapola* Lottery is more equitable, more statelike than the state itself.

Norwegians are the world's heaviest gamblers on state lotteries, venturing some $125 per person each year; Sri Lankans by contrast bet very little, averaging only 4¢ (Rs. 1.60) per person each year. But lotteries are preeminently a poor person's game – some 90 percent of the bettors, I would say, are very poor people – and those who bet wager considerably more than Rs. 1.60 each year. The class origins of lottery players have more instructive implications for the way lottery wagering is connected to development. The poor people who are the nominal beneficiaries of the development projects that government pursues are also the chief source of lottery revenues. It is thus no accident that advertisements emphasize not simply the good fortune of the winners but also their life situations. Consider a print ad 'Housemaid to Millionairess' – which plays on the dreams of one Sri Lankan woman, her picture at the center of the advertisement, who left the island to help her family:

> The streets of Kuwait were not paved with gold after all.
>
> Chandrawathi returned home after two heart-break years there, with barely a fraction of the fortune she had hoped to find.
>
> That was five years ago, and what with 3 fast growing daughters to fend for, and a home in Maligawatte which always went under water with the least shower of rain, things were bad, but not too bad for this housewife who believed in taking the rough with the smooth – always with a smile.
>
> She told us that she had always had a premonition that good days were round the corner.
>
> Last week she turned that corner.
>
> The Wheel of Fortune Jackpot which had eluded 22 others was hers. All Rs. 1,655,000/= of it!
>
> 'Kuwait was not where the pot of gold was at the end of the rainbow. It was at this end – at home all the time'.
>
> > (*Daily News*, November 16, 1989)

The advertisement's punchline reads, 'Wheel of Fortune – the second of the 3 chances you get with the same ticket in the DEVELOPMENT LOTTERY'. The self-development Chandrawathi had envisioned when she joined other Sri Lankan housemaids in the Middle East yields to the extraordinary development that a good heart and a lottery ticket can bring at home. The optimism that allowed her to take 'the rough with the smooth' in both Kuwait and Sri Lanka also kept her trying her luck in the lottery. Her new fortune will not go to waste, the advertisement concludes, for Chandrawathi intends to find a better place to live and to educate her three daughters. And while she will move on in life, she will not forget her neighbor, who discovered Chandrawathi's Wheel of Fortune ticket. She found the ticket in the appropriate place – lying forgotten under the television set Chandrawathi bought with her Gulf savings.

Another favored life story depends on the lucky winner's own efforts at economic enterprise, now serendipitously helped along by winning the lottery, his life a metonym of the lottery's commitment to development. Well-to-do people play the lottery, and they obviously win on occasion, but when such a person wins a big prize – for example, the Development Lottery jackpot – he will be profiled in a news article, but he is unlikely to appear in subsequent advertisements for the lottery. For advertising the moral qualities of the Development Lottery, the winning ticket is the ticket held by either a poor person or someone who has started a small business:

Mr. Don Norbert Jayamaha of Kandana West, the second winner of the top prize of Rs. 500,000/ + in the new Development Lottery is living proof that life does not end at retirement.

When 58-year old Mr. Jayamaha retired from the State Pharmaceutical Corporation a little over 3 years ago, it signalled the beginning of a new career as vigorous as the one that had just ended.

He set up a thriving poultry farm at Kandana and continues to be as active as ever.

On this red-letter day in his life, Mr. Jayamaha had gone marketing to Ja-ela. A regular feature on every marketing trip is that he buys a Development Lottery ticket and that day was no exception. Just one ticket as on all previous days – but today that ticket turned out to be a half-million rupee winner.

He plans to use his money constructively. He hopes to expand his poultry farm and also to build a house for one of his children.

Development Lottery   Keeps Its Promises.

('Yet Another 5 Lakh Winner for the Development Lottery',
Daily News, 15 January 1987.)

Advertising puts lottery tickets in a variety of what Stephen Greenblatt (1990:161–63) calls 'zones of display'. Some of those 'zones' exploit the everyday-ness of winners' lives. Here, a thoughtful neighbor finds a ticket lying ignored under a television set, and urges its owner, a poor woman recently returned from the Gulf, not to give up on her luck; there, an elderly entrepreneur buys a ticket in the midst of the careful business of marketing, where he is equally disciplined in buying just one ticket. Television drawings by contrast display those lottery tickets in a 'zone' that is literally theatrical, the viewer holding the ticket in hand, the *Wasana Chakra* spinning on the screen. That peculiar kind of engagement – the reality of sitting in a waterlogged home in Maligawatte while watching some very unreal doings in the television studio – constitutes a kind of circulation between 'zones of display' that Greenblatt cannot have encountered in Elizabethan England. Where is the lottery number to be read – on the television screen or in the player's hand? What is the 'zone of display' – the broadcast studio or the shack?

If television gaming produces an order of excitement that links together a nation of television sets, print advertisements try for a radically different effect, putting lottery tickets in zones of display that are serious and moral. When Greenblatt emphasizes capitalism's capacity for creating and then violating discursive domains, he speaks of capitalism in an early moment of its development. Once capitalist enterprise becomes a branded, advertised activity, and once television comes to complement print advertising, the oscillation becomes virtually a blur. It took Cardinal Wolsey's hat – to use Greenblatt's example – hundreds of years to move from sign of high office to theatrical prop to a memento of the founder of an Oxford college. Through all of these zones of display, Greenblatt never explains capitalism's role in these transformations. The lottery ticket moves between these domains on a daily basis, and the role of capitalism, at least the role of the 'official art' of capitalism, is transparent.

Lotteries, Nation, and War

What is more striking than the connection between lotteries and development is the way the Sri Lankan government wants to use lotteries for political purposes. If the Bank of Ceylon can characterize its Visa card as a 'Visa for the People from the Bankers to the Nation', lottery gambling can be directly linked to the nation. And while the Bank of Ceylon's campaign is the work of an advertising agency, government bureaucrats and elected officials – as much as advertising agencies – make the connection between lotteries and building the nation. The mutual interest shared by government and the advertising business suggests another way postcolonial governments rearrange the relationship between polity and economy. Sri Lanka, a nation by virtue of well-to-do people charging purchases with their Visa cards and poor people betting on the Development Lottery?

Let this example suggest the circumstances that have overtaken lottery gambling in the politically-troubled Northern and Eastern Provinces, where the civil war has been concentrated. After 1983, when Tamil guerrillas ambushed and killed a lorry full of Sri Lankan soldiers at the approach to the Jaffna Peninsula, armed conflict became the primary social fact in the north and east. Over 100,000 Tamils fled to refugee camps or to south India, public services were eliminated or reduced to their most minimal form, and daily life became increasingly dangerous for most people, now trapped between suspicious, if not hostile Sri Lankan troops and roving bands of suspicious and mutually hostile guerrilla groups. The various national lotteries continued to sell lottery tickets in the contested parts of the island, never knowing exactly who was marketing the tickets or whether revenues would make it to Colombo. In January of 1986 the first Rs. 100,000 winner of the *Sevana* lottery from Jaffna walked into the *Sevana* Secretariat in Colombo. The staff was delighted, not because the winner had survived the perilous trip from the north but because the northernmost point which had produced a winning ticket previously was Vavuniya.[8] Now the lottery had been pushed into the Tamil heartland.

But the chairman of the *Sevana* board of management, Ajantha Wijesena, faced a problem peculiar to paying off winners in besieged parts of the island. To exploit the publicity value of a Tamil winner of the lottery, he needed to announce the man's name; to make known a Jaffna winner's name was to subject him to grave risks. He made the obvious choice, not revealing the winner's name or address, but he also began arrangements for him to receive his Rs. 100,000 directly from the prime minister, then publicizing the event while hiding the identity of a man who otherwise would be visited by guerrillas as soon as he returned to Jaffna. According to Wijesena, the prime minister was personally delighted that tickets were selling in Jaffna and that a jackpot winner had emerged from there. Why the prime minister would find time to give out a lottery prize, in this case a relatively small one, makes sense only because of the national purposes that lotteries serve – the nation that gambles together stays together. And more was at stake than simply Tamils' participation in a national institution such as a lottery: 'The one million houses programme had penetrated terrorist

42

bound areas and was going on virtually at the same pace as in the rest of Sri Lanka. "This", Wijesena added, "was why the people in the North and East were also participating in the Sevana activities"'.

I have not discovered exactly when Tamil terrorist groups started to sell their own lottery tickets, but by 1987 they had extended sales into the northwestern and north-central parts of the island from their previous base in the Northern and Eastern Provinces (Haniff 1987). In so doing, terrorist lotteries moved from the areas directly contested by the several Tamil guerrilla groups and Indian Peace Keeping Forces – at least Indian troops were not selling Indian lottery tickets! – into areas that stand between the Tamil provinces and the balance of the island where Sinhalas predominate. The pattern had been established previously that terrorist groups attempted to supply many of the same services in the Jaffna Peninsula that government had once supplied, setting up rubbish-collection services, local policing, banking facilities, not to mention their own brutally efficient version of the Inland Revenue Service. Lotteries were a logical addition, another technique of government to create an economy at the level of the entire state (see Foucault 1991). Talk about the *jatika cintanaya* aside, lottery gambling has become such a regular part of Sri Lankan life that a terrorist lottery reestablishes a bit of the normal order of things in a part of the island where there is little normalcy. Lotteries provide another source of revenue for hard-pressed terrorist groups, but the governmental aspirations, the presumption to rule by imitating the state, are worth noting.

A national government does not sit by willingly and let citizens gamble with terrorists, but there was not much the national lotteries could do but ship tickets to the north and east and hope that beleaguered Tamils and Muslims would do their gambling with the state. In August of 1987 the *Sevana* Lottery took a small step to sustain sales in terrorist areas by launching a new advertising campaign: 'From Dondra [at the southern tip of the island in a Sinhala area] to Point Pedro [at the northern tip in a Tamil area], *Sevana* a way of life'. Proponents of the *jatika cintanaya* had difficulty with the idea that playing any lottery constituted their 'way of life', but the idea that Sinhalas and Tamils might find some common ground by wagering on the same prizes suggests the desperate straits to which 'nation-building' has been reduced.

The war of the lotteries continues, for what is at issue is not simply revenues but whether the Tamil guerrillas will be able to create an alternative 'way of life', an alternative nation, Tamil Eelam. The national government recognizes as much – when a million-rupee winner was reported from Jaffna, the spokesman for the awarding of the *Sevana* prize said that the way that Jaffna gamblers continued to bet in troubled times proved that the 'Sevana message of peace for all would be spread island-wide'. He added, 'Some of the residents in the North and East have even sent money orders requesting tickets to be posted to them and they have always been obliged as gratitude for their participation and goodwill'.[9]

What he did not say is that, when Sri Lankans in besieged areas play the lottery by mail, they do so because traveling to a market town risks being blown apart by a land mine or killed by a terrorist ambush and buying a ticket in public can mean being identified as either a government loyalist or a terrorist sympathizer. Advertising and television drawings create the 'national' character of Sri Lankan lotteries, but the 'national' character of consumption enters human lives when bettors decide whether to play with the nation or the guerrillas, to play by mail or buy a ticket in person. Where lottery gaming is tied as much to development as to desire, purchasing lottery tickets is an extreme example of what Douglas and Isherwood (1979:67) mean by consumption – using 'goods and services to make firm and visible a particular set of judgments in the fluid processes of classifying persons and events' – and a peculiarly modern test of citizenship.

Sri Lanka is having great trouble creating citizens, and I do not want to be read as expecting too much from lottery gaming. I do want to suggest that lotteries have a kind of portentous materiality – a thing linked to the prospect of winning an infinitely greater number of things – that concentrates the mind wonderfully, and by blurring the line between a political act and a consumption decision, a lottery ticket puts the nation in the hands of ordinary people. Viewing a lottery drawing creates the simultaneity and common world that Anderson finds important in the reading of newspapers. Yet because drawings are televised and because unimaginable value is at stake, drawings take Anderson's prospect of a 'league of anonymous equals' one step beyond anything newspapers ever created. Most of all, lotteries require bettors to take action, make choices, and keep their eyes fixed on the prize, for the next spinning of the *Wasana Chakra* may be the lucky one. In a way that is at least formal, this kind of everyday engagement forces people to think the nation.

To conclude with an example: Talking to an advertising executive who had put together Sri Lanka's first birth-control campaign in the

44

1970s, I asked how he had managed to popularize the use of condoms in a society where advertising condoms on television is still so delicate that commercials are constructed to afford parents 'deniability'. They can explain to an inquiring child that condoms are 'medicine'. He told me he made the campaign an exercise in acting on the national welfare both for condom users and the local merchants who sold the product. To this end, he had convinced *mudalalis* (small-scale merchants) that they were not so much selling a new product as dispensing medical and political advice about the national welfare and enlisting their customers in a good cause. Buy a condom as a favor to the nation! Do it at my suggestion! Looking back on the campaign, the executive quoted Lenin. I heard what he said, but I remember being preoccupied with the transnational irony – a Roman Catholic advertising executive tells a Western academic how he convinced a South Asian nation to use condoms by quoting the moving force behind Soviet communism. His reference to Lenin now strikes me as an example of how much an anthropologist can learn from an advertising executive: If you want to enlist a person in the Communist Party, he said Lenin said, you do so not by asking him outright to join but by asking him to put up a banner or pass out leaflets. Once you have got the person to carry out the favor, he has recruited himself. I suspect the making of national identity is similar, a negotiated process by which people recruit themselves through everyday acts of 'national' resonance.

Notes

1 This paper by Steven Kemper first appeared in *Public Culture*, vol. 5, no. 3 (1993), pp. 377–93. Reproduced with permission of the University of Chicago Press. ©1993 by The University of Chicago. Figure 1 (development lottery advertisement) was not available for reproduction in this volume. Minor stylistic changes have been made for the sake of editorial consistency.

2 I owe this reference to Tim Burke.

3 That same month the Banque Francaise du Commerce Exterieur concluded agency agreements with Lao Bank and Mongolia's State Bank, allowing Visa cards to be honored in two even less likely countries; *Far Eastern Economic Review*, May 9, 1991, p. 57.

4 The shape of economic interests was veiled but less than entirely hidden in the early Sri Lankan nationalist movement. See, e.g. Wickremeratne (1969:123–50).

5 Development theory itself has often been willing to sacrifice tradition in the cause of economic growth. See Binder (1986:3–33). I mean only that the popular representation of development promises a better future that emerges seamlessly from the local way of life.

6 Casinos are especially anomalous because they are controlled by foreign capital and principally serve foreigners in Sri Lanka on holiday or on business usually related to the Muslim-dominated gem trade. Without a word of warning, the government outlawed casino gambling in June, 1991. It returned a few years later.

7 The Development Lottery also depends on Western production, for tickets are shipped into Sri Lanka from the United States once a week. Lotto is organized by the National Lotteries Board, working in conjunction with a British Management company, De La Rue Systems, Ltd., that runs the game throughout the world.

8 'First Sevana Winner from Jaffna', *Daily News*, 10 January 1986.

9 'Sevana Lottery' Sales to Be Boosted in North and East', *Sun*, 27 August 1987.

References

Alavi, Hamza 1972 'The state in post-colonial societies-Pakistan and Bangladesh', *New Left Review* 74 (July/August).

Anderson, Benedict 1983 *Imagined Communities*, London: Verso.

Appadurai, Arjun 1990 'Disjuncture and difference in the global cultural economy', *Public Culture* 2 (2) (Spring).

Binder, Leonard 1986, 'The natural history of development theory', *Comparative Studies in Society and History* 28 (1).

Clifford, James 1988 *The Predicament of Culture*, Cambridge, Mass.: Harvard University Press.

Douglas, Mary and Baron Isherwood 1979 *The World of Goods,* New York: Basic Books, 1979.

Escobar, Arturo 1988 'Power and visibility: development and the invention and management of the third world', *Cultural Anthropology* 3 (4) (November).

Foucault, Michel 1991 'Governmentality', pp. 87–104 in Graham Burchell, Colin Gordon, and Peter Miller (eds.), *The Foucault Effect*, Chicago: University of Chicago Press.

Gellner, Ernest 1983 *Nations and Nationalism*, Ithaca, N.Y.: Cornell University Press, 1983.

Greenblatt, Stephen 1990 'Resonance and wonder', in Greenblatt (ed.) *Learning to Curse*, New York: Routledge, 1990.

Gunewardena, Rickardo 1988 'Five years of cash-in-a-flash', Advertising Supplement on Lotteries, *Sunday Times*, 22 May.

Haniff, Jehan 1987 'Terrorist lotteries in NW and NCP', *Island*, 10 January.

Kohn, Hans 1955 *Prelude to nation-states: the French and German experience, 1789–1815*, Princeton, N.J.: Van Nostrand.

Sahlins, Marshall 1988 'Cosmologics of capitalism: the trans-Pacific sector of the world system', *Proceedings of the British Academy*, 74.

Sahlins, Peter 1989 *Boundaries: the making of France and Spain in the Pyrenees*, Berkeley and Los Angeles: University of California Press.

Schama, Simon 1989 *Citizens*, New York: Knopf.

Tennekoon, Serena 1988 'Rituals of development: the accelerated Mahaväli development program of Sri Lanka', *American Ethnologist*, 15 (2) (May).

Weber, Eugen 1976 *Peasants into Frenchmen: the modernization of rural France, 1870–1914*, Stanford, Calif.: Stanford University Press, 1976.

Wickremeratne, L. A. 1969 'Religion, nationalism, and social change in Ceylon, 1865–1885', *Journal of the Royal Asiatic Society* (Great Britain and Ireland).

3

REPRESENTING NATIONALITY IN CHINA

Refiguring Majority/Minority Identities[1]

Dru C. Gladney

The following statement was made by a private taxi driver as I was on
my way into the city from the Beijing Capital Airport shortly before the
1991 Chinese New Year's Spring Festival. It raises many of the issues
addressed in this chapter:

> I try to stay clear of politics. On New Year's Eve, I'm not going to
> light fireworks like everyone else, and that's how I'll show that I
> don't support the government. If I don't set off fireworks, all my
> neighbors will know that I don't give a damn about this country.
> I'm just going to sit at home and watch the special New Year's
> program on TV. They'll have a lot of acrobats, singers,
> comedians, and minority dances. Those minorities sure can sing
> and dance . . . . I really like to watch those minority girls, they're
> a lot 'looser' (*suibian*) than our Han women. They bathe naked in
> the rivers and wear less clothing. Our women wouldn't act that
> way. . . Some of my friends have even gone down to Yunnan . . .
> or was it Guizhou? . . . to see if they could meet some minority
> girls, they are very casual, you know. Han women aren't free like
> that. It's frustrating. Just like our politics, we can't do anything
> about it (*mei banfa*). So why try?

This chapter will argue that the representation of the 'minority' in
China reflects the objectivizing of a 'majority' nationality discourse
that parallels the valorization of gender and political hierarchies.[2] This
process reverses subject/object distinctions and suggests the following
parallels: Minority is to the majority as female is to male, as 'Third'
World is to 'First', and as subjectivized is to objectivized identity. The
widespread definition and representation of the 'minority' as exotic,
colorful, and 'primitive' homogenizes the undefined majority as united,
monoethnic, and modern. The politics of representation in China

reveals much about the state's project in constructing, in often binary minority/majority terms, an 'imagined' national identity (Anderson 1983). While this dichotomization may not be as meaningful in social life, it is through reading the representation of minorities in China that we can learn much, perhaps more, about the construction of majority identity, known in China as the 'Han' nationality.

Following the tragedy of the 1989 Tiananmen massacre, there has been an onslaught of scholarly publications attempting to define and redefine China's 'quest for a national identity' in various terms including: Confucianism or neo-Confucianism (i.e., recent suggestions in the political economy literature that it is Confucian culture that has led to the rapid industrial successes of the East Asian economies of Japan and the 'four little dragons': Taiwan, South Korea, Hong Kong, and Singapore), language (the popular notion that those who speak and read Chinese are Chinese), Han Chinese sedentary agriculturalism (contrasted with 'minority' nomadism, see Fei Xiaotong 1989), the geophysical space of the country occupied by the PRC (*Zhongguo*, the central kingdom centered in the territory of China, see Thierry 1989), or a bio-genetic neoracist notion of pan-Chinese yellowness (as the Su Xiaokang 1989 television series *River Elegy* seemed to suggest).[3]

By contrast, a burgeoning literature on the anthropology of the Self has argued for movement away from reified definitions of Self to emphases upon 'multiplicity, contextuality, complexity, power, irony, and resistance' (Kondo 1990:43). Similarly, studies of ethnicity and nationalism have begun to move away from either culturally or primordial-based formulations, to the analysis of power relations, particularly in contemporary nation-states (Anderson 1983:16; Comaroff 1987; Hobsbawm 1990; Gladney 1991; Keyes 1981). The connection between the relationally described identities of nationalism and gender was made most clearly in the conference volume *Nationalisms and Sexualities* (Parker et al., 1992). The authors convincingly argue that 'like gender – nationality is a relational term whose identity derives from its inherence in a system of differences' (Parker et al., 1992:5; compare also Caplan 1987:10). In this chapter, I wish to extend this argument to address the issue of relational identity in China through analysis of the politics of minority/majority representation.

Perceptive China scholars have noted the colorful portrayal of minorities in China as often derogatory, colonial, and useful to the state (Diamond 1988; Thierry 1989), but this extends to imperial times and

49

is not particularly new (see Eberhard 1982). Studies of modern Chinese art have also drawn attention to the important place of minorities in the formation of art history in the PRC (Chang 1980; Laing 1988; Lufkin 1990). I would like to suggest here (and I believe that this is a new direction) that the objectified portrayal of minorities as exoticized, and even eroticized, is essential to the construction of the Han Chinese majority, the very formulation of the Chinese 'nation' itself. In other words, the representation of the minorities in such colorful, romanticized fashion has more to do with constructing a majority discourse, than it does with the minorities themselves. This minority/ majority discourse then becomes pervasive throughout Chinese culture, art, and media.

In *Woman and Chinese Modernity*, Rey Chow (1990:21) also makes the important connection between ethnicity and the construction of Chinese womanhood, but Chow's is an external argument about the Western construction of China as feminine, while I am linking internal constructions about the gendered minority Other within Chinese society. In conclusion, I also extend the argument to popular culture in general, with a reference to the interesting continuance of the discourse in the recent film, *Ju Dou*, by Zhang Yimou. Significantly, and here this study makes a contribution to those discussions that attempt to move beyond Edward Said's Eurocentric 'orientalist' critique, the representation of minority and majority in Chinese art, literature, and media will be shown to have surprising parallels to the now well-known portrayals of the 'East' by Western orientalists. This 'oriental orientalism', and the objectification of the minority Other and majority Self in China, will be shown to be a 'derivative discourse', in Partha Chatterjee's (1986:10) terms, stitched from Chinese, Western (namely Morganian and Marxist), and Japanese ideas of nationalism and modernity.

This approach rejects the traditional center-periphery construction of Chinese society, with the so-called 'minorities' on the distant margins of Chinese society and nationality. It also challenges the dominant idea that 'cultural change [in China] was overwhelmingly one way' (Naquin and Rawski 1987:129), or that anyone who came into China, foreigner, minority, or barbarian, was subject to 'Sinicization' (Ch'en 1966, Lal 1970). In these more traditional configurations, Chinese culture functioned simultaneously, to quote James Hevia,[4] as both 'sponge and eraser' of foreign cultures: China not only absorbed outsiders, it dissolved them, and the few that survived on the 'periphery' were generally thought 'marginal' to the understanding of

Chinese society. During my fieldwork, I was often surprised to find that many of the reforms in China, whether they be in spheres related to the market economy, privatized agriculture, or religious and political freedom, were first allowed in minority areas, and these often directly influenced the nature and force of change among the Han (see Gladney 1990a). In this chapter, I want to extend the argument further and show that even in the areas of popular culture, art, film, and moral value, the so-called 'peripheral minorities' have played a pivotal role in influencing and constructing contemporary Chinese society and identity. I am addressing public culture in its often state-sponsored production and reproduction, concerning myself more with representations in nationally distributed media and film, rather than with a specific field site.

I also suggest that the commodification and objectification of minorities in China represent something more than a response to Western consumer tourism, providing the state with not only hard currency, but also important symbolic capital, to use Bourdieu's (1977:6) construction. The exoticization and representation of minorities is an enterprise that took on enhanced importance with the rise of the Chinese nation-state and is central to its nationalization and modernization project: The homogenization of the majority at the expense of the exoticized minority. The so-called minorities, long confined to the margins of Western and Chinese theoretical discourse on Chinese society, are no longer marginal, and perhaps never should have been, to our understanding of contemporary China.

The Public Display and Commodification of the Minority Other in China

One cannot be exposed to China without being confronted by its 'colorful' minorities. They sing, they dance; they twirl, they whirl. Most of all, they smile, showing their happiness to be part of the motherland. The four-hour Chinese New Year's program is a yearly special broadcast throughout China to its 1.1 billion population. And, even though only eight percent of that population is supposed to be minority (the *Han* majority occupy 91.96 percent of China's population according to the 1990 census), fully one-half of the evening's programming is devoted to smiling minority dancers. A brief examination of the opening minutes of the evening's program immediately reveals the crucial role minority peoples play in the contemporary construction of the People's Republic of China.

51

The program begins with a view of the clock tower on Beijing's Central Radio and Telegraph Building striking 8 o'clock, the time for the start of the show that lasts until midnight. It is the most popular program on television during New Year's, carried on the CCTV Central Broadcasting System that is received throughout China, including Tibet, Mongolia, and even Taiwan and Hong Kong. In my several years of field work in China, I noted that most families from Beijing to Xinjiang preferred to stay at home on New Year's Eve and watch this program with relatives and a few close friends. During the 1991 broadcast, I was with Chinese friends in their apartment in Beijing, and was repeatedly told to sit and watch the program with the rest of the family, even though I preferred to catch up on local gossip. After the television clock struck 8 p.m., the doors to the elaborate stage opened to reveal a wide array of colorfully dressed minorities advancing onto the stage. After a brief introduction to the evening's program, four well-known television hosts wished the audience a 'Happy New Year' and initiated the first choreographed program of the broadcast by stating: 'China is a multi-national country, fifty-six different nationalities, fifty-six different flowers. The many nationalities wish to extend to all of you a Happy New Year through a special Tea and Wine Happy New Year's Toast!' The program followed with Tibetans, then Mongols, Zhuang, Uzbek, Korean, Wa, Hui and other minority dancers presenting Buddhist 'hata' (scarves), other minority gifts, and cups of tea and wine to the studio audience, singing their native songs in their native languages, with a Chinese translation superimposed on the television screen.[5] The program had well over half its time devoted to minority songs and dances.[6] In striking resemblance to the 'tribute' offerings of the ancient Chinese empires, the minorities performed, sang, and presented ritualized prostrations as they offered greetings to the studio audience, who appeared to be largely members of the Han majority. They appeared so, because the studio audience was uniformly (as if in uniforms) dressed in conservative suits with ties, Mao jackets, or other formal, dark 'Western' attire, in marked contrast to the 'colorful costumes' of the minority entertainers. Nonminority entertainers and hosts exclusively wore Western-style suits and dresses.

After the People's Republic of China was founded in 1949, the state embarked upon a monumental endeavor to identify and recognize as nationalities those who qualified among the hundreds of groups applying for national minority status. The question of a person's nationality, which is registered on passports and all official documents, is decoded by Stalinist and historical criteria that determine if an individual is a member of a group that was ever linguistically, economically, geographically, or 'culturally' distinct from the so-called Han majority population (see Fei 1981; Yang 1992). This recognition may make a considerable difference in obtaining certain entitlements accorded to minorities, in some cases including permission to have more than one child, obtaining entrance to a university, access to local political office, special economic assistance, and tax relief programs. Those who were recognized by the state are always portrayed in the state-sponsored media as happily accepting that objectivized identity, as the caption for a photograph of several minorities in traditional costume pictured in a brochure introducing the 'Nationalities Cultural Palace' (*Minzu Wenhua Gong*) in Beijing reads: 'The Happy People of Various Nationalities' (*Minzu Wenhua Gong* 1990:12). Significantly, Tiananmen, the Gate of Heavenly Peace, is bordered on both sides by the slogans: 'Long Live the Chinese People's Republic' (*Zhonghua Renmin Gongheguo Wansui*) and 'Working Peoples of the World, Unite!' (*Shijie renmin gongren tuanjie*). These state-sponsored signs on public buildings and in the media emphasize for the Chinese populace over and over again that China is a multiethnic and multinational state – a point that is critical to China's representation of itself to itself, and to the international sphere. China regards itself as a multinational nation-state that must be reckoned with by other multinational, 'modern' nation-states.

As multinational, China portrays itself as democratic, claiming 'autonomous regions, prefectures, counties, and villages' based on the Soviet model, but in name only, since the Chinese constitution does not allow true geopolitical secession – something perhaps the conservative Russian right wing now wishes Stalin would have thought of when he approved a Soviet constitution that allowed for political secession of the (now former) republics. The myth of democratic representation is critical to China's construction of itself as a modern multinational state, distinguishing and distancing itself from the ancient feudal Chinese empires that did not allow for representation. As Spivak (1990:105) argues, 'One of the gifts of the logic of decolonization is parliamentary democracy'. Given public criticism over China's treatment of Tibet, it is not surprising that Tibetans are often represented as the most willing subjects of Chinese 'democratic liberation'. In one state-sponsored pictorial, a Tibetan is portrayed as happily voting, as if Tibetans really did control their own destinies. The caption reads: 'Happiness Ballot' (*Nationality Pictorial* 1985:10). In another published painting, several minorities are portrayed on the Great Wall, happily proclaiming in the caption, 'I love the Great Wall' (*China Islamic Association* 1985:28) – although the Great Wall was primarily built to keep nomadic peoples out. It is also interesting to note that in this figure, probably geared for school children, the figures on the Great Wall, with one exception, are clearly Muslim: the men wear Turkic and Hui (Muslim Chinese) Islamic hats, and the woman is veiled. The other man, strangely enough, is an African. Perhaps he is represented on the wall with the other minorities to represent their ethnic solidarity; more seriously, perhaps it is to emphasize their corporate 'primitivity' (i.e., promoting the idea that China's minorities are like 'primitive' Africans), which is key to understanding the position of the minorities in the Marxist-Maoist evolutionary scheme (see below).

The commodification of minorities is accomplished through the representing, packaging, and selling of their images, artworks, and 'costumes' in the many pictorial-gazeteers, such as *Nationalities Unite* (*Minzu Tuanjie*) and *Nationality Pictorial* (*Minzu Huabao*), as well as in museum displays, such as in the 'Nationality Cultural Palace', an enormous exhibition hall and conference center on Changan Avenue that houses a store selling minority artifacts and costumes as well as temporary exhibitions on minority nationalities. It is bordered by the Nationality Hotel and offices of the State Commission for Nationality Affairs, the ministry charged with administrating all dealings with minorities in China. Minority areas have boutiques, open markets, tourist stores, and even 'cultural stations' (*wenhua zhan*, see Schein 1990) where minority goods are collected, displayed, sold, and modeled. Books and sets of photo cards (*minzu kapian heji*) published by the state introduce the fifty-six nationalities of China and are widely distributed to school children, foreign students and tourists, and carried by officials on trips abroad as gifts to their host institutions. In baseball card fashion, the back of the card has each group's statistics summarizing the nationality's distinctive history, language, and culture. The nationalities themselves are portrayed on the front by a 'representative' iconographic image, generally a photograph, of that group, colorful and usually female.

It is noteworthy that of the fifty-six nationalities introduced in the state-sponsored English language pictorial *Chinese Nationalities* (1989), only three nationalities are represented in the first picture as males. All fifty-three others are represented as females, by a beautiful, alluring young woman, in a colorful 'native' costume. The minorities are almost always portrayed in natural, romantic settings, surrounded by fauna and flora. Significantly, however, the Han are represented in the same book by conservative, middle-aged women in an urban setting, with what is generally thought to resemble 'modern', Western-coiffured hair, dressed in Western-style sweaters, modest pants and long-sleeved outfits. This displays what the authors perhaps considered to be their modernity, and by extension, their normality, civility, and subjectivity. The authors of *Chinese Nationalities* chose a 'modern' photo to represent the Han, not one that bears any resemblance to a 'traditional' Chinese society, even though the minorities are always shown in their 'traditional' dress. Instead of being represented as singing and dancing, one photo has the Han women with single infants in strollers. The caption reads: 'It's good to have only one child' (*Chinese Nationalities* 1989:20). When minority men are portrayed, and then rarely, they are generally exoticized as strong and virile, practicing strange and humorous customs, or possessing extraordinary physical abilities in sport, work, or the capacity to consume large amounts of alcohol much more than a typical Han (*Chinese Nationalities* 1989:16). 'To drink like a Mongol' is a compliment often heard about prodigious drinking ability in China.

The state, through commodifying and representing its minorities as colorful and exotic, engages in a project familiar to the representation of colonized peoples by colonial regimes. By publishing an extraordinary collection of 'orientalist' erotic post-cards, the Algerian Malek Alloula (1986) examines French observations of Algeria, and claims to be sending the Orientalist postcard back 'to its sender' (Alloula 1986:5), unveiling the role of the 'colonial harem' as both orientalizing the Other and subjectivizing the European Self. Through state-sponsored representation of the minority Other as exotic, much the same is accomplished in China, only in the context of what Michael Hechter (1975) has termed 'internal colonialism'.[7]

Essentializing the Han

The representation of the Han as 'normal' and 'un-exotic' is critical for understanding the construction of present-day Chinese identity. Just as Peter Worsley has shown that the discourse of First and Third Worlds helps to confirm the so-called First World's superiority (see Worsley 1984),[8] the subordination of nationalities in China leads to the clear promotion of the Han to the vanguard of the peoples of the People's Republic. While research on the rise of Russian nationalism has been popular in Soviet studies since the 1970s, both by foreign and Russian scholars, as yet no larger studies of the creation of Han nationalism have emerged – perhaps because it is often assumed that 'Han' is generally equivalent to 'Chinese'. Few have questioned how the Han became the 91.96 per cent majority of China. Yet in China, identity papers register a person not as 'Chinese' (*Zhongguo ren*), but as Han, Hui, Manchu, or one of fifty-six stipulated identities. In China, national identity is not only 'imagined'; it is stamped on one's passport.

The notion of '*Han ren*' (Han person) has existed for many centuries as referring to descendants of the Han dynasty (206 B.C.–A.D. 220), which had its beginnings in the Wei River valley. However, I submit that the notion of *Han minzu* or *Han min* (Han nationality) is an entirely modern phenomenon – it arises with the shift from empire to nation. While the concept of a Han person (*Han ren*) certainly existed, the notion of a unified Han nationality (*minzu*) that occupies 91.96 per cent of China's population gained its greatest popularity under Sun Yatsen. The leader of the Republican revolution that toppled China's last empire, Sun was most certainly influenced by strong currents of Japanese nationalism during his long-term stay there (the Chinese term *minzu* derives from the Japanese *minzoku*). More practically, Sun needed a way to mobilize all Chinese against the imperial rule of the Qing, a dynasty founded by a collection of northeastern nomadic peoples who became known as the Manchu. Although he certainly did not invent the idea, by invoking the argument that the majority of the people in China were Han, Sun effectively found a symbolic metaphorical opposition to the Manchu and all 'foreigners', against whom the vast majority of peoples in China would easily rally. Sun advocated the idea that there were 'Five Peoples of China' (*wuzu gonghe*): the *Han*, *Man* (Manchu), *Meng* (Mongolian), *Zang* (Tibetan), and *Hui* (a term that included all Muslims in China, now divided into the Uygur, Kazakh, Hui, and so on).

It is not at all surprising that Sun himself would find personally appealing the idea of the Han as the national group, which included all the regional peoples and Sino-linguistic speech communities. He was Cantonese, raised as an Overseas Chinese in Hawaii. As one who spoke Mandarin with a Cantonese accent, and lacking strong connections in Northern China, he would have easily aroused the traditional northern suspicions of southern radical movements extending back to the Southern Song dynasty (A.D. 960–1279). Sun found a way to rise above these deeply embedded north-south ethnocentrisms. The use and perhaps invention of the term *Han minzu* was a brilliant attempt to mobilize other non-Cantonese, especially northern Mandarin speakers, and the powerful Zhejiang and Shanghaiese merchants, into one overarching national group pitted against the Manchu and other foreigners threatening China during the unstable period following the Unequal Treaties.

In Benedict Anderson's (1983:87) poignant terms, Sun was engaged in a project of 'stretching the short tight skin of the nation over the gigantic body of the empire'. The 'imagined' Han majority nationality and derivative minority nationalities that were created, not unlike Victor Mudimbe's (1988:23) 'invention of Africa', led to the invention and legitimization of the Han. It is cultural difference between Mandarin and Cantonese, Shanghaiese and Sichuanese, that most Chinese feared would pull China apart, and the notion of the Han was one fiction encouraged to hold them together.[9] Yet, it is interesting to note that while Sichuanese, Mandarin, Hunanese, and Cantonese restaurants are considered 'ethnic' cuisines in Los Angeles, Hong Kong, and elsewhere, in China the people who produce and consume these foods are somehow not what they eat – they are not ethnic, but all considered Han. Neither the Nationalists in Taiwan nor the Communists on the mainland have challenged this generic ethnonym; it proved too fundamentally useful. The invention of Han Chinese nationalism is perhaps one of the closest realizations of Julian Huxley and A.C. Haddon's (1936) perceptive definition of a nation 'as a society united by a common error as to its origin and a common aversion to its neighbors'. It is surprising, however, that this concept of the Han as one 'ethnic' group occupying 91.96 per cent of China's population has never been seriously challenged by China scholars.

Han Modernity and the Construction of Primitivity

The Han are frequently represented as somewhere near the 'modern' end of a Marxist historical trajectory upon which China's minorities must journey. Much of this derives from a continued commitment in Chinese social science to the study of minorities as 'living fossils' indicating the origins of 'primitive communism'. Matrilineality, communal living and property holding, and even extra-marital sexuality among the minorities all become 'proofs' of how far the Han have come. Chinese Marxist social science has been heavily influenced by stage evolutionary theory, particularly as represented in the writings of the American anthropologist Lewis Henry Morgan (see Yang 1992). In his famous 1878 treatise, *Ancient Society*, Morgan described in his first chapter, entitled the 'Ethnical Period', the development of society from savagery, to barbarism, and then to civilization. Tong Enzheng, the Sichuanese anthropologist and museologist, criticized Chinese anthropology's heavy reliance, almost to reverence, upon this theory of societal evolution:

Because of the esteem in which both Marx and Engels held [Morgan's] works, and especially because Engels, in *The Origin of the Family, Private Property, and the State*, affirmed many of his views, there has been a tendency among scholars to mistakenly equate his positions with specific positions taken by Marx and Engels, positions which themselves were mistakenly equated with the fundamental principle of Marxism. As a result, Morgan's most representative work, *Ancient Society* has been canonized, and for the past 30 years has been regarded as something not to be tampered with . . . . therefore, to cast any doubt on it would be to cast doubt on Marxism itself.

(Tong 1989:182, 184)

In China, minority studies became an avenue for proving Morgan (and it was believed, Marxist thought in general) to be right, over and over again, through the examination of minorities as representatives of earlier forms of society, 'living fossils' of savagery and barbarism (Tong 1989:185). The Han, as representative of 'higher' forms of civilization, were clearly more evolved, and were to lead the way for minorities to follow. As if to underline the continued dominance of this theory, Fei Xiaotong (1989), China's most revered social scientist, presented a 1988 Tanner lecture in Hong Kong entitled 'Plurality and Unity in the Configuration of the Chinese Nationality', which was later published in the Beijing University Journal. In the article, Fei traced the rise of the Han people from multiethnic origins prior to the Qin dynasty, and their almost unilineal descent down to the present day, despite absorbing and being conquered by various foreign tribes and nations.

As soon as it came into being, the Han nationality became a nucleus of concentration. Its people radiated in all directions into the areas around it and, centripetally, absorbed them into their own groups and made them a part of themselves . . . . As the non-Han rulers' regimes were mostly shortlived, one minority conqueror was soon replaced by another, and eventually all were assimilated into the Han . . . . But as the national minorities generally are inferior to the Han in the level of culture and technology indispensable for the development of modern

58

industry, they would find it difficult to undertake industrial projects in their own regions, their advantage of natural resources notwithstanding . . . . Therefore, our principle is for the better developed groups to help the underdeveloped ones by furnishing economic and cultural aids.

(Fei 1989:39, 45, 47, 52)[10]

Fei Xiaotong's understanding of national identity and social development is based on a strong commitment to Stalinist-Leninist nationality policy, based on Morgan's theory of stage development evolutionism, and Engel's prediction of the withering away of class and national identity with the removal of private property.[11] While there are many nationalities in China, the Han are defined to be in the cultural and technical vanguard, the manifest destiny of all the minorities. While some Chinese scholars, like Tong Enzheng, are beginning to challenge the dominance of the Marxist-Stalinist-Morganian paradigm, it still heavily influences the popular discourse regarding nationalism and Han superiority in China, as well as state policy.

The popularity of this discourse is evidenced by a recent film, *Amazing Marriage Customs* (*Jingu Hunsu Qiguan*, literally, 'Strange modern and ancient marriage customs'), distributed by the Nanhai Film Company. Filmed entirely in China with government approval, the film is a survey of marriage customs throughout China, with a heavy dose of minority practices, especially in Yunnan. What is noteworthy about the film is not the typical exoticization and eroticization of minorities as described below, but the deliberate structuring of the film along stage evolutionary theory. At the beginning of the film, we are shown primeval visions of a neolithic past and the emergence of primitive mankind. The narrator intones:

Getting married is natural, but during long period [sic] in history, men had no idea of 'love' and 'marriage'. From 'childhood' of human history, 3,000,000 B.C. to the end of matrilineal society in 5,000 B.C., marriage history transits from group marriage, polygamy, to monogamy stage [sic]. Each stage has its own development, traces of which could be found, only three decades ago in China . . . . From 3,000,000 B.C. to 1,000,000 B.C. human society began to form. There was nothing called marriage, or it was called primitive promiscuity [*yuanshi luanhun de jieduan*, lit., 'stage of primitive confused marriage']. From 1,000,000 B.C. to 100,000 B.C. human society divided into blood families

59

[*xueyuan jiazu*]. Promiscuity existed, called consanguine group marriage. In matrilineal society, group marriage outside tribe [sic] started. In ancient society, nothing called marriage could be found in group marriage. The relationship was casual.[12]

The film then presents a succession of minorities in various stages of transition from 'matrilineality' to 'patrilineality', including intimate scenes of marriage and mating rites among the Naxi, Dong, Bouyi, Yao, Hani, Wa (Va), Moso, Zhuang, and Miao (Hmong). Several of these groups are described as practicing 'free love' and very 'open to sex'. In one scene, Dong women literally become the 'scenery'. They are shown bathing in the river, only barely covered by their triangular tops, and as the camera focuses on exposed breasts, the narrator states: 'The (women) take a bath in the river after work, what a lovely scene. The scenery is beautiful enough, they make it more fascinating'. In one particularly explicit bathing section featuring Miao (Hmong) women, the camera zooms in on a group of women disrobing completely in the river, and with long-lens shots taken through the grass in a voyeuristic fashion, the narrator notes the arrival of several men:

They've asked their lovers to come. What for? To watch! A thorough examination indeed! If he's satisfied, must do something [sic], in a very polite way of course. He present her a red ribbon, in a serious manner. Very happy indeed! The ribbon is a token for engagement. With this token she is somebody's. How romantic!

Following the 'matrilineal' section, the film introduces the more conservative and covered Uygur Turkic Muslims of Xinjiang. 'Islam', we are told, 'respects patriarchy and husband right', and 'women are subordinate', as if the Muslims represent an intermedial stage between primitive promiscuity and 'modern' Han conservatism. The final scene begins with views of Tiananmen Square and the Forbidden City, and, against a background of Han couples dating in the park, the narrator states:

The characteristic of modern marriage is freedom, monogamy, and equality between sexes. The law of marriage stipulates . . . . No force on either side. Or a third party interfering! Love is most essential in modern marriage. Having love affairs [*tan lianai*, lit., 'speaking about love relations'] is a prelude of marriage. In the countryside of Beijing you may observe this wonderful prelude.

The film then notes that in a 'modern, large city' it is often difficult to find a mate, and computerized dating is featured as a 'modern' solution for finding a spouse. The film culminates with a grand mass wedding of 100 couples, dressed in formal Western attire, who were actually married at the Beijing Hotel as a result of successful computerized matchmaking. The narrator concludes: 'Monogamy means equality between the sexes. This harmonious union of love, marriage, and sex life notes the result of evolution in history'.[13]

The minorities play an important role in China's official vision of history, nationality, and development. Their 'primitivity' contrasts with supposed Han 'modernity'. Minorities become a marked category, characterized by sensuality, colorfulness, and exotic custom. This contrasts with the 'unmarked' nature of Han identity. 'Han-ness' for the Chinese connotes civility and modernity, and this is perhaps why the more 'educated' minorities, such as the Manchu and Koreans, are never exoticized as sensual or primitive.[14] The Han, although they supposedly comprise nearly 92 per cent of China's population, are rarely described or studied as Han per se, whereas whole research centers and colleges are devoted to the study and teaching of minorities in China. Anthropologists of Euro-American society have begun to note a similar process in the unmarked majority category of 'whiteness'. Majorities, according to Virginia Dominguez's (1986) revealing study of Louisiana Creole identity, become 'White by Definition'. It is only the so-called 'ethnics' (a term in the Oxford English Dictionary that came into the English idiom denoting 'heathen') who are marked by 'culture'. Majorities by extension, become denaturalized, homogenized, and essentialized as 'same'. This is particularly true, according to Hobsbawm (1990:66), of Asia, where large blocks of Chinese, Japanese, and Koreans are thought to be 'homogeneous'.[15] In the West, it is 'whiteness' that is beginning to be problematized in the effort to scrutinize and come to terms with minority/majority discourses.[16] This has yet to be done with 'Han-ness' in China.

Exoticizing and Eroticizing Minorities in China

While minorities are no longer portrayed as barbarians in China, and many of the disparaging Chinese ideographs that formerly scripted their names with 'dog' and 'bug' radicals were changed in 1949, their portrayal in public the media is not only much more 'colorful' and 'cultural' than the Han (thanks, perhaps, to Stalin, whose four criteria adopted by the Chinese state for recognizing a people as a nationality included 'culture'), but also much more sensual. One of the favorite themes is that of minority women, especially the Dai (Thai), Hani, and Li, bathing in the river.

The image of Dai (Thai) and other minority women bathing in the river has become a *leit-motiv* for ethnic sensuality and often appears in stylized images throughout China, particularly on large murals in restaurants and public spaces. School children are often encouraged to make wood-block prints of Thai bathers and other exotic representations of minorities. One of the most famous incidents regarding the public portrayal of minority nudes in China was that at the Beijing Capital Airport.[17] Yuan Yunsheng returned from sixteen years of exile in Manchuria to be assigned by the state to paint a mural at the Beijing airport in 1979. He chose for his subject the Dai (Thai) people of Xishuangbana, whom he portrayed in his *Water Festival, Song of Life* on the background of a floral jungle motif, working, dancing, and, of course, bathing. However, the bathing mural on one side of the room eventually proved too problematic, and it was covered up in March 1980. Although the mural was proudly displayed in many official Chinese publications from October 1979 to early 1980, minority cadres from Yunnan began to object that the bathing mural was simply too offensive for public displayal and denigrating to minorities. It had also been causing a disruption in the dining room where it was exhibited because of the crowds of people who came to view it.

While the nudes eventually proved so controversial that the mural was covered up, and has since been uncovered, covered, and perhaps uncovered again, I would argue that as the murals were commissioned and approved in the first place – and displayed for nearly half a year – this indicated that the nude and even erotic portrayal of minority women was officially sanctioned.[18] Partly as a result of this popular image, many northern Chinese, like the friends of my taxi driver, have flocked to minority areas to voyeuristically gaze upon this minority 'custom', to the extent that few minority women now continue to bathe this way in the more densely populated areas. From the statement of the driver at the start of this chapter, and the reported presence of 'sex tours' to Yunnan and other minority areas, it can be argued that Thai and other minority women in China have become at a popular level, in Camille Paglia's (1990:40) terms, the ultimate 'sexual personae' for the 'Eastern Eye' of the broader Han Chinese society. This objectified minority woman exudes sexuality, the very opposite of the Nefertiti-like portrayal of chaste, reserved, and bound women, which Paglia argues became the model for the Western woman, but also came to denote 'modernity' for Chinese women as well, similarly restrained in their 'ritual bonds' (Paglia 1990:71). While it may be argued whether the images of minority women bathers are actually 'erotic' or 'sensual' in the eye of the beholder, they are clearly images that do not apply to Han women, who are generally represented as covered, conservative, and 'civilized' in most state publications. Nudity is often idealized and romanticized in China as being natural, free, and divorced from the constraints and realities of 'modern' life. Minorities become likely subjects for such romantic yearnings. Here the audience becomes an important issue, but as in any discussion of public culture, this is difficult to assess. Suffice it to note that in official public arenas, such as airports, hotels, and government offices, images of naked Han women are rarely found. Yet representations of unclothed minority women are frequently found in the official public sphere.[19]

In her perceptive article on the popular David Henry Hwang play, *M. Butterfly*, Marjorie Garber (1992:123) stresses the importance of clothing in making the link between gender representation and transvestism. The link between clothing and nationality, in which minorities are generally dressed in 'costumes', while the majorities merely wear 'clothes', is clearly made in Chinese museums, popular culture, and film. The changing of clothes and the altering of a restricted Han Self is precisely the basis for the 1985 movie, *Sacrificed Youth (Qing qun ji)*. In this film by the Beijing film studio's woman director, Zhang Nuanxin, a young Han woman from Beijing is sent down during the Cultural Revolution to the Thai (Dai) minority region of Yunnan in Xishuangbana, near the border of Burma and Thailand, where she is confronted by more 'liberated' Thai female customs. She wishes that she could be as free, and in a moment of rebellious assertion and self-transformation, she exchanges her drab, blue worker's clothes for a Thai sarong, whereupon she is pronounced 'beautiful' by her Thai hosts and girlfriends. This leads her further on the road to self-criticism and the cultural critique of repressed Han identity. In this instance of retailoring the nation, to borrow a phrase from Parker et al. (1992:120), for Duoli, the Han woman, cross-dressing becomes a transnational political act.[20]

In another scene of *Sacrificed Youth*, Thai women are shown in the classic cultural trope as freely bathing nude in the river – a rare bit of soft porn for a 1985 film in China. The protaganist of the film observes the Thai women swimming from a distance and wishes that she was not so inhibited by her Han mores that she did not feel she could join them without her swimsuit. 'Later', she declares, 'I learned to swim like they did, and I never wore a swimsuit again'. The bathing scene is prefaced by an encounter between a group of Thai young working women and men, who stop to sing antiphonal sexually suggestive songs to each other. Here, too, the sent-down Han observer says, 'I could not join them, which made me feel inhibited and culturally behind'. Admiration for minority sexual freedom and a 'natural' state of being becomes the foil by which Han majority and state-supported values are criticized. Both scenes are introduced and concluded by long shots of verdant, rushing waterfalls, suggesting perhaps that it is the natural sphere, with its cleansing element of water, that transforms what the state denigrates for Han as erotic and perhaps 'pornographic' into what is natural and unfettered.

Pornography in any form is restricted in China as illegal.[21] This includes any publication, foreign or domestic, that the state censors regard as morally inappropriate for its broader population. Foreign visitors in the past were regularly searched upon entry for magazines, books, and videos regarded as pornographic, and there are regular police raids upon a burgeoning black market industry of underground (literally) video parlors and markets for erotic literature.[22] While there has been a profusion of illicit pornographic material in the 1990s and it has become much more widely available in urban areas, it is still illegal and arrests may be made. In the mid-1980s a wide variety of magazines and books with sexually suggestive titles and scantily clothed men and women proliferated throughout the nation's bookstores and newsstands. Particularly popular was the *jian mei* ('make, or establish, beauty') genre of athletic magazines and playing cards which portrayed mainly Han Chinese and foreigners lifting weights or posing in skimpy bathing suits.[23] State censors prohibit depiction of total nudity and these publications were frequently reviewed and confiscated. Yet despite this severe restriction upon and preoccupation with the sale of nude representations of foreign and Han Chinese women, throughout China, in state-sponsored media as well as foreign and domestic tourist shops, images of nude minority women are publicly displayed, *National Geographic*-style, in various suggestive poses. Not only are nude representations of minorities displayed in galleries and public spaces like the Beijing Capital Airport, but they are readily available for sale in hotel tourist boutiques and minority crafts shops, such as the Central Institute for Nationalities Minority Handicrafts Store and the Nationalities Cultural Palace.

Scholars of traditional China are quite familiar with the long and widespread tradition of erotic art and literature, which had little to do with minorities. In *Sex in China*, the Chinese 'sexologist' Ruan Fangfu (1991:2) notes that the earliest sex manuals came from China, where one could find a classic sexological text dated in 168 B.C., *He Yin Yang Fang* (Methods of Intercourse between Yin and Yang), as well as the pre-Tang *Important Methods of the Jade Chamber, Book of the Mysterious Penetrating Master*, and other classical texts that now are found in comic book form through Taiwan and Southeast Asia, but are still restricted in China.[24] After surveying this abundant traditional literature, Ruan (1991:29) groups them in three categories: descriptions of the mystical benefits of sexual intercourse; the health benefits of intercourse if following certain theories and texts; and the inherent pleasurability of sex. The Dutch sinologist, Robert Van Gulik, collected hundreds of Chinese erotic sex manuals that proliferated in the late Qing, and popular classics like *Dream of the Red Chamber* and *Water Margin* are extremely explicit and rarely published in their unabridged forms.[25]

If erotic images and public portrayals of Han Chinese sexuality are an acknowledged aspect of everyday life in pre-1949 China, Taiwan, Hong Kong, and Singapore, why have they been so absent, so repressed, in the China mainland since 1949? George Mosse's (1985) argument linking totalitarianism and sexuality might have some bearing here. Mosse argues that unlicensed sexuality represents a threat to totalizing regimes. If Foucault (1980:24) is correct that the 'policing of sex' is an important component in maintaining the unmitigated power of the central state, then China's repressive prudishness is perhaps the best example of this endeavor. The policing of sex tends also to coincide roughly with radical leftist authoritarian campaigns in China: for example, the 1966–1976 Cultural Revolution, the 1984 Spiritual Pollution campaign, and the more recent post-Tiananmen 1989–90 Six Evils campaign, in which public sexuality, pornography, and prostitution were all condemned as 'feudalist' and thought to be an insidious part of the 'democratic' or liberal movements that led to the crackdowns. In July 1990, the Vice President of China's Supreme People's Court, Lin Zhu, issued a new decree that traffickers in prostitution and pornography would be subject to the death penalty.[26] China is one of the few non-Islamic nations where prostitutes, pimps, and purveyors of pornography are routinely rounded up, imprisoned, and even, perhaps, executed under the 'hoodlum offenses' statute.[27] Slightly explicit films such as Zhang Yimou's *Red Sorghum* and more recently *Ju Dou*, all proposed, approved, funded, and produced by the state during more liberal periods, are routinely banned once more radical political winds prevail.[28] In other studies, Ardener (1987:114) and Mayer (1975:260) have shown how 'prudery' serves to reinforce, and even invent, social hierarchies. In China, enforced prudishness and controlled fertility among the Han, as opposed to represented minority sensuality, serves the state's national project of emphasizing Han solidarity, civility, and modernity.

Sex becomes one of the most public of private contested political spaces in China. In a state that regularly monitors the monthly menses of its women workers, engages in Malthusian birth-planning programs, and strictly regulates the age at which one can marry (21 for women, 22 for men), it is not surprising that sexuality has become highly politicized. Elsewhere, I have discussed the role that liberated sexuality played in the Tiananmen Square student protest, particularly in the students' public attempt to wrest political control of their bodies away from the state (Gladney 1990c). Here, I am arguing that it is the repression and control of sexuality among the Han, and its open representation among the minorities, that demonstrate the important role eroticization of the engendered minority Other plays in the Han construction of Self.

Painting Minorities: The Invention of the Yunnan School

In the early 1980s, several northern Han painters were assigned to Southern China to paint minorities and other 'appropriate' subjects, leading to what has since been called the 'Yunnan School' (*Yunnan Huapai*) of modern Chinese painting. The Yunnan School has been regarded as one of the first distinct 'schools' to emerge in contemporary Chinese art and has had a tremendous influence on the current generation of artists in China. In the early 1980s, Jiang Tiefang, Ting Shao Kuang, and He Neng became known in China for challenging accepted norms of painting, particularly including nudes with accentuated breasts in brilliant colors. This led, according to Joan Lebold Cohen, critic and dealer of Chinese art, to the founding of the 'Yunnan School of Heavy Oil Painting in 1982' (Cohen 1988). It is significant that Ting Shao Kuang, one of the most prominent and successful members of the 'school' has stated repeatedly that there is no such organized 'school'; rather, his and other similar work represents a style of art that is new in its subject matter (mainly minorities), and style (use of heavy oil and bright colors in abstract forms). In a 11 July 1992, taping interview with Ting Shao Kuang by the Los Angeles Chinese television station, Channel 18, Ting stated:

'There is no such thing as the Yunnan Art School. We are all different artists from China trying to revolutionize the repressed mainland Chinese painting through the use of minority subjects, sexuality, and heavy oil colors, in often Western-influenced styles'. It is revealing that Ting should now say this, since one of his well-known paintings is entitled 'Dawn of the Yunnan Art School' (Ting 1990:11), and he has become one of the wealthiest and most successful representatives of the Yunnan Art School style. The 'Yunnan School' may very well exist only in the West, where it has met with tremendous financial success. Cohen (1988), claiming that the school represents a 'renaissance' in Chinese painting, suggests that the most significant event in the development of the Yunnan School was when He Neng, Jiang Tiefang, and Liu Shaohui were commissioned to produce paintings for a documentary film project 'featuring the costumes, habits and environment of the various minority peoples living in Yunnan' (Cohen 1988:5). By travelling to the minority areas, Cohen explains, the northern Han artists found that they could express many of their artistic interests through the color and style of minority representation.

Liu Bingjiang's *Nude* (in Cohen 1987:46), shown at the Oil Painting Research Association Exhibition in Beijing 1979, is clearly a minority representation, indicative of early Yunnan School tendencies. On a colorful background, a dark-skinned female nude is realistically portrayed kneeling with her hands on the ground in a submissive posture, wearing nothing but her jewelry. Given the tapestry background, her jewelry, and most importantly, the posture, the painting is one of the earliest works in the Yunnan School style. According to Cohen (1987:46), her kneeling position is not within the officially sanctioned 'academic painting repertoire' and thus suggests to Cohen a 'South Asian' influence. It is important to note that the bracelets she wears clearly resemble shackles and, combined with the posture, the painting evokes erotic subservience and submission.

Unlike abstract Han figure paintings, it has been and still is officially acceptable to vividly and realistically paint, exhibit, and sell minority nude artwork. In another example, Chen Zhangpeng's oil of a nude is appropriately titled *Innocence*. Reflecting Western influence, especially Gauguin, Picasso, and even Andrew Wyeth, this painting situates the exoticized minority subject in both the past and the present. Cohen's caption explains: 'Chen's sketchy study of a nude kneeling next to a tiger expresses the ancient Chinese idea that the untrammeled nature of the wild creature is innocent. Likewise, *primitive* people, uncorrupted by civilization, are innocent, a concept similar to Rousseau's romantic notion of the noble savage' (Cohen 1987:65, emphasis in original).

The 'innocence' of minorities in China contrasts well with representations of Han Chinese women as the modern workers of the industrialized nation, who Chairman Mao once declared, 'Hold up half the sky'. The notion that the minorities represent the 'primitive' and beautiful 'noble savage', unsullied by Chinese political machinations and the degradations of modern society, is an important theme for China's modern artists. It may very well represent a Gauguinesque romanticization of the 'savage' in contrast to the modern alienation of Chinese urban life. It may also be viewed as a cultural critique, or rejection, of modern Han China; an accepted venue for criticizing the depersonalizing, totalizing state.

In an interview with the Yunnan painter, Xiao Jiahe, a former student of Jiang Tiefang, and himself a minority, the son of an intermarriage between a Han and a Jingpo, stated that he liked to paint minorities because 'They are pure and beautiful. It makes me feel peaceful when I paint them'. When I asked him why seven of the ten paintings in his exhibition, with such titles as *Ancient Girl*, *Tara's Toilette*, *Summer Solstice*, *Blossoms*, *Morning Prayers*, and *Homage to the Spring*, portrayed minority women in kneeling, submissive poses, with voluptuous scantily clothed figures, he said: 'Because I like the human body, and I think this portrays the essence of female beauty. It's also difficult to capture an entire woman's body in a small painting if she is standing' (personal interview, 30 July 1991). It is significant that in later conversations, Xiao explained that when he came to the United States, he was urged by American gallery owners and agents, particulary the Allen H. Fingerhut Group, who strongly promote most of the Yunnan Art School paintings (and published Cohen's 1988 book on the 'Yunnan School'), to increase his use of motifs and colors popularized by the Yunnan Art School, since these works sold well in the U.S. 'They told me to use more pastel, gold, and bright colors; to paint beautiful, large-breasted women in elongated form, and to use 'ethnic' clothing. I even included a lot of African clothing because of my interest in Africa. I tried to make my art look more erotic (*xing aide*) but not pornographic (*se qing*)' (personal interview, 30 July 1991). Though most of his artwork was enthusiastically received, comments from viewers at one of his exhibits were critical of his representation of minority women and caused him to reevaluate the Yunnan Art School style. 'I have since rejected the Yunnan Art School', he told me in a later interview (29 February 1992). 'They are only interested in making money, repeating the same old salable paintings. It is too repetitious. It is not art . . . I refuse to jeopardize my artistic career just to make money'.[29]

By objectifying minority women as colorful, exotic, and erotic, by denying them their individuality and subjectivity, these Chinese artists are engaging in an anthropological enterprise well established by Lewis Henry Morgan, Franz Boas and other early American historicists who posited a 'common psyche' shared by all 'primitives'. Though Boas and later anthropologists stressed individual contributions to the construction of cultural artifacts, and through painstaking ethnographic work brought to light the individual contributions of many 'primitive artists', his commitment to the notion of a common cultural determinism and psyche in artistic construction nevertheless contributed to the objectification of the minority Other. In his pathbreaking 1927 study of *Primitive Art*, Boas revealingly wrote: 'The same motif recurs over and over again in the tales of primitive people, so that a large mass of material collected from the same tribe is liable to be very monotonous, and after a certain point has been reached only new variants of old themes are obtained' (Boas 1927 [1955]:330). It is precisely the repetitive nature of 'primitive' art construed as generic, unsigned, and anonymous, that makes it so attractive to the 'modern' collector: Since primitives are all similar in their artistic representations, their artwork and thought patterns homogenized by a uniform culture, why should one piece of art need a signature? According to Sally Price, it is its anonymity and timelessness that make primitive art so attractive to the time-bound, modern individual: 'In the Western understanding of things, a work originating outside of the Great Traditions must have been produced by an unnamed figure who represents his community and whose craftsmanship respects the dictates of its age-old traditions' (Price 1989:56).

Significantly, the use of 'traditional' minority art, colors, and styles may be said to have paved the way for the public reintroduction of the Han nude in China, but only in a highly stylized, Picasso-like form. Western motifs, styles, and color, with minority subjects, become a thinly veiled means of challenging traditional Chinese artistic conventions. Han female nudes, when they are officially and publicly represented at all, are generally in highly stylized forms, often in the Picasso genre, as a famous oil, *Daughter of the Sea*, by Jiang Tiefang demonstrates. An exhibit brochure features a print of Jiang's 1988 *Playing Water*, an eroticized and Picassoesque portrayal of the Yunnan Thai water festival, including black sensuous dancing figure, with large breasts and nipples accentuated in bright red. The back of the promotional brochure reads:

> Jiang Tie-Feng is the most influential contemporary artist of the People's Republic of China. His 'Yunnan School' represents the first new Chinese art movement in 700 years, and the rebirth of artistic traditions that have been repressed since the Ming Dynasty.
>
> (Fingerhut Group Publishers, painting brochure, 1992)

The Picassoesque portrayal of Han women and the abstract representations of the minority women have become so popular now in the West that not only have Chinese artists like Jiang Tiefang, He Neng and Ting Shao Kuang become extraordinarily successful and wealthy, purchasing houses in Bel Air and Beverly Hills, but they have spawned a whole lucrative industry now sweeping the upscale art industry in China and abroad. After he visited a Shanghai exhibition of his work in Spring 1992, Ting told me that he was literally mobbed by his fans. 'If I had painted Han that way when I was in China before, they probably would have arrested me. Now I am a hero' (personal interview, 11 July 1992).

The Austin Galleries is a series of chic art dealerships with galleries in Chicago, Detroit, San Francisco, Carmel, and Laguna Beach. At the well-appointed Chicago gallery, I was attracted in November 1991 by a large Yunnan School painting of a minority dancer prominently displayed in the glass case fronting onto Michigan Avenue. Not only were there several Yunnan-School-style paintings by a Han Chinese immigrant, Wu Jian, but there were similar versions by a certain artist, Wong Shue, who turned out to be originally from Jamaica. The gallery consultant, Bella Cipkin, explained that the genre is the best-selling artwork in the gallery, with large paintings selling for $8,000–$10,000, and that many artists are beginning to copy the flowing, colorful style. Cipkin noted: 'The mauve colors and liberating minority art in its breathtaking sensuality go well with the furnishings in professionals' homes'. She also went on to suggest that one of the reasons the art might be becoming more popular in the U.S. was that it represented minority art: 'What with the problems in Tibet and all, Americans want to support the ethnic people in China all they can'. Again, it is important to note here that very little of the Yunnan-School art is produced by minorities themselves.

Marginalizing the Center of Chinese Film

'Minorities film' has followed oil painting in reforming the accepted norms of Chinese taste. Paul Clark (1987a:20), critic of Chinese film, argues that it is the 'propensity of minorities film to explore normally avoided subjects' that made them so successful and influential. In a Channel 4 documentary on 'New Chinese Cinema', Wu Tianming, the director of the now-famous Xi'an Film Studio, where many of the influential 'fifth generation' filmmakers were working (including Zhang Yimou, Tian Zhuangzhuang, and Chen Kaige), quoted a Chinese proverb: 'When there's no tiger on the mountain, the monkey is king', indicating that it is distance from the centers of power such as Beijing and Shanghai that allowed his studio the freedom for exploration. In the Channel 4 documentary, the young director of the new, more realistic minority films, *On the Hunting Ground* (1985) and *Horsethief* (1986), Tian Zhuangzhuang, explained why he chose to film in minority areas:

> I had several reasons. For one, Beijing Film Studios wouldn't let us direct when we were assigned there . . . . *On the Hunting Ground* and *Horsethief* may deal with regional minorities [lit: minority nationalities], but they're actually about the fate of the whole Chinese nation.
>
> (*New Chinese Cinema* 1988)

According to Paul Clark in his analysis of *Chinese Cinema*, it is the search for a 'national style' (*minzu fengge*) that was lacking among the Han that directors found among minorities. 'Paradoxically, one of the most effective ways to make films with "Chinese" style was to go to the most "foreign" cultural areas in the nation' (Clark 1987b:101). The search for a national identity in China, apparently became more readily understood in opposition and contrast to minority cultures thought to be more vibrant and easily objectified than that of the amorphous, invented Han Chinese Self. Through the representation of minorities as sensual, liberated, and colorful, Chinese filmmakers and artists found a 'metaphorical resource':[30] They were able to introduce taboo and often illegal art into the Chinese cultural mainstream. These artistic motifs then eventually influenced the broader Han majority-accepted cultural repertoire of artistic convention, leading to the establishment of a 'national' style and identity.

Through the national medium of officially approved film, Han national identity becomes clearly objectified. In Zhang Nuanxin's *Sacrificed Youth*, two scenes depict an explicit rejection of sensual involvement by the female protagonist, precisely because she is a 'Han'. In the first instance, Duoli, the Beijing Han woman sent down to the countryside, is teased while gathering firewood in the forest by her Thai coworkers about an ox-cart ride home from a Beijing male she had met in the marketplace. When she protests that there is nothing between them, her coworkers chide, 'Don't be afraid to tell us!' She replies: 'We are Hans, you know, we don't start love affairs that young' [*literal translation*: 'We are Han people, we don't talk about love that early'].[31]

In the second instance, she is sitting alone with the very same Han youth late at night in the dark, romantic forest, listening to the enchanting music of a distant Thai celebration.

> *Duoli*: What are they singing?
> *Male friend*: Can't you tell? 'My lover's hands are tender and fair'.
> *Duoli*: Don't they find it embarrassing?
> *Male*: Why should they? Isn't it better to speak out one's feelings? Unlike we Hans, always beating around the bush.
> *Duoli*: Speak out yourself then, no one tries to stop you.
> *Male*: But can you?
> *Duoli*: Why not?
> *Male*: OK. What's on your mind now?
> *Duoli*: I . . . I find . . . it's getting cold. Let's go home.
> *Male*: Is that all?
> *Duoli*: Yes.
> *Male*: [while gazing at her in her sarong]: You are a Han from head to toe.
>   [*Literal*: No matter what you say, you still are a Han]

In an interview with Zhang Nuanxin, the director of *Sacrificed Youth*, published in *Camera Obscura*, Zhang states that she made the film to encourage the expression of Han female subjectivity and beauty:

> After I read the original short story by Zhang Manling, I felt there were many things in it that I'd experienced myself. I'd been down in the countryside, too. I'd felt that the older and less attractive clothes were, the better. When we were very young, we couldn't make ourselves attractive, nor could we express love.
>
>   (Zhang Nuanxin 1989:21)

Indeed, it is the need for self-discovery, awareness, and expression that Chris Berry (1991:6) has argued pervades much of 'women's cinema' in China. Yet it is only by going to minority areas and contrasting the repressed, bounded Han female self to the constructed minority Other as unrestrained and beautiful that these goals can be explored on the screen. This goes against Julia Kristeva's (1986:45) utopian construction of the position of women in Confucianized Chinese society, and though it is framed as a Western critique, I agree with Rey Chow (1990:6) that it nevertheless idealizes the position of women in China to an inexcusable degree.

There are important parallels here to the *National Geographic* tradition of the sexual portrayal of the Other for a conservative readership, which generally regards such portrayals of its 'own' as pornographic.[32] Clearly, in both cases there is a hierarchy of self: voyeurism of the Other is permissible when they are regarded as less familiar, less civilized, than one's own. As Paul Clark has argued in an *East-West Film Journal* article, 'Ethnic Minorities in Chinese Films: Cinema and the Exotic', film in China from the beginning was regarded as a foreign medium, a venue for viewing the exotic and strange. When China became closed to the outside world after 1949, minorities for the first time *took the place of foreigners* as subjects of the exotic. As Clark (1987a:15–16) explains: 'Film audiences could travel to 'foreign' lands without crossing the nation's borders'.

But I would go farther than Clark's emphasis on fascination with the exotic. In China there is more to it than the typical *National Geographic*-style romanticization of the primitive, which one might argue is found in almost any society. Here, the state is intimately tied to, in control of, and provides funding for the politicized process of portraying the Other. In Said's (1978) terms, the state has turned its gaze upon the internal other, engaging in a formalized, commodified oriental orientalism, that may be focussed on the minorities but represents a long tradition of fascination with the outsider in Chinese society.[33] The real issue here is why the state should choose to explicitly support such an enterprise. I argue that the politics of this representation of the minority Other are both an extension of power-relation practices in the traditional Chinese state, as well as a product of China's rise as a nation-state.

Contesting and Coopting Otherness: Eroticizing (Even) the Muslims

While minorities appear to have had little choice in the way they have been exoticized in the media, and Han must also deal with their *de-*

exoticized essentialization, there have been several attempts at contesting that restricted space. Not only did the student democracy movement emphasize the sensual, the unique, and the individual, but recent films such as *River Elegy* (*He Shang*), *Sacrificed Youth*, *Red Sorghum*, and *Ju Dou* all represent various popular levels of contestation (see Wang 1989:32). Minorities have also attempted to voice their objections. The covering up of the nude bathing portion of Yuan Yunsheng's Beijing Capital Airport painting was partly due to complaints from Yunnan minority cadres. In Urumqi, Xinjiang, I witnessed a large group of Uygur Muslim artists rallying in protest in 1987 over an exhibition at the Overseas Chinese Hotel of portrayals of Uygurs and other Central Asians by Han artists that they claimed denigrated them as either too humorous or too sensual. Paintings primarily by Han artists portrayed the Uygurs singing, dancing, riding donkeys and balancing watermelons on their heads. Worse yet, many paintings portrayed Uygur women in revealing skirts engaged in erotic dances, such as Ting Shao Kuang's *Silk Road*, which portrays a bare-breasted minority woman on a background of deserts and camel caravans. For many Uygurs, these representations are particularly offensive, as they regard themselves as conservative Muslims.

While one might be prepared to allow for the possibility that southwestern minorities may have more 'open' sexual practices than the typical Han in China today, they are not the only minorities portrayed as sensual and erotic. While Thai women did traditionally bathe in the nude (though many may fear to now), and the Moso as a possible matrilineal society may very well have allowed extramarital sexual practice at the matrilocal residence, the Uygurs and other Muslim peoples can hardly be said to be more publicly erotic or sensual than the Han in their traditional culture (see Gladney 1990b). Uygur women are widely known throughout China to traditionally cover themselves with *purdah*-like head scarves and wraps that envelop their entire faces and hair (known as *chumperdah* in Uygur). Unlike the Middle East *purdah*, where eyes are generally exposed, Uygur *chumperdah* cover the entire face. As Muslims, they are generally much more conservative than Han Chinese in the public sexual sphere. Despite their protestations, these representations continue, underscoring the extraordinary contrast between the Han and the minority spectacle in China.

Like many tourist hotels, the Sheng Tang ('Flourishing Tang') Hotel in northeast Beijing has a tile mural of a Tang-dynasty minority dancer, with accentuated nude breasts, in the center of its main dining hall. On the opposite walls, erotic stylized murals from the Dunhuang Buddhist grottoes grace the dining room. Like many public places in China, the sensual 'Flying *Absarases*' are an officially sanctioned art subject (Cohen 1987:17–20). I once asked a group of Han scholars viewing this mural if they thought the dancers were minorities or Han, and they all said minorities, even though the theme is from the Buddhist caves of Dunhuang, supposedly the cradle of *Chinese* Buddhist religious tradition. While Buddhism became transformed into a 'Chinese' religion, its sensual representation in art and absarases has apparently retained the attributes of foreigners and minorities, not Han.

In the Chinese tourist pictorial, *A Picture Album of Turpan Landscape and Custom* (1985:16), a Han artist, Gu Shengyue, portrays the sensual images of the Dunhuang caves, with floating female absarases and their accentuated breasts, hovering above him, almost as if to say: 'Though these Uygur claim to be Muslim, we know what they are really thinking about when they sing and dance'. They have become yet another landscape in the national repertoire of China. In another portrait from the same pictorial, sensual Buddhist figures are portrayed hovering above ecstatic Uygur dancers (*Picture Album* 1985:18). Central Asian dance and artistic display come to represent a metaphor of sensuality and eroticism for Han China, even though the region is now dominated by Muslims.

Extremely realistic is the figure painting *Nude with Apples* (in Cohen 1987:101) by Tang Muli, a Han artist who has travelled widely abroad. With a Central Asian *doppa* hat, sitting upon a Xinjiang carpet and eating apples, often produced in China's dry, cold northwest, the realist painting of a complete frontal nude is clearly meant to portray a Central Asian minority, although the model may very well be Han. Perhaps Tang Muli knew that a Han woman could rarely be portrayed so vividly and realistically. Yet, this is despite the fact that Muslims are the most conservative of all peoples in China.

The last painting of eroticized Muslims I will note is also the most startling: Zhao Yixiong's 1979 oil, *The Awakening of Tarim*. Of this controversial painting, Cohen (1987:54) writes: 'Tarim symbolizes the beginnings of modernization on the edges of the great Takla Makan, China's most terrible desert. She awakens on a vibrant patchwork of Silk Road images: camels, mosques, oil derricks, Buddhist deities, oases, grapes, gourds, and pomegranates'. While paintings of Uygur and other Muslims by Han artists such as Huang Zhou have had a long history in China, they were never so eroticizied as Zhao Yixiong's. His painting makes clear the dramatic linkage between nationality, woman, and modernity: By depicting his nude Uygur female subject as 'awakening' from the midst of her traditional life to a 'modern' world filled with oil rigs, airplanes, and nuclear installations, Zhao Yixiong perhaps suggests that it is only in throwing off the traditional minority culture of Islam, with its covered women, mosques, and caravans, that Tarim, the woman and the region, can be modernized. With a mosque minaret, and camel caravans emerging from between her thighs, this painting would, of course, be extremely offensive to Uygurs. Nevertheless, it was commissioned to be painted by Zhao Yixiong, who, as a painter for the Chinese Museum of Chinese History and Revolution, is employed by the state to represent the Other in strikingly similar orientalist fashion to that of Alloula's *The Colonial Harem*.

Cohen informs us that Zhao's painting was not allowed to be exhibited by the Chinese authorities. One might assume this was because of its explicit, erotic nature. Yet, according to Cohen (1987:54): 'The [Oil Painting Research Association] excluded it because of the green streak on the woman's buttocks – an Expressionist gesture that was apparently thought to be offensive'. Extraordinarily, *expressionistic representation* was rejected as improper for minority portraiture in favor of explicit realism. By contrast, *realistic representation* of the Han female body has been restricted by the Chinese state. Just as the subordination of Chinese women reifies the elevated position of men, so the exoticization of minorities essentializes the imagined identity of the Han and reaffirms Han feelings of superiority. Public, state-sponsored minority representation as both more sensual and more primitive than the Han supports the state's agenda: With the proper educational and economic progress they will eventually attain the modernity that the Han have attained, and enter into the same civilized restrictions under the authority of the state as vanguard. Symbolic tribute by minorities becomes an important link with China's past, establishing their own feudal pasts, and a signal of who will lead the future. It also legitimates the state's authority to enforce homogeneity, morality, and 'civility' among the nearly 92 per cent Han majority, while difference is 'temporarily' tolerated among the 'backward' minorities. In a socialist society that claims to be post-Confucian, gender and ethnic hierarchies continue to be articulated in a discourse of morality – the proper ordering of the social universe. It is precisely resistance to that order that makes the film *Ju Dou* so controversial.

Conclusion: Woman as Minority and Other in China

The furor over the nominating of the film *Ju Dou* for an academy award in 1991 was primarily due to its offensiveness to Chinese moral and hierarchical sensibilities, according to the press (Wu Dunn 1991:B1). Not surprisingly, *Ju Dou* was made by a product of the Xi'an film studio, director Zhang Yimou, who starred in Wu Tianming's iconoclastic film *Old Well*. Ju Dou, a young bride, is physically abused for not being able to become pregnant by her elderly, probably impotent, husband. She is beaten repeatedly, tied, and even pinned down by a horse-saddle on which her elderly husband sits while he sexually abuses her, in what may probably be China's first, and perhaps last, bondage-style film. In order to save herself (the old man had already beaten to death two previous wives), she seduces his adopted son, and the resulting story of their infidelities is what many Chinese found offensive. Just as Ju Dou is expected to accept her fate, even at the point of death, so are Han Chinese women required to restrict their sexuality in the service of the state. Similarly, minority women are allowed to be portrayed erotically because that, too, serves the interests of the regime. This may also be a contributing factor in the state's general exemption of most minorities from the birth-planning program.[34] Minority women are encouraged to be fecund, their bodies are less controllable than those of the ritually bound Han women. Although minority under-population is the main reason usually given for their exemption from birth-planning restrictions, perhaps an additional metaphorical reason is that minorities represent uncontrolled sensuality, fertility and reproductivity; Han represent controlled, civilized productivity. Yet it is primarily not women's bodies that are at issue, it is the state's (and by extension, the patriarchal male's) control of them.

In a fascinating parallel to the 'Thai-bathers' motif pervading much of minority art, there is a critical moment in *Ju Dou* in which Yang Tianqing, the adopted son, voyeuristically observes Ju Dou bathing through a hole in the washroom wall. This scene bears striking resemblance to the voyeurism of the Miao men and film viewers of Miao women bathers in the *Amazing Marriage Customs* film and the bathing scene in *Sacrificed Youth* described above. In each case it is water and bathing that lead to the voyeuristic gaze and the construction of the sexual object. As he enlarges the hole for a better view, she discovers him and covers the hole with straw from the inside of the washroom. Later, she once again finds that he has removed the straw from the inside for an unobstructed view. This time, however, in a radical departure from traditional Chinese female modesty (but more like the Miao and Thai bathers), she actually attracts his attention by deliberately making washing sounds, and then allows him to view her naked body, savagely marked by his adopted father's beatings. The shock engendered by her beautiful but grotesquely bruised body both compels and humiliates the viewer. Similarly, Han voyeurism of minority women and the submission of Han women to the patriarchal social order are what the state, for its own self-perpetuating reasons, considers proper in China.

Zhang Yimou's reversal of those roles in *Ju Dou* delegitimates the state's authority to objectivize the Other, both woman and minority, and this may be an important factor in the state's attempt to prevent its nomination for an academy award. By turning her gaze directly back on the adopted son, Ju Dou both humiliates him and establishes her subjectivity, resisting his use of her as an object of sexual desire. By taking her affairs into her own hands, and later seducing him, she establishes her own identity and asserts individuality.

Minorities, too, by allowing the objectivizing gaze of the state-sponsored media, establish their identity and right to a voice in their own affairs, appropriating and turning, whenever possible, these objectivizing moves to their own benefit. In this way, the maintenance and assertion of minority 'culture', no matter how exoticized or contrived, may be seen as a form of resistance. By participating in their 'training' by the Han Chinese state, supporting minority art and culture, they often find ways to promote values that may be contrary to the state's modernizing program. These glimpses of a more naturalized, colorful, liberated and sensual lifestyle, that urban Han Chinese now find so alien to their own living situations, contributes to their popularity as colonized and gendered subjects (see Chatterjee 1989:624). It also might explain why minorities and their exoticized portrayal in the Yunnan Art School are extremely popular in the West, where many long for a similar naturalized lifestyle, often as a way of critiquing China's image as a totalitarian homogenizing state. Successful marketing of these images in the global capitalist economy perpetuates minority/majority discourses in China and abroad. The appearance within and without China of books, courses, and institutions devoted to the study of 'China's Minorities' reflects this homogenization: the pretense that one could draw a clear line between the minorities and the rest of 'Han' China. This chapter has argued otherwise, attempting to directly link minority with majority discourses in the public sphere. In China and elsewhere, constructing minority identities is directly related to that of the majority. As Han-ness is related to 'whiteness', so the majority in China is invented as an unmarked category, courtesy of a subjugated, stigmatized, and identified minority.

Though alienated moderns may wax nostalgic over exoticized representations of imagined pasts, the belated arrival in China of Hobsbawm's (1991:163) universalized 'nationality principle', coupled with the government's expressed desire to be reckoned as a 'modern nation-state', indicates that the identification, and exploitation, of minorities for tourist dollars and nationalization programs will mean their continued stigmatization as exoticized subjects – a stigmata that they may only infrequently turn to their own benefit. Minority co-optation of these motifs may help increase their own autonomy, turning the tables of representation. Yet these attempts at subjectivity and independence will always be threatening to any totalizing, objectivizing state that seeks homogeneity of the majority at the expense of the minority. It is no surprise that *Ju Dou* was banned and that minorities are encouraged to do little more than sing and dance in the People's Republic.

Notes

1 This paper by Dru C. Gladney first appeared in *The Journal of Asian Studies*, vol.53, no.1 (February 1994), pp. 92–123. Reprinted with permission of the Association for Asian Studies, Inc. The original photographs and photographic plates are not reproduced here. Minor stylistic changes have been made for the sake of editorial consistency.

2 This paper has benefited from presentations at the following institutions: The University of Wisconsin-Milwaukee; the Tri-University East Asia Area Committee Seminar at the National Humanities Center, Chapel Hill; the Regional Seminar of the Center for Chinese Studies, University of California, Berkeley; the China Seminar of the University of California, San Diego; the Anthropology Colloquium, University of Washington; and the Visual Anthropology Seminar of the University of Southern California. For critical comments and thoughtful suggestions, I am particularly indebted to Benedict Anderson, Wimal Dissanayake, Thomas Gold, James Hevia, Janet Hoskins, Huang Hai-yen, Ira Lapidus, Nancy Lutkehaus, Frederick Wakeman, and Geoffrey White. My 1991 trip to China was supported by grants from UNESCO and the American Academy of Arts and Sciences. The views expressed in this chapter are the author's alone and do not represent any organization.

3 For recent explorations of Chinese identity, see the Dittmer and Kim (1993) collection, *China's Quest for a National Identity*; three chapters on China in Harumi Befu's (1993) collection, *Cultural Nationalism in East Asia*; as well

as two special issues of the journal *Dædalus* (Spring 1991 and Spring 1993). The 'Confucianist' argument has been most recently rearticulated by Samuel Huntington (1993:25), and more classically by Mary Wright (1957). Interestingly, none of these authors has problematized the connection between 'Han' and 'Chinese', which, historically suspicious as it will be shown, nevertheless still dominates Chinese discussions of majority/minority national identity (see Yang Kun 1992).

4 Personal communication. For my earlier critique of the 'marginalizing' discourse regarding minorities in China, and its reliance upon Shils's (1975) center-periphery model, see Gladney (1991:94–96); see Appadurai (1986:745–55) for a general theoretical critique of the model and its influence upon social theory.

5 Although the Hui do not possess their own separate language, and are known for eschewing the 'songs and dances' by which many minorities are iconographically represented in China (see Gladney 1991:21–30), in this program they sing and dance like the rest of the performers. Instead of detailed lyrics from a traditional New Year's folk song (of which there are none), the Hui sing their traditional Arabic greeting, *A'salam Alei Cum* ('peace be with you'), over and over. The Chinese subtitles translated this formulaic greeting as '*Pengyou Nihao*' (Friend, hello).

6 In her informative M.A. thesis, Lufkin (1990:3) observes that minority folk tales, like performers, are similarly disproportionately represented. Seventy-five per cent of the more than 70 published folk tales in the magazine *Chinese Literature* from 1951–1976 were by national minorities. I am grateful for her making the M.A. thesis available to me after my presentation of an earlier version of this paper.

7 For a discussion of Hechter's theory regarding 'Internal Colonialism' and its relevance to understanding the minority situation in the former Soviet Union and China, see Gladney (1994 a).

8 In Aijaz Ahmad's (1992) controversial critique of the 'Three Worlds' notion, he accuses Edward Said, Fredic Jameson, and Salman Rushdie of subscribing to an essentialized 'third world' of non-Western literatures. For a response to Ahmad, see the Fall 1993 issue of *Public Culture*, especially Sprinker's (1993) critical assessment.

9 For a description of the rising salience of the new 'politics of difference' in China, see Edward Friedman (1994) and Gladney (1994c).

10 These excerpts from Fei's 1989 article are taken from the English transcript of the Tanner lecture, which has not yet been published.

11 The 'national question' was hotly debated in the Second and Third Internationals, and strong differences of interpretation about national identity, social evolution, and the relation between class and ethnicity emerged between Stalin and Lenin. China was most influenced by Stalin's conclusion that nationalist self-determination was a strategic, but temporary, necessity for the Bolshevik cause (see Connor 1984:67–101). For an excellent summary of this debate, see Blaut (1987).

12 From *Amazing Marriage Customs*, directed by Suen Wan and Guo Wuji (1992). The text cited here and below is taken directly from the English subtitles, with Chinese and some literal translations provided in brackets. A similar film survey of minority marriage customs produced in Hong Kong by

Wah Ngai Film Production and King Video is entitled 'The Inside Story of the Great Southwestern Forbidden Borderlands' (*Da Xinan Jinjing Tanmi*, 1990). This film, however, includes an incident in which the Bai nationality in Yunnan is described as being so 'hospitable' that the host offers his wife to the guest as a sexual partner. The 'custom' is then enacted explicity on film. *Y Na Na: Woman of a Thousand Places* (1992), a film by Yvette M. Torell, replicates this exoticized portrayal of Dai, Naxi, Bai, and Tibetan women in Yunnan and Tibet, complete with the now mandatory Thai bathing scene. In a well-worn, inaccurate representation of the 'Naxi' matrilineality (see McKhann's 1989 excellent critique of this characterization), Torell's introduction invites the viewer to learn from their 'matriarchy'. It is noteworthy that these films, like minority representation in general in China, focus almost exclusively on women and sexual relations.

13 The linkage of matrilineality with existing 'primitive' minorities is supported by descriptions of several groups in *China's Minority Nationalities* (Ma Yin, 1989, the translation of the standard text, *Zhongguo shaoshu minzu*). For example, 'The Jino matriarchal society gave way to a patriarchal one some 300 years ago. But the Jinos were still in the transitional stage from primitivity to a class society at the time the People's Republic was founded in 1949' (Ma 1989:334).

14 I would like to thank one of the anonymous reviewer for bringing this point about Koreans and Manchu to my attention. The Korean minority is the most educated and one of the most economically advanced groups in China (see Lee 1986).

15 Eric Hobsbawm supports this widely accepted idea of Asian majority mono-ethnicity in his classic work, *Nations and Nationalism Since 1780* (Cambridge: Cambridge University Press, 1990), p. 66, '. . . China, Korea, and Japan, which are indeed among the extremely rare examples of historic states composed of a population that is ethnically almost or entirely homogeneous'. Hobsbawm continues: 'Thus of the (non-Arab) Asian states today Japan and the two Koreas are 99% homogeneous, and 94% . . . of the People's Republic of China are Han' (p. 66, n. 37).

16 Dominguez (1986:140ff.) chronicles the 'veritable explosion' of defenses of white Creole ancestry in New Orleans once increasing polarization of white/black racial categories called attention to their identification with 'blacks' despite their physical appearance as 'whites'. For problematizing 'whiteness', see also Frankenberg's (1993) excellent *White Women, Race Matters: The Social Construction of Whiteness*.

17 See Lufkin's (1990:35ff.) interesting analysis of the offensive and controversial nature of this mural. Unlike most more subdued minority art, this mural, she argues, was too confrontative and too publicly exposed. For photographs of Yuan Yunsheng's airport murals, see 'Magnificent Paintings: The Murals of the Beijing International Airport', *China Pictorial* 1980 (1):18–31; and Cohen 1987:28–36.

18 I was recently told that Yuan Yunsheng's mural was uncovered in 1990, and has now been restored to its original eroticized form. Given the post-1989 political climate in Beijing, this may reflect another attempt to repress difference among the majority by emphasizing the erotic, exotic ways of the minority.

19 The rationale for such behavior is illustrated by a comment made by a Hong Kong Chinese academic, who, appearing at a dinner party in a Hani minority costume, began to move rhythmically and sensually. When asked why she acted so out-of-character, she stated: 'All of us Han from Yunnan have some minority blood in us, and the clothes just bring it out!'.

20 It is noteworthy that in the original book by Zhang Manling upon which this film was based, the protagonist is sent down to the rural countryside in a *non-minority* area, and the issues have less to do with dress and sensuality than with an affirmation of the naturalism of peasant life to which the Han woman must become accustomed. *Sacrificed Youth* relocates the episode to a minority area, where Han/minority issues come to the fore, further dramatizing the conservative repressiveness of dominant Han Chinese culture.

21 I use the word 'restricted' here because, though prohibited as pornographic for the general populace, it is possible to view foreign films with sex and nude scenes in various elite universities and training institutes. In 1983 I viewed the thought-to-be very *'huang'* ('yellow', or pornographic) uncensored version of *Kramer vs. Kramer* at the Beijing Foreign Languages Institute with a group of Chinese English students, their spouses, friends, and several cadres of the university. Chinese friends frequently complained to me that literature and films regarded as pornographic and illegal for common people were readily available to elite government officials and their families. Explicit foreign films are also widely shown in the joint-venture hotels throughout China, and such access to these and other 'Western' luxuries is one reason Chinese youth envy those who can obtain jobs there. Here, I must make very clear, the difference between what is erotic and pornographic in China is defined by what the state regards as legal and illegal. The point here is not about eroticism in general; it is that in China representations of Han subjects classed by the state as pornographic would not be illegal, and thus only erotic, if the Hans were *dressed* as minorities. In China, 'erotic' is generally glossed as *xing aide*, (that which influences or encourages sexual love), or *xinggan* ('sexy') , whereas 'pornographic' is generally translated, *se qing*, (lit. 'colorful sentiment') obliquely referring to the color yellow, which refers specifically to the pornographic press.

22 Legalized 'private video rooms' (*geti luxiang yuan*) are found in most cities and towns in China, showing films imported from Hong Kong, Taiwan, and the West, which are frequently monitored by the local police. They are also known to show slightly risque or even 'hardcore' erotic films late at night when the authorities are not around. Even in remote rural areas, where the police are fewer and farther between, these parlors are not unusual. I recall late one night in May 1985 passing one such parlor with a long line out front, where ticket prices had been increased from 15 *fen* (cents) during the day to 5 *yuan* (Chinese currency, equivalent then to slightly less then $2.00 U.S.) due to what I was told was the very 'yellow' nature of the Hong Kong film. This parlor was quite popular, even though it was located in a Muslim minority area, within the Hezhou Hui Autonomous Prefecture in Gansu.

23 See Orville Schell's (1989) humorous portrayal of this burgeoning industry of sexually suggestive publications, which led in part in 1989 to a

widespread series of protests by Muslims offended by their depiction in a Chinese book, *Sexual Customs* (*Xing Fengsu*). In response to what was termed China's 'Salman Rushdie' incident, the state banned and burned the book, closed the publication house, and arrested the authors (see Gladney 1991:1–15 and 1994a). Many of these publications have been strictly curtailed as 'bourgeois liberalism' since 1989.

24 I am grateful to John Ollsen for directing me to this source.

25 The 1988 Exhibition of Nude Art (*Luoti Huaxiang Zhanlan*) shown at the Beijing Fine Art Museum was the first since the founding of the People's Republic to specifically exhibit nudes. Although it also included many minority nudes, it was closed after less than two weeks, despite enormous ticket sales at more than ten times the normal price (5 *yuan* instead of 10 *fen*, equal to U.S. $2.00 instead of the normal .03 U.S.). The state justified the early closing of the exhibition because it claimed that many of the female models had objected to the public exhibition of their nude portraits as immoral. The models' husbands publicly complained of being the brunt of others' jokes, and claimed that their wives were no longer safe from attack. The state apparently has never been worried about this problem where minority women models and their husbands are concerned.

26 *Sing Pao Daily*, 18 July 1990, cited in Ruan (1991:180).

27 Ruan (1991:83, citing a *People's Daily* 15 February 1990, article) reports that a crackdown on prostitution and pornography announced by Li Ruihuan in September 1989 netted 103 prostitutes in Beijing alone between 25 November and 15 December. The Vice Minister of the Public Security Bureau reported that by January 1990, 35,000 separate cases had been prosecuted, involving 79,000 prostitutes and their customers. On 16 April 1993, Reuters reported a *Beijing Evening News* story that Wang Shuxiang was sentenced to death by the Beijing Intermediate Court for selling pornography and illegally trading in publishing quotas. A *Far Eastern Economic Review* (18 November 1993:40–41) story, entitled 'Reining in Erotica', reported on Beijing's most recent attempt to crack down on widespread pornography, including banning two books. Jia Pingao's *Fei Du* ['Defunct Capital'] and another popular book, *White Deer Park*, were both banned for their 'pornographic' subject matter and 'gratuitous sex scenes'. The article noted that the immediate effect of the ban was to triple the sales of the books and turn the authors into national celebrities. The article also reported that Madonna was recently granted permission to perform in China if she guaranteed there would be no nudity in the show.

28 *The New York Times* (Kristof, 13 February 1992:A7) reported the arrest of Pan Weiming, the 42-year-old former Chief of Propaganda in Shanghai, for trying to 'philander with woman'. A well-known pro-democracy advocate, the Chinese Public Security Bureau managed to arrest him one year ago and give him a four-year sentence for soliciting a prostitute in Sichuan. Supporters argue it was a set-up, however, as the entrapment procedure involved videos in the hotel room and long-term surveillance of his activities, with subsequent interrogation reportedly focusing more on his pro-democracy contacts than his well-known sexual dalliances. In a recent crackdown, the Sichuan Fine Arts publishing house was closed down for printing obscene books, and two others were cited (*Turkish Daily News*,

April 22, 1993:2). The reporter noted: 'Chinese authorities have a very broad definition of pornography that often includes just about any depiction of the human body that is not in a medical or scientific context'.

29 Exhibition comments on Xiao Jiahe's works included the following: 'Your work reminds me of Gustav Klimt's gold period, Picasso's colors after Cubism, Kokoschka's hands, Miro's organic shapes, Native American Indian women . . .'. 'An enthralling body of works, full of magical shapes and curves, flowing like everlasting rivers. A joy to see'. 'Talented, yes! Evocative, yes! But because your main subject in this exhibition is young, nubile women (one model?), I could see you having commercial success in advertising art'. 'I feel that the two best paintings were the one of the peasant and the weaver's daughter. You unquestionably have tremendous talent, however, what distinguishes these two over the others was the subject. The beautiful young woman in each painting offers no insights into the female human being. She is more object than an exploration of the subject . . .'. (Hand-written comments from the 5–30 July 1991 exhibition, 'Works by Chinese Artist Xiao Jiahe', Memorial Union, University of Wisconsin-Madison).

30 James Hevia, personal communication.

31 In this chapter, 'literal' refers to my translation of the original spoken or written text, while the translated or subtitled versions are given where available, unless otherwise noted.

32 For an excellent deconstruction of the eroticized, exoticized image of the 'primitive' in *National Geographic*, see Lutz and Collins' (1993) *Reading National Geographic*.

33 Louisa Schein (1990), in a provocative analysis, uses the notion of 'internal orientalism' to describe this project. In China, this fascination with the exotic has extended not only to the minority nationalities, but to representations of foreigners as well.

34 Until recently, minorities were allowed to have one or more children than the Han in their area. I found that this policy in practice meant that in most rural areas, minorities had as many children as they wanted (Gladney 1991). Post-1989 attempts to institute birth-planning in Mongolia and Xinjiang have led to riots among the minorities who argue China's policy of encouraging Han 'assimilation through immigration' had led to excessive Han population growth in their areas.

References

Ahmad, Aijaz 1992 *In Theory: classes, nations, literatures*, London: Verso.

Allworth, Edward 1980 'Ambiguities in Russian group identity and leadership of the RSFSR' in Edward Allworth (ed.), *Ethnic Russia in the USSR: the dilemma of dominance*, New York: Pergamon Press.

Alloula, Malek 1986 *The Colonial Harem*, Minneapolis: University of Minnesota Press.

Anderson, Benedict 1991 (1983) *Imagined Communities*, London: Verso Press.

Appadurai, Arjun 1986 'Theory in anthropology: center and periphery,' pp. 745–61 in *Comparative Studies in Society and History* 13.

Ardener, Shirley 1987 'A note on gender iconography: the vagina', pp. 113–42 in Pat Caplan (ed.), *The Cultural Construction of Sexuality*, London: Routledge Press.

Arkush, R. David 1981 *Fei Xiaotong and Sociology in Revolutionary China*, Cambridge: Harvard University Press.

Barthes, Roland 1983 *A Roland Barthes Reader*, Susan Sontag, ed. New York: Hill and Wang.

Befu, Harumi (ed.) 1993 *Cultural Nationalism in East Asia: representation and identity*, Berkeley: Institute of East Asian Studies.

Berry, Chris (ed.) 1991 *Perspectives on Chinese Cinema*, London: BFI Publishing.

Blaut, James M. 1987 *The national Question: decolonising the theory of nationalism*, London: Zed Books.

Boas, Franz 1955 *Primitive Art*, (1st edition, 1927), New York: Dover Publications.

Bourdieu, Pierre 1977 *Outline of a Theory of Practice*, Cambridge: Cambridge University Press.

Cahill, James 1983 'Figure, bird, and flower painting in China today', in Lucy Lim (ed.) *Contemporary Chinese Painting*, San Francisco: Chinese Culture Foundation.

Caplan, Pat 1987 'Introduction', pp. 1–30 in Pat Caplan (ed.), *The Cultural Construction of Sexuality*, London: Routledge.

Chang, Arnold 1980 *Painting in the People's Republic of China: The politics of style*, Boulder: Westview Press.

Chatterjee, Partha 1986 *Nationalist Thought and the Colonial World: a derivative discourse*, London: Zed Books.

Ch'en Yüan 1966 *Western and Central Asians in China Under the Mongols: their transformation into Chinese*, Monumenta Serica Monograph XV, Los Angeles: Monumenta Serica at the University of California.

Chinese Nationalities 1989 Beijing: China Nationality Photography and Art Press.

Chow, Rey 1990 *Woman and Chinese Modernity: The politics of reading between East and West*, Minnesota and Oxford: University of Minnesota Press.

Clark, Paul 1987a 'Ethnic minorities in Chinese films: cinema and the exotic', pp. 15–32 in *The East-West Film Journal* 1 (2).

—— 1987b *Chinese Cinema*, Cambridge: Cambridge University Press.

Cohen, Joan Lebold 1987 *The New Chinese Painting 1949–1986*, New York: Harry N. Abrams, Inc.

—— 1988 *The Yunnan School: a renaissance in Chinese painting*, Minneapolis: Fingerhut Group Publishers.

Comaroff, John 1987 'Of totemism and ethnicity: consciousness, practice and the signs of inequality', pp. 301–23 in *Ethnos* 52 (3–4).

Connor, Walker 1984 *The National Question in Marxist-Leninist Theory and Strategy*, Princeton: Princeton University Press.

Diamond, Norma 1988 'The Miao and poison: interactions on China's southwest frontier', pp. 1–25 in *Ethnology* 27(1).

Ding Shaoguang 1990 Hiestand Gallery portfolio brochure. Miami University, Oxford Ohio. 15 September–12 October.

Dittmer, Lowell and Samuel S. Kim (eds.) 1993 *China's Quest for a National Identity*, Ithaca: Cornell University Press.

Dominguez, Virginia R. 1986 *White by Definition: social classification in Creole Lousiana*, New Brunswick, N.J. Rutgers University Press.

Fei Xiaotong 1981 'Ethnic identification in China', in *Toward a People's Anthropology*. Beijing: New World Press.

―― 1989 *'Zhonghua minzu de duoyuan jiti juge'* (Plurality and Unity in the Configuration of the Chinese Nationality), pp. 1–19 in *Beijing Daxue Xuebao*.

Frankenberg, Ruth 1993 *White Women, Race Matters: the social construction of whiteness*, Minneapolis: University of Minnesota Press.

Foucault, Michel 1980 *The History of Sexuality*. Trans. Robert Hurley, vol. 1. New York: Vintage Press.

Gansu 1982 Lanzhou: Gansu People's Publishing Society.

Friedman, Edward 1994 'Reconstructing China's national identity: a southern alternative to Mao-era anti-imperialist nationalism', pp. 67–91 in *The Journal of Asian Studies* 53 (1).

Garber, Marjorie 1992 'The occidental tourist: *M. Butterfly* and the scandal of transvestism', pp. 121–46 in Andrew Parker, Mary Russo, Doris Sommer, and Patricia Yaeger (eds.) *Nationalisms and Sexualities*, London: Routledge.

Geertz, Clifford 1963 'The integrative revolution: primordial sentiments and civil politics in the new states', in Clifford Geertz (ed.), *Old Societies and New States*, New York: Free Press.

Gladney, Dru C 1990a 'The peoples of the People's Republic: finally in the vanguard?', pp. 62–76 in *The Fletcher Forum of World Affairs* 12 (1).

―― 1990b 'The ethnogenesis of the Uighur', pp. 1–28 in *Central Asian Survey* 9 (1).

―― 1990c 'Bodily positions and social dispositions: sexuality, nationality and Tiananmen', Paper presented at the Social Sciences Seminar, The Institute for Advanced Study, Princeton, 19 April.

―― 1991 *Muslim Chinese: Ethnic Nationalism in the People's Republic*, Cambridge: Harvard University Press, Council on East Asia.

―― 1994a 'Salman Rushdie in China: religion, ethnicity, and state definition in the People's Republic', pp. 255–78 in Helen Hardacre, Laurel Kendall, and Charles F. Keyes (eds.), *Asian Visions of Authority: Religion and the Modern States of East and Southeast Asia*, Honolulu: University of Hawaii Press.

―― 1994b 'The making of a Muslim minority in China: dialogue and contestation', pp. 115–142 in *Etudes Oriental* (13/14).

―― 1994c 'Ethnic identity in China: the new politics of difference', in William A. Joseph (ed.), *China Briefing, 1994*, Boulder: Westview Press.

Hobsbawm, Eric 1983 'Mass-producing traditions: Europe, 1870–1914', in Eric Hobsbawm and Terence Ranger (eds.) *The Invention of Tradition*, Cambridge: Cambridge University Press.

―― 1990 *Nations and Nationalism since 1780*. Cambridge: Cambridge University Press.

Huntington, Samuel P. 1993 'The clash of civilizations?', pp. 22–49 in *Foreign Affairs* 72 (3).

Huxley, Julian S. and A.C. Haddon 1936 *We Europeans: A Survey of 'Racial' Problems*, New York: Harper.

Jin Binggao 1984 'The Marxist definition of nationality, its origin and influence', pp. 64–7 in *Minyuan Xuebao* 3.

Keyes, Charles F. 1981 'The dialectics of ethnic change', in Charles Keyes (ed.), *Ethnic Change*, Seattle: University of Washington Press.

Kondo, Dorinne 1989 *Crafting Selves*, Chicago: University of Chicago Press.

Kristeva, Julia 1993 *About Chinese Women*, Anita Barrows, trans. original French edition, 1974, *Des Chinoises*, New York: Marion Boyars Publishers, Inc.

Laing, Ellen Johnston 1988 *The Winking Owl: art in the People's Republic of China*, Berkeley: University of California Press.

Lal, Amrit 1970 'Sinification of ethnic minorities in China', pp. 1–25 in *Current Scene* 8 (4).

Lufkin, Felicity 1990 *Images of Minorities in the Art of the Peoples Republic of China*, M.A. Thesis, University of California, Berkeley.

Lutz, Katherine and Jane L. Collins 1993 *Reading National Geographic*, Chicago: University of Chicago Press.

Ma Yin (ed.) 1989 *China's Minority Nationalities*, Beijing: People's Publishing Society.

Mayer, Iona 1975 'The patriarchal image: routine dissociation in Gusii families', pp. 260–76 in *African Studies* 34 (4).

McKhann, Charles F. 1995 'The Naxi and the nationalities question', pp. 39–62 in Stevan Harrell (ed.) *Cultural Encounters on China's Ethnic Frontiers*, Seattle: University of Washington Press.

Minzu Wenhua Gong (The Cultural Palace of Nationalities) 1990 Full color brochure, Beijing: Beijing Xingguang Caiyinchang.

Mosse, George L. 1985 *Nationalism and Sexuality: middle-class morality and sexual norms in modern Europe*, Madison: University of Wisconsin Press.

Mudimbe, V.Y. 1988 *The Invention of Africa: gnosis, philosophy, and the order of knowledge*, Bloomington: Indiana University Press.

Naquin, Susan and Evelyn S. Rawski 1987 *Chinese Society in the Eighteenth Century*, New Haven: Yale University Press.

Paglia, Camille 1990 *Sexual Personae: art and decadence from Nefertiti to Emily Dickinson*, New York: Vintage Books.

Pan, Lynn 1992 'A Chinese master', pp. 30–7 in *The New York Times Magazine*, 1 March.

Parker, Andrew, Mary Russo, Doris Sommer, and Patricia Yaeger (eds.) 1992 'Introduction', pp. 1–20 in Andrew Parker, Mary Russo, Doris Sommer, and Patricia Yaeger (eds.) *Nationalisms and Sexualities*, London: Routledge.

A Picture Album of Turpan Landscape and Custom 1985 (*Tulufan Fengqing Huaji*) Urumqi: Sinkiang People's Press.

Population Census Office of the State Council of the People's Republic of China and the Institute of Geography of the Chinese Academy of Sciences 1987 *The Population Atlas of China*, Oxford: Oxford University Press.

Price, Sally 1989 *Primitive Art in Civilized Places*, Chicago: University of Chicago Press.

Ruan Fangfu 1991 Editorial assistance provided by Molleen Matsumura, *Sex in China: studies in sexology in Chinese culture*, New York: Plenum Press.

Said, Edward 1978 *Orientalism*, New York: Random House.

Schein, Louisa 1990 'Barbarians beautified: the ambivalences of Chinese nationalism', paper presented at the Annual Meetings of the American Anthropological Association, New Orleans, 2 December 1990.

Schell, Orville 1989 *Discos and Democracy: China in the throes of reform*, New York: Anchor Books.

Shils, Edward (ed.) 1975 *Center and Periphery: essays in macro-sociology*, Chicago: University of Chicago Press.

Spivak, Gyatri Chakravorty 1990 'Women in difference: Mahasweta Devi's "Duoloti the Beautiful"', pp. 96–120 in Andrew Parker, Mary Russo, Doris Sommer, and Patricia Yaeger (eds.) *Nationalisms and Sexualities*, London: Routledge.

Sprinker, Michael 1993 'The national question: Said, Ahmad, Jameson', pp. 3–30 in *Public Culture* 6 (1).

Stalin, J.V. 1953 *Works*. 1907–1913. Volume 11. Moscow: Foreign Languages Publishing House.

Su Xiaokang, Director 1989 *He Shang* (River Elegy), 6-part television series, Beijing.

Suen Wan and Guo Wuji 1992 *Amazing Marriage Customs*, Hua Nan Film Company.

Sun Yatsen 1924 *The Three Principles of the People: San Min Chu I*, Taipei: China Publishing Company.

Thierry, François 1989 'Empire and minority in China', in Gérard Chaliand (ed.) *Minority Peoples in the Age of Nation-States*, London: Pluto Press.

Ting Shao Kuang 1990 Hiestand Gallery, Miami University, Oxford, Ohio, 15 September–12 October, Oxford, Ohio: Segal Fine Art.

Tong, Enzheng 1989 'Morgan's model and the study of ancient Chinese society', pp. 182–205 in *Social Sciences in China*, summer.

Wang, Yuejin 1989 'Mixing memory and desire: *Red Sorghum*: A Chinese version of masculinity and femininity', pp. 31–53 in *Public Culture* 2 (1).

Wright, Mary Clabaugh 1957 *The Last Stand of Chinese Conservativism*, Stanford: Stanford University Press.

Worsley, Peter 1984 *The Three Worlds*, Chicago: University of Chicago Press.

WuDunn, Sheryl 1991 'China opposes Oscar nomination of film it suppresses at home', *New York Times*, 25 February: B1, B3.

Yang, Kun 1992 *Minzu Xue Diaocha Fangfa* (Nationality Studies Research Methodology), Beijing: CASS.

Zhang Nuanxin 1989 'Interview with Zhang Nuanxin', *Camera Obscura* 10(2): 21–22.

4

REPRESENTING ABORIGINES

Modelling Taiwan's 'Mountain Culture'[1]

Shih-chung Hsieh

Tourism as a social institution exerts a powerful influence on shaping cultural images of ethnic groups (see Van den Berghe and Keyes 1984). It not only plays a major role in constructing images of a particular ethnic group among tourists but provides tourists themselves with an opportunity to re-define their own cultural identity. In Taiwan, indigenous people are the only group who have become the subject of ethnic tourism. Nonetheless, anthropological and sociological research has not yet realized the full academic significance of this phenomenon. This chapter is intended to pioneer such a work.

Nelson H.H. Graburn (1989 [1977]:31–32) has pointed out that so-called ethnic tourism has qualities of both natural and cultural tourism. Ethnic tourism generally refers to the process of visiting an 'other-community' or a tourist site whose inhabitants or performers differ from visitors in term of race, culture, language or customs. Besides enjoying natural scenery at a tourist site, tourists are given opportunities to observe the 'staged' lifestyle or culture of particular ethnic groups. This is considered one of the most important activities in any dynamic form of ethnic tourism (see Cohen 1996; Sweet 1989; Dearden and Harron 1994; Hsieh 1994a). 'Indigenous tourism' is one sub-category of ethnic tourism. Since 'indigenous tourism' always involves relationships between tourists from the highly industrialized and capitalist world and tribal indigenes themselves, it is bound to attract the special interests of anthropologists and sociologists (see e.g. Van den Berghe 1992; Adams 1984, 1990; Nason 1984; Van den Berghe and Keyes 1984; Esman 1984; Swain 1990; Cohen 1996).

In many Asian countries, the state is quite often a main power in establishing the 'nuclei' or 'attracting centers' (a term borrowed from Leiper 1990) of tourism of indigenous minority groups. The state manipulates patterns of tourism in terms of its domination ideology.

Robert E. Wood (1984) defines the state as a collective middleman. While he stresses the role of the state as a middleman for a particular cultural or ethnic group, he does not seem concerned with the ways in which the state acquires cultural information. The state quite often depends on academic and other relevant materials in achieving its goal. Thus, academics, especially anthropologists, emerge as a main actor in transmitting cultural information to the state and, for that matter, tourist industries in general. I would therefore like to pay attention to the role of academics in promoting knowledge about indigenous groups through tourism as well as the broader contexts in which academics are placed in Taiwan.

In Taiwan, even though one third of the so-called 'mountain people' live in plain areas, indigenous people are generally called 'mountain people' and their culture 'mountain culture' by both the indigenous people themselves and Han-Taiwanese/Chinese. Han-Taiwanese/Chinese are the dominant ethnic group in Taiwan. The state, commercial enterprises, academics and individual urbanites, who together stand for the Han-Taiwanese/Chinese in the urban center, participate in the construction of an imagined 'primitive' world of the indigenous people in Taiwan. In the following discussion, I will describe how these groups interact with one another to create the past, present and even future stories of Taiwan's indigenous people. The state and entrepreneurs as well as academics, who provide them with cultural information, are the key role-players in directing visitors to recognize an 'original type' of the indigenes. In his study of the Polynesian Culture Center in Hawaii, Stanton (1989 [1977]:251–255; 1974) defines this kind of original type as a 'model culture', in which traditional forms of material culture are always altered or even distorted for the satisfaction of tourists. The contents of an exhibited model culture are, for the most part, static and lacking in aspects of cultural change. In the future, the indigenous people will have to face the demands of showing a model, or 'original type' of 'mountain culture' to strangers.

The process of exhibiting model culture is not an easy one. The representatives of nine indigenous groups stay together at a tourist site to build old-style houses, dance, sing, wear formal costumes, weave, sculpture, light fire, cook, and speak the native languages. These staged acts may represent part of the real life of indigenous people, part of the imagination of the managers of the enterprise, part of a vision of the anthropological specialist, and part of a propagandized aspect of the national culture. Whichever aspect is closer to reality, display of a 'model culture' has become a way of making a living. But visitors may not be conscious of such a deliberate process. They tend to accept what the model presents them to construct, thereby strengthening or ensuring a 'real picture' of their own definitions of the culture of the indigenous groups.

My case studies will take up the two main institutions of ethnic tourism in Taiwan, the Taiwan Aboriginal Cultural Park and the Formosan Aboriginal Culture Village. The case studies look at activities of various participants such as the owners of institutions, unit leaders, designers, academic consultants, indigenous workers and tourists in terms of their respective roles in representing the model culture. The relationship between the operation of the model culture and the process of forming cultural images among visitors will be a focal point of analysis.[2] Particular attention is drawn to anthropologists' active participation in the promotion of indigenous tourism and its meanings in Taiwanese society. This is a critical analysis of how the 'model culture' represents indigenous people in contemporary Taiwan.

The Taiwan Aboriginal Cultural Park

The Taiwan Aboriginal Cultural Park (TACP), which is under the administration of the Provincial Government, is located at Fuguwan of Majia, Pingdong County.[3] The Park was opened in 1987. In Taiwan, the word 'park' usually brings to mind leisure, play and sight-seeing. This state-owned 'cultural park' is designed to exhibit the 'culture items' of the 'mountain people'.[4] A number of indigenous people work in the park in order to successfully dramatize the local color of 'mountain culture'.

A brochure published by the Park emphasizes that 'traditional mountain cultures . . . are important and precious cultural and tourist resources' and that this Park has been created to 'maintain and develop' mountain culture. Since the maintenance of the culture is one of its most critical missions, experts were consulted and hired to design this institution. They have created an exhibiting area for the 'traditional culture of housing and dwelling among mountain people'. In other words, visitors see what are 'officially' recognized as 'original' buildings and part of the traditional lives of the mountain people. At present, these traditional buildings have been carefully protected within the exhibition area, and large numbers of aborigines are hired to live and work there. According to the Institute of Ethnology of Academia Sinica, one of the original designers of the TACP, all exhibited buildings had to be built following the rule of re-constructing a traditional structure selected from a tribal village or an earlier ethnographic picture. This was done in order to maintain an 'authentic' style.

The buildings are also designed to authenticate the tradition of a tribal village for the satisfaction of tourists. A high evaluation of these perceived traditions is evident in the attitudes and behavior of almost all the managing staff and host performers. Many ethnologists participated in the planning of the cultural performances, and various anthropological terms such as 'social institution', 'inheritance by the eldest', 'ancestor worship', and 'aristocratic ranks' were adopted as one medium of transmitting knowledge about indigenous society to visitors. Academic words have thus been organized to become a particular aspect of traditional culture. There is also a plaque beside the front door of every building which describes the origin of the house, its basic structure, decoration and furnishings. When people look at these plaques, they might perceive that a systematic knowledge of exotic 'mountain culture' has been codified already.

The infrastructure of the Park is well-constructed to attract tourists. Tour buses painted with indigenous symbols wait by the gate of the park where visitors walk in. People can enjoy beautiful scenery as the buses drive around the hills on high quality paved roads. The park is divided into three sections: first, Tamaluwan, which displays the architecture of the Atayal, Saisiat, Puyuma, Ami and Yami tribes; second, Fuguwan, which displays items of material culture derived from Bunun, Tsou, Paiwan and Rukai; third, Naluwan, which comprises a performing field, a restaurant and an exhibition hall extolling indigenous lifestyles. The bus stops at each of these three sections. Tourists may decide to get off at one stop and take a look there or continue their journey to the next stop. The ideal route planned by the Park authorities is to see the architecture in the Tamaluwan area first, then to watch dancing performances and have lunch or buy artifacts, and finally to Fuguwan for photo opportunities in front of the classic buildings. When tourists walk in the park, which occupies a few hills, they climb up and down slopes, and see the wooden, bamboo, thatched or stone-built houses. These experiences match the image of the wild ecological niche of the mountain people's dwelling. After absorbing these first impressions, tourists gather around the dancing platform, the area where the dynamism of the mountain culture is best expressed. The mountainous surroundings are tranquil, but the dancing is energetic and exciting. This contrast between quietness and vivacity seems to convey to visitors the unique cultural traits of the mountain people.

The dancing programs, like the other two locations where the housing models of the nine ethnic groups are exhibited, claim to contain only indigenous elements. When the performance starts, a host and a hostess come out to make an introduction:

> *Host*: I am a young person from A tribe of B township of C county. My original name is DEF, and Han-Chinese name is GHI.
>
> *Hostess*: I am a young person from J tribe of K township of L county. My original name is MNO, and Han-Chinese name is PQR.
>
> *Host*: We welcome you.
>
> Hostess (salute to audience): We appreciate your visiting.
>
> *Host*: Now, let me teach you some tribal words. 'Yila O'.
>
> *Hostess*: Mali! Mali! (Greetings!)
>
> *Host*: The costumes, languages, customs, rituals, folk songs and dances of the nine indigenous groups are very different from one another. Today, we are going to perform special features of each based in order of the northern, central, eastern and southern parts of the island.
>
> *Hostess*: Not only that, we also wish to introduce several exciting and interesting activities which belong to the different groups. We expect to narrow the distances between you and us within the short span of sixty minutes. Let us appreciate and respect each other.
>
> *Host*: Now, please relax and applaud enthusiastically for our coming performance.
>
> *Hostess*: Mali! Mali! (Greetings!)

The hostess explains that *mali mali* is a word for extending cordial greetings in the Paiwan community. She requests audiences to repeat it aloud twice. Before each programme, all the dancers wearing costumes of the nine groups come out onto the stage. At the very outset of each programme, the host usually teaches a few native words of each group, and goes on to provide ethnological information about the main cultural characteristics of the people. All visitors at this moment have been led to a situation which is full of 'mountain flavour'.

The host then gives a description at the beginning of each program in which each group is highlighted by one or two particular cultural traits. In this way, the audience may form at least a general image of indigenous culture. One may think of indigenous culture in terms, for example, of Atayal's weaving, Saisiat's Rite of Little Spirits, Tsou's patrilateral power and four-step movements, Bunun's chorus, Puyuma's Spartan training of young men, Ami's Harvest Festival, Yami's Dance of Swinging Hair and Spiritual Dance, Rukai's snake symbol, and Paiwan's social hierarchy. (For the complete text of the description of each tribe, see Appendix). Such a simple introduction may not be enough for people with a keener interest, for whom a detailed brochure is available.

After listening to the host's talk, learning nine different ways to say 'How are you', and having watched colorful dancing performances, the activity reaches its climax. The host indicates that a swing supported by four long poles on the ground is characteristic of the Paiwan or the Rukai cultures. He says: 'Only the daughters of the chief or noble can play on a swing in a wedding . . . A new-made swing becomes sacred after a priest's practice. A legend has it that there are two important taboos. First, a man may never play on the swing because he may become unable to father a child. Second, the girl who prepares to play on the swing must be carried by her man on his back when he is running. As regards the ways of carrying and swinging, we will show you.' When two dancers finish the demonstration, the host asks a man and a woman from the audience,who are in high spirits by this time, to act as bride and bridegroom to play the swing. The two invited to join in the performing party are representing the watchers' side. The fact that Han-Taiwanese/Chinese (more than 98 per cent of audiences) take part in this activity seems to symbolize that members of the 'civilized world' have entered into the traditional or primitive world. This is an important phenomena of ethnic tourism in areas outside of Taiwan as well. In the central highlands of Sulawesi, Indonesia, for instance, originally the people of Toraja prohibited the public presentation of the rituals and dances associated with birth and death. Now they publicly perform these two rituals under arrangement with the government. Tourists therefore can watch two of most important ritual performances in the personal life of the Toraja, and are even invited to wear a traditional one-piece skirt in order to get a feel of the exotic social world (Adams 1984, 1990:31–34).

There are other important features of the TACP. One of them is the establishment of a restaurant serving indigenous food. Several famous native sculptors also put their products there for sale. A brochure for the restaurant says: 'This restaurant is built in accordance with the style of Paiwan's stone house. We are sure that it is the biggest stone house in

Southeast Asia. The inner portion of it is decorated with expensive wood. The dining room is beautiful and supplies various kinds of luxurious dishes, fast food, and indigenous snacks . . . .' Stone plates, wood and indigenous food, especially the kinds of food called by original names, such as *chuluge, qinafu,* and *jinbole,* help to create the exotic impression. Tourists eat such food and have a direct experience of 'mountain tastes'. In addition, the Park once offered courses on the traditional cooking methods of the nine groups feautured in the TACP and published 'Recipes of Taiwanese Indigenous Food' which introduced many formal dishes supposedly popular in indigenous communities. Traditional architecture, old style food, tribal songs and dances, and a variety of classic artifacts are all aspects of expressive culture presented in formulating and shaping the model characteristics of particular ethnic groups.

Han tourists are more or less satisfied with a cultural park like this one which presents 'mountain culture' in well-organized ways. In this administrative unit responsible for the preservation and development of 'mountain culture', most cultural interpretations relating to food, clothing, housing, artifacts and rituals are strongly associated with 'mountain', 'primitiveness', 'tradition' and 'nature'. The Park demonstrates a reality for those curious tourists who are encouraged to tap into their previously held beliefs and imagination. Indeed, the KMT (Nationalist Party) Government was wise to assimilate the indigenous people into the Han-Taiwanese/Chinese dominated national culture under a self-righteous pretext of having preserved traditional indigenous culture at the TACP (see Hsieh 1986; 1994b; 1994c). Han tourists may therefore completely ignore the serious extent to which the real life in tribal communities had been essentially changed under the unchallengeable policy processes and the Han's intensive economic and population invasion.

The Formosan Aboriginal Culture Village

The Formosan Aboriginal Culture Village (FACV) is called *Jiu Zu Wen Hua Cun* in Chinese, which means the 'Cultural Village of Nine Groups'. It is located at Yuchi, Nantou County, and is often mentioned in conjunction with TACP. This is not because they came into being about the same time (FACV in 1986, TACP in 1987), but because even though TACP is a state-owned local unit and FACV is a private enterprise they show similar attitudes toward indigenous culture. There are a number of similarities between the two. One of these concerns the role of academics in supplying cultural knowledge to elites in the metropolitan center – political elites in the case of TACP, or economic elites in the case of FACV. The FACV as well as the TACP has followed the pattern of finding a place with beautiful scenery and building houses of each tribe on each site. The TACP was established in the ancestral lands of the Paiwan, whereas the FACV was located on a broad slope near the Sun Moon Lake, the homeland of a small tribe named Thao. It is probably because of its geographical proximity to the Thao that one can see not only the 'Thao spot' exhibiting traditional houses which cannot be found at the TACP, but one can also enjoy a performance of the ritual of pounding millets with pestles, which is believed to be a tradition of the Thao.

The Village has printed various brochures. There are at least three different designs for introducing the enterprise: a folded sheet of paper; a sixteen-page pocket handbook, and a 160-page monograph. All of the three papers are entitled 'the Formosan Aboriginal Culture Village'. The company makes many versions in languages such as Chinese, Japanese, and English.[5] Everyone receives a 16-page brochure when entering the village. Here is a paragraph from the brochure:

> The Formosan Aboriginal Culture Village is based on the primitive tribal architecture and artifacts of every group . . . The layout of the Village has been directed in consultation with scholars and specialists. We attempt to protect the environment and maintain traditional 'mountain color' . . . We would like to concretely exhibit the special features of mountain culture.

Use of terms and phrases such as 'primitiveness', 'consultation with scholars and specialists', 'tradition' and 'special features of mountain culture' reflects the ways in which mountain culture is represented by the FACV. First, the oldness of the culture is emphasized. As in the founding process of the TACP, the owner of the FACV requested a number of academics to present the 'genuine tradition'. In introducing the nine groups and their cultures, the 160-page book borrows many descriptive phrases of cultural traits from ethnological materials. Examples of such ethnological phrases include: the 'bilateral kinship' and 'institution of social control' of the Yami, the 'matrilineal society' and 'age hierarchy' of the Ami, the 'tattooing' and 'organization of worshipping groups' of the Atayal, the 'totemic clans' and 'rite of worshipping little spirits' of the Saisiat, the 'meeting hall' of the Tsou and 'song of pestles' of the Thao, the 'fine-note chord' and 'digging teeth' of the Bunun, the 'men's house' and 'eldest daughter inheritance' of the Puyuma, the 'social ranks' and 'Agkistrodon acutus snake as ancestors' of the Rukai, and the 'five-yearly worshipping ritual' and 'three ranking system' of the Paiwan.

Normally, academics make their knowledge of other cultures accessible through writing. The FACV also utilizes academic writings – but only to a limited extent. Rather, it displays traditional culture through concrete objects which become efficient tourist resources. When people look at the styles and interior arrangements of the houses of a particular group, they are exposed not just to the physical materials. Rebuilding a house is not merely a case of asking indigenous workers to do it by traditional techniques, because a rebuilt house open to the public must also be approved by specialists whose profession is to explain old ethnographic records and books in the first place. Plaques written by specialists are put near the main door, and the contents of well-printed brochures for tourists' consumption are all based on anthropological reports. Furthermore, a complete cultural scene is recreated by hiring indigenous elders wearing formal traditional costumes on which anthropologists supervise invisibly, or behind the scenes so to speak. Therefore, one could say that tourists have seen the 'tradition' and regard their impression of the mountain people as 'authentic' although that 'tradition' is constructed by specialists. Through its role as a copier of unchallengeable academic works, I would suggest that the FACV produces powerful influences in directing visitors to shape an image of the 'mountain people'.

The infrastructure of the FACV is composed of a convenient transportation system, food and artifact shops, and exquisite planning for presenting the natural and artificial scenery. The entire area is divided into nine villages. Visitors can either take tour buses or walk. There are three main visiting spots: 'Watch Mountain Tower' which is good for enjoying a view of the distant landscape; 'Spirit Stone of Ten Thousand Mountains' next door to a temple of Earth God; and 'Naluwan Theater' where people can enjoy dancing performances. The Spirit Stone is named for a huge rock near the Rukai tribe's Ten Thousand Village which is related to the legend of a snake-ancestor. However, the Earth God Temple of the traditional Han-Taiwanese/ Chinese folk religion next to the stone is worshipped as a base for supporting the enterprise. This is obviously a syncretic religious approach: on the one hand, we can see a Han God standing at the peak of the hill overlooking everything else and extending his grace to protect the FACV; on the other we can see him transferring 'spiritual energy' to the indigenous representative – the Stone. Moreover, in seeking supernatural power to enhance the successful running of the company, the businessmen involved have practiced a trans-cultural action where they believe in and worship spirits of both the Han-Taiwanese/Chinese and the indigenous people. However, the real power is presumably the Earth God, whom the enterprise owner and his Han Chinese workers ordinarily worship. One may also interpret this relationship to be a reflection of the asymmetric relationship between the Han dominator, symbolized by the Earth God, and the dominated indigenous people, symbolized by the Stone.

The company not only presents a couple of manikins in front of many tribal houses but also requests older indigenous men and women in traditional costumes to sit both indoors and outside. They toast yams, cook glutinous rice, make sculptures and weave clothes. Arranging 'classic people' to do 'classic works' certainly is a process of declaring tradition. Originally, the company asked ethnic troupes from different tribes to perform traditional dances at least twice a day but later found out that many tourists were not interested. The enterprise's profit margin for paying a troupe NT$10,000 (about US$300) was insufficient, and the dance was discontinued. At present, dancing performances are concentrated on stage at the Naluwan Theater.

Because of the active involvement of academic specialists as consultants and designers, most of the dancing programmes, just as in the case of TACP, are always preceded by descriptions of populations, distribution, cultural characteristics, and the contents of songs and dances among all ethnic groups in terms of ethnological terminology. The following is a summary of the ethnic features and songs or music that appear in the brochure 'The Naluwan Theater':

> *Rukai*: This is a patrilineal society. There are four social ranks: chief, noble, gentry, and commoner. Their songs and dances include 'Love Song', 'Song of Four Seasons', 'Love Song of the Rukai', 'Song of Curing Disease by Witch', 'Song of Catching Crabs by Rukai Children', 'Song of Girl's Praying', and 'Song of the Good Year'.
>
> *Yami*: Half fishing and half cultivation is their subsistence. Fishing in coastal waters has been well-developed. Their songs and dances include 'Hya-Bo-Rea, A Traditional Song' and 'Dance of Spiritual Power'.
>
> *Tsou*: Rubbing animal's skin and making leather is well-known. They have a significant religious life. Their songs and dances

include 'worshipping the god', 'song of triumphant return', and 'song of sending the spirit to leave'.

Ami: Besides the tradition of matrilineal inheritance, the Ami's music and dance is the most rich and varied among the nine groups. Their songs and dances include 'Song of Welcoming Guests in Naluwan', 'Ami's Beautiful Girl', 'Love Song of the Ami', 'Celebrating Good Year in Yiwan Tribe', and 'Blue Moon and Night Scenery–A Folk Song'.

Puyuma: Witchcraft is very popular in this group. Moreover, they adopt a spartan way of training soldiers. Their song and dances include 'Song of Puyuma Girl', 'Song of Unification', 'Song of Triumphant Return', and 'Happy Days in the Good Year'.

Atayal: They emphasized military power, people practiced head-hunting for revenge or winning honor. Tattooing is a mark of a particular sub-group. Their songs and dances include 'Love Song of the Atayal', 'Dance of Expressing Love by Bamboo Plates', 'Song of Worshipping the Spirit', 'Dance of Welcoming Guests', and 'Song of Happiness'.

Saisiat: The rite of worshipping the Little Spirits whose 'little ritual' is practiced every two years, and the 'great ritual' conducted every ten years, is the most evident feature in this group. 'The Song of Blessing and Praying' is the typical one which can be heard often.

Paiwan: Wood and stone sculpture and weaving are the main elements composing the primitive arts of this group. They are a bilateral society, the class system is much more strict than the Rukai. Their songs and dances include 'Song of Satirizing Enemies', 'Song of the Good Year', 'Love Song of the Paiwan', 'Song of the Rite of Wishing for Rainfall', and 'Song of Seeing Friends Off'.

Bunun: They are famous for music traditions. For example, they are one of the two peoples in the world who still preserve the technique of the eight-note chorus. The Bunun are also good at hunting; they used to hunt enemy's heads, and practice a custom of tattooing and digging teeth. Their songs and dances include 'Song of Greeting', 'Song of Watch's Praying', 'Soldiers Report of Meritorious Military Service', and 'Song of Drinking'.

Just like the introductory series at the TACP, the dancing programme designer at the FACV also wishes to help tourists to construct a basic impression of indigenous culture. The FACV obviously prefers to emphasize Rukai's social ranks, Yami's fishing, Tsou's leather making, Ami's matrilineal trait and varied dance, Puyuma's witchcraft and spartan training, Atayal's head-hunting and tattooing, Saisiat's rite of worshipping the Little Spirits, Paiwan's sculpture and class system, and Bunun's eight-note chorus. A tourist who has watched the entire show has, without question, a good chance to form his or her own image about indigenous people and culture through these key introductory remarks.

The programmes, representing each group described above, are performed on different days. However, the first one, 'Dance of Welcoming Guests', and the closing one, 'Play with My Friends', seem to appear every time. As in the TACP, the FACV arranges a high swing of Paiwan or Rukai style to be a medium of connection with the dancers and audiences. In addition, the FACV adds adventurous and exciting elements into the manner of play. There is a ditch located in between the platform of the Naluwan Theater and the seats for visitors. The host of the programme sometimes may ask a woman to weave on a raft, or have an old man drill a piece of wood and make a fire. Following the performances, the host invites several guests to take a swing to hop across the ditch, and the audience laugh delightedly if someone falls into the water. Those who have passed over the ditch to the platform have a chance to learn the bamboo pole dance, and then take the swing to jump back to their seats. The programme then ends.

After seeing the performances at the Naluwan Theater, many tourists follow a trail down to the Thao village to enjoy the 'Song of Stone', i.e. pounding pestles. A plaque hung there says: 'It is a special music played on the New Year's day for worshipping Spirits. They take advantage of the different length and weight of pestles to strike stones and make a beautiful melody filled with various scales and tempos. It is really amazing'. There is also a pond in front of platform. Usually they have a woman sitting on a raft to demonstrate a witch's ritual. Visitors are again invited to join dancers or play a traditional music instrument. Furthermore, if the number of tourists is large enough, dancers may perform a broad Tsou ritual dance in scale beside the Tsou and Thao villages.[6]

Since the TACV was founded in the south of Taiwan, several training programs in association with indigenous cultures seek advice from the Park. Similarly, the FACV has established a reputation for its ability to represent indigenous cultures. A KMT-sponsored organization has requested the FACV more than three times to hold a program in which young people can experience 'mountain culture'. Dancers in the program serve as assistant instructors, teach primary techniques for making tools, and accompany the participants staying in wooden or stone houses several nights. Although 'mountain culture' is a general and vague concept, it is felt to be experienced by anyone who has actually had contacts with it, however limited. Entering the Village, visitors, especially those joining the training program, can get a secured sense of experiencing the natural and traditional 'mountain' life, which is mediated through the perception of the FACV and the discussion of 'correct information' regarding mountain cultures.

Finally, the artifacts should be carefully described too. There are more than five stores within the Park. All of the clerks are Han-Taiwanese/Chinese. They are requested to read relevant materials concerning indigenous culture in preparation for tourists' inquiries. However, almost all artifacts, except for a small amount made by old indigenous workers, are manufactured by Han-Taiwanese/Chinese from urban areas. A desire for consumption may be stimulated when tourists see and feel these 'indigenous things' under the atmosphere created by and transmitted through the concept of 'mountain culture', and the name 'Formosan Aboriginal Culture Village'. A decorative cloth found in one of the stores which is presented as brilliantly reflecting mountain color is in reality made by a Han artist. In addition, imitation glazed necklaces are from stores in Pingdong, southern Taiwan. However, the time and location of purchase are meaningful to the visitors who have bought souvenirs. The artifacts themselves may not be valuable, but the reason why the chosen souvenir is significant to the buyer is the fact that it was bought from the FACV. Throughout the process of choosing, buying, and keeping this sort of souvenir culture, it enables the buyer to retain a memory of having experienced mountain culture (Moore 1985:630; Moeran 1983:99). Nelson H.H. Graburn (1984:409–14) points out that the motivation for keeping evidence of contacts with authentic, alien, or other worlds is obvious in the process of mass tourism among the middle class. Therefore, they keep souvenirs at home, especially those which are perceived to represent 'the other' and this creates the phenomenon of museumification of their own houses.

Both the FACV and the TACP have an admired model of representing indigenous culture in Taiwan. Operating on a limited scale, the FACV enriches understanding of the synchronic cultural life and the diachronic historical evolution of Taiwan's indigenous people. Along with the TACP in Pingdong, it creates a contemporary-style 'mountain culture tourism' or 'mountain people tourism'.

101

Anthropologists and Representation of Indigenous Culture in Taiwan

Previously, people had to visit tribal areas if they wanted to see indigenous people. Today, new and fashionable enterprises of ethnic tourism have shifted the representation of the nine groups to new locations which have no direct connections with the indigenous people. Tourists ever hardly inquire about the relations between the locations of the 'ethnic theme parks' and the original dwelling communities of the indigenous people. As long as they can enjoy well-established infrastructures, they feel secure and satisfied. Both the Taiwan Aboriginal Cultural Park in Majia and the Formosan Aboriginal Cultural Village in Yuci are such institutions. These theme parks exhibit 'mountain culture' with beautiful natural scenery as their background. These are huge institutions which have collected 'cultural traits' as the expressions of Taiwan's aboriginal culture. The creation of such institutions more or less reflects the economic power of Taiwan in both public and private spheres. The economic development of Taiwan in the 1980s has had a direct influence on the transformation of the pattern of indigenous/ethnic tourism. It has brought about the creation of a more elaborate model culture for tourists, who can now observe the systematic design of the housing of the nine groups and attend performances of elders weaving or baking yams at tourist sites. In addition to some older and smaller commercial organizations, where people can have a taste of mountain culture by watching dance performances for example, much larger institutions such as TACP and FACV have been founded to represent indigenous culture in more dynamic ways.

Both 'mountain culture' and 'culture of the nine groups' are general names that refer to Taiwan's indigenous culture as a whole. The use of these words indicates the desire of these two institutions to effectively demonstrate the similarity of all 'mountain people'. 'Naluwan' is another important concept to be mentioned here. It is a way of yelling that creates an exciting 'primitive' atmosphere, but most aborigines themselves do not know the meaning.[7] In Taiwan, the non-Han 'mountain people' are regarded as a special people who have the 'natural' right of developing, preserving or performing their traditions. Thus, 'Naluwan' is seen as a 'mountain' word, and is linked to an experience of 'mountain people' or 'mountain culture.' Furthermore, since Naluwan represents 'mountain culture' as an inclusive concept, a synthetic performance containing elements of all nine groups naturally can be expected. Tourists expect to encounter a sort of 'synthesis of the nine groups' or 'the whole of mountain culture' at these sites.

It may be noted here that the present characterization and categorization of indigenous people was established in the 1960s. The first ethnic labelling and categorization of the Formosan indigenous peoples is reported to have been done by Japanese ethnologists at the end of the nineteenth century. Because they found similarities among different groups in material culture, social organization, language and physical characteristics, they applied the general ethnic name, *Takasagozoku* (in Madarin *Gaoshazu* and in Taiwanese *Goshuazo*).[8] Later, in the middle of the twentieth century, Taiwanese/Chinese anthropologists generally followed the Japanese-created ethnic map. They, however, changed the Japanese term into a similar Chinese word, *Gaoshanzu* (mountain people) . It was in the second half of the 1960s that people in Taiwan, including indigenous intellectuals themselves, generally accepted this characterization of the indigenous people and its categorization into 'jiuzu' or 'nine groups' (see Hsieh 1987, 1994a, 1994b).[9] Later, in 1994, *yuanzhumin* (lit. original inhabitants) became an official name for the indigenous people of Taiwan. The two ethnic theme parks, as illustrated in this chapter, are a product of this intellectual development. We may also say that they play an important role in promoting such characterization and categorization of Taiwan's indigenous people.

We have seen that the new form of ethnic tourism is a product of the cooperation between bureaucrats, entrepreneurs and academic specialists. Scholars have taken part in the designing of mountain culture tourism and in this process many ethnological terms have been utilized to describe as well as shape the culture of the indigenous people. Preservation and transmission of indigenous culture, which had long appealed to Taiwanese anthropologists, as well as academic attempts to anthropologize the cultural exhibitions of TACP and FACV clearly reflected the tradition of salvage anthropology in Taiwan since the 1950s (see Hsieh 1987; Li Yih-yuan et al 1975).

Many scholars (e.g. Shih Lei 1971;Chen Chi-lu 1958, 1978; Li Yih-yuan et al. 1975) were concerned about the prospect of rapid disappearance of traditional indigenous culture. Thus, working in the field with the aid of interpreters, they always asked elders about the past instead of observing their contemporary daily lives. Furthermore, anthropology in Taiwan has long been a neglected discipline because of the limitation of occupational positions (see Li Yih-yuan 1996). Most Taiwanese anthropologists have tried to call attention to the social significance of anthropology. Anthropologists' participation in the creation of these two huge indigenous culture parks was a good opportunity for them to express their desire and their ability to preserve culture through productive use of their academic knowledge. In Taiwan, the overwhelming majority of anthropologists conduct their research by applying for grants to the National Science Council of the Executive Yuan or by taking up projects entrusted by particular governmental agencies. In general, anthropologists who conduct NSC-supported research projects are better respected by colleagues. In contrast, because state-initiated projects tend to stress more applied and pragmatic aspects, anthropologists engaged in such projects are judged poorly by fellow researchers and accumulate little credit in terms of academic achievement. Nevertheless, there were anthropologists who still wished to participate in the project of creating indigenous theme parks in the hope of changing the stereotype of anthropology as a discipline which has little practical use. One interesting fact is that anthropological knowledge has been successfully popularized by public and private tourist-oriented enterprises instead of through written ethnographies. One might recall that classifying and exhibiting artifacts has always been an important tradition of anthropology. The effectiveness with which anthropological knowledge is diffused via tourism in comparison with various kinds of 'serious', more formal educational means is evident in our examples.

Tourist institutions continue to stress the 'tradition' of the 'mountain people.' This so-called tradition can be discovered in the contents and arrangement of their exhibitions. Table 1 shows most of the traits of the model culture found in these institutions.

The contents of the exhibition accompanied by words such as 'tradition', 'natural', 'real', 'enthusiastic' and 'primitive' in brochures and plaques, or spoken by programme hosts, become a way of representing indigenous culture in Taiwan at present. 'Mountain people' thereby can be formulated as a group of happy primitive people who are distributed in remote mountainous areas, live in straw or stone made houses, and hunt and fish for a living; the young girls show enthusiasm to visitors, old women are tattooed and the daily work is dancing and drinking. Emphasis on 'traditions' such as these functions to promote ethnic tourism. In Xishuangbanna, Yunnan, China, homeland of the Tai people ('Dai' in Chinese pinyin), several major towns such as Yunjinghong and Ganlanba have been decorated by yellow or golden colors on the walls of new buildings after the local government opened the area to tourists in 1985. The yellow or golden

Table 4.1 Displayed cultural items at TACP and FACV

Categories	Cultural Traits
People	1. tattoos 2. colorful garments 3. T-shaped short pants of Yami male 4. shouting and enthusiastic songs and dances 5. weaving exhibition by old women
Location	1. Indigenous tribal land (TACP) 2. beautiful scenery (TACP and FACV)
Material	1. realistic and abstract patterns 2. canoes 3. houses made of straws, wood, or stone 4. classic tools for hunting and cultivation 5. wild animal symbols, such as snake, deer, boar 6. sculptures
Activities	1. songs and dances 2. worshipping spirits and drinking 3. making fire, weaving, pounding pestle 4. dance or play with tourists to prove the primitive warmth of the indigenous people
Food	1. meals with indigenous names 2. special products from mountainous areas

color is a key symbol in the Tai tradition that reminds visitors that they have reached real Tai country. Most higher officials feel that the display of this 'yellow tradition' is the most effective means of attracting tourists (Hsieh 1989; 1993a: 93–112). Moreover, indigenous people in the contemporary industrial world are expected by the majority society to continue their 'tradition' – a tradition which can be sampled by members of the majority society, especially those urbanites eager to temporarily leave their artificial world (see Graburn 1983:11–15; Cohen 1988:37–41; Hsieh 1993b).

In both TACP and FACV, institutions designed to preserve and develop 'mountain culture', all cultural symbols relating to food, clothing, housing, artifacts and ceremonial activities deliberately retain their connection to the terminology of 'mountain', 'tradition' or 'nature'. Tourists arrive there to confirm their imaginations, and these institutions make every effort to satisfy them by providing the 'cultural facts' to the curious visitor. Wherever tourists go, they find either impressive mountain scenery or traditional architecture. After enjoying quietude in sightseeing, visitors begin to participate in the energetic dancing performances. The dual experiences of tranquillity and activity give urbanites satisfaction of their inner mind and release from stress. To most of the tourists, the 'mountain people' are an alien people. The purpose of their visit is to see their 'otherness'. For indigenous workers at these tourist sites, especially for the dancers, training is doubtlessly hard and the duty of representing model mountain culture is always a heavy responsibility. They 'learn', 'memorize' and 'perform' dances, rituals and lifestyles in a process of 'digesting' culture. The two institutions described in this chapter should provide an idea of what it means to preserve culture in the context of ethnic tourism. It is a model, or to put it more precisely, the creation of a nearly perfect cultural landscape.

Appendix

The following is the description of every indigenous tribe the host gives at the beginning of each dancing programme at the Taiwan Aboriginal Cultural Park.

> *Atayal*: 'Ankalasigubi' means 'How are you' in Atayal. The Atayal are good at weaving. What the dancers wear are made by Atayal women. Traditionally, people judge the social status of any mature woman by means of the weaving patterns. Let's enjoy the programme 'Love Story in Tailuge'.

> *Saisiat*: 'Souxialahai' means 'How are you' in Saisiat. The Saisiat are well-known for the 'Rite of Little Spirits'. What you are listening to is a song of worship. The song is for memorializing Da-ay, an agricultural god, who has helped the people to receive more harvest. They practice the rite every two years at Xiangtianhu of Nanzhuang. And every ten years, the Saisiat have to hold an expanded ritual. Today, the Saisiat will use bamboo poles, abundant in the mountainous area of central Taiwan, as performing equipment to play the impressive 'Dance of Bamboo Poles'.

> *Tsou*: 'Abeibeiyou' means 'How are you' in Tsou. The Tsou is a typical patrilineal society. People attach more importance to men. The sexual division of labor is evident as both political affairs and military activities have been monopolized by the male. Tsou people have the virtue of respecting their forebears. Let's enjoy some performance aspects of the ritual

of worshipping spirits. What you are watching is the so-called four-steps' dance which has been found among all nine groups. The only difference for the Tsou in comparison to the others is their movements are from left to right instead of right to left. This special feature has an intimate connection with the traditional idea of right superiority and left inferiority. You are watching a dance of seeing the god off. Their dancing gaits look very simple, but they utilize great physical strength and patience'.

Bunun: 'Maxialasiha' means 'How are you' in Bunun. The Bunun are not only skillful at hunting, but famous for musical expression, i.e. the song for praying for a good millets' harvest. Let's relax and listen to a beautiful song of the Bunun. Please enjoy the melodious chorus'.

Puyuma: 'Simahulan' means 'How are you' in Puyuma. The Puyuma maintained a strong military power in the past. All young males had to pass a long process of Spartan training at a men's house. Today, we will enjoy a rite of passage to celebrate the coming of age and its accompanying dance'.

Ami: 'Wuayshi' means 'How are you' in Ami. The Ami's costume is the most dazzling. In Hualian, the Ami wear red clothes, but in Taidong, black becomes the major color for the same ethnic group. A great amount of varied songs and dances also can be found in almost all Ami tribal communities. The Harvest Festival usually attracts thousands of visitors each year. Now, let's enjoy a soft and light Ami dance, 'the Bamboo Stick Plays Spring Wind'.

Yami: 'Ayouyi' means 'How are you' in Yami. You are enjoying a Yami women's Dance of Swinging Hair. It celebrates their healthy and brilliant hair. Let's continue to watch the males' Spiritual Dance. The Yami call it 'Malidun'. Traditionally, the elders trained the younger generation to strengthen their physical power by using this particular dancing action. When men perform this dance on the beach, it is filled with masculine energies'.

Rukai: 'Shabaoniaw' means 'How are you' in Rukai. The handmade clothes by Rukai weavers are always admired because of their ingenious skills. The Agkistrodon acutus, a kind of krait snake, is a godlike protector of the Rukai. People thus prefer to have the snake symbol on their clothes. However, only headmen and aristocrats are qualified to put the snake image on their costume. Now we are enjoying the singing of a love song, named 'Song of the Rest on the Paddy'. It describes young persons singing of sending love to one another'.

Paiwan: 'Tawaytaway' means 'How are you' in Paiwan. Social hierarchy in Paiwan society was very strict. Class distinction between noble and headmen and commoners appeared in costume styles, the naming system, and housing decoration. Now, let's enjoy the God Harvest Year, which expresses the people's celebration by dancing and singing'.

Notes

1 I am indebted to my students Hsinchuan Su, Fengyi Cheng, Shanshan Wu, Lingpo Lin and my wife, Sally, for their co-participation in my field work. Research funding came from the National Science Council of the central government of Taiwan, and the proof reading load for the revised version of this chapter fell on the shoulders of my research assistant Yu-ling Juliane Su. I also give them my heartfelt thanks.

2 The TACP and FACV are not the first nor the only two modellized indigenous tourist spots in Taiwan which integrate cultural features of all groups into a delimited space. In the 1970s, the Government of Nantou County collected part of the traditional cultivation land of the Thao Tribe next to the Sun Moon Lake of central Taiwan to establish the first of these centers named the Center of Taiwan's 'mountain culture'. However, it was abandoned due to failed management. In addition, there is another spot located at Hualien County named Eastern Hawaiian Resort which was founded in 1990 by personal investment. Research should include this institution if one expects a more complete picture of indigenous tourism in Taiwan. Due partly to its limited scale and resrtrictions of time on my part, I have decided to focus on the two main institutions.

3 Fuguwan was originally part of the Beiye village of the Paiwan people.

4 To use the buildings as an example, one will find the dwelling-houses, watch towers, barns, chicken farms, men's houses, spiritual halls, cowsheds, graves, trenches, swings, boat-houses, earthenware-making stands, balconies, delivering houses, goat sheds, smelteries and pigsties of the nine indigenous groups.

5 A young anthropologist once wrote book drafts which describe each ethnic group. The company has never published them because of similarities with the 160-page book they already had and the marketing problems that would result.

6 My fieldwork data are insufficient to inquire into the question why Tsou and Thao, and not others, are chosen.

7 Some Amis tribesmen insist that it comes from an Amis's exclamation of admiration. Indeed, the earliest company to have arranged staged performance of indigenous dancing for tourists was in the Amis area, i.e. Hualian County on the eastern coast of the Island, opened in the 1960s. It is

possible that subsequent tourist institutions have emulated the way of yelling 'Naluwan' from the Hualian's program.

8 The other term used to refer to indigenous people was *fan*, which came into use from the seventeenth century, when the Han Chinese migrated to Taiwan. They called its aborigines *huan* or *fan* (barbarians).

9 The linguistic theory that all aboriginal dialects in Taiwan belong to the Austronesian or Malayo-Polynesian family strengthened the 'one people theory' both among academics and ordinary people. Like American aborigines who have long been uniformly characterized as Indians, all tribes were driven to develop a common identity. Many aboriginal intellectuals in Taiwan called for a united spirit in order to pursue common objectives. I once called this the 'pan-indigenous social movement' (Hsieh 1987).

References

Adams, Kathleen M. 1984 'Come to Tana Toraja, "Land of the Heavenly Kings": travel agents as broker in ethnicity', pp. 469–485 in *Annals of Tourism Research* 11.

—— 1990 'Cultural commoditization in Tana Toraja, Indonesia', pp. 31–34 in *Cultural Survival Quarterly* 14 (1).

Chen, Chi-lu 1958 'Taiwan de bowuguan he renleixue de fada' (The development of museums and anthropology in Taiwan), pp. 1–8 in *Taiwan shengli Bowuguan xue Niankan* 1.

Cohen, Erik 1988 'Traditions in the qualitative sociology of tourism', pp. 29–46 in *Annals of Tourism Research* 15.

—— 1996 *Thai Tourism: hill tribes, islands and open-ended prostitution*, Bangkok: White Lotus.

Dearden, Philip and Sylvia Harron 1993 'Alternative tourism and adaptive change', pp. 81–102 in *Annals of Tourism Research* 21.

Esman, Marjorie R. 1984 'Tourism as ethnic preservation: the Cajuns of Louisiana', pp. 451–467 in *Annals of Tourism Research* 11.

Graburn, Nelson H.H. 1983 'The anthropology of tourism', pp. 9–33 in *Annals of Tourism Research* 10.

—— 1984 'The evolution of tourist arts', pp. 393–419 in *Annals of Tourism Research* 11.

—— 1989 [1977] 'Tourism: the sacred journey', pp. 21–36 in Valene L. Smith (ed.) 1989 *Hosts and Guests: the anthropology of tourism*, Philadelphia: University of Pennsylvania Press.

Hsieh, Shih-chung 1986 'Ethnic contacts, stigmatized identity, and Pan-Taiwan aboriginalism: a study on ethnic change of Taiwan aborigines', a paper presented at the 2nd International Sysmposium on Taiwan Studies, University of Chicago, July 7, 1986.

—— 1987 *Rentong de wumin: Taiwan yuanzhumin de zuqun bianqian* (Stigmatized Identity: ethnic change among Taiwan's aborigines) Taipei: the Independent Post.

—— 1989 'Ethnic-political adaptation and ethnic change of the Sipsong Panna Dai: an ethnohistorical analysis', Ph.D. dissertation, Seattle: University of Washington.

—— 1993a 'Daile: Xishuang ban na de zuqun xianxiang' (The Tailue People: the ethnic phenomenon in Sipsang Panna), Taipei: The Independent Post.

—— 1993b 'Ximeng rensheng' (Life is like a play), *Zili Zaobao*, June 28, 1993.

—— 1994a *Shanbao guanguang: dangdai shandi wenhua zhanxian de renleixue quanshi* (Mountain people tourism: an anthropological interpretation on the performances of contemporary mountain culture), Taipei: the Independent Post.

—— 1994b 'From Shanbao to Yuanzhumin: Taiwan Aborigines in transition, pp. 404–419 in Murray A. Rubinstern (ed.) *The Other Taiwan: 1945 to the present*, Armonk, N.Y.: M. E. Sharpe.

—— 1994c 'Tourism, formulation of cultural tradition, and ethnicity: a study of Daiyan identity of the Wulai Atayal', pp. 184–201 in Stevan Harrell & Huang Chun-Chieh (eds.) *Cultural Change in Postwar Taiwan*, Boulder: Westview Press.

Leiper, Neil 1990 'Tourist attraction systems', pp. 367–384 in *Annals of Tourism Research* 17.

Li Yih-yuan et al. 1975 'Gaoshanzu yanjiu huigu yu qian zhan zuotanhui zonghe taolun jilu' (Final discussions at the symposium on 'Taiwan's Aborigines: retrospects and Prospects'), pp. 107–117 in *Bulletin of the Institute of Ethnology, Academia Sinica* 40.

Li Yih-yuan 1996 'Taita kaogu renleixuexi yu Zhongguo renleixue de fazhan' (The department of anthropology and archaeology and the development of anthropological research in China), pp. 1–5 in *Bulletin of the Department of Anthropology* 51.

Moeran, Brian 1983 'The language of Japanese tourism', pp. 93–108 in *Annals of Tourism Research* 10.

Moore, Alexander 1985 'Rosanzerusu is Los Angeles: an anthropological inquiry of Japanese tourists', pp 619–643 in *Annals of Tourism Research* 12.

Nason, James D. 1984 'Tourism, handicrafts, and ethnic identity in Micronesia', pp. 421–449 in *Annals of Tourism Research* 11.

Shih, Lei 1971 *Su-paiwan: yi ge Paiwanzu buluo de minzuxue tianyie diaocha baogao* (Su-paiwan: an anthropological investigation of a Paiwan village), Taipei: Academia Sinica.

Stanton, Max E. 1989 [1977] 'The Polynesian cultural center: a multi-ethnic model of seven Pacific cultures', pp. 247–262 in Valene L. Smith (ed.) *Hosts and Guests: the anthropology of tourism*, Philadelphia: University of Pennsylvania Press.

Swain, Margaret Byrne 1990 'Commoditizing ethnicity in southwest China, pp. 26–29 in *Cultural Survival Quarterly* 14 (1).

Sweet, Jill D. 1989 'Burlesquing the other in Pueblo performance', pp. 62–75 in *Annals of Tourism Research* 16.

Van den Berghe, Pierre L. and Charles F. Keyes 1984 'Introduction: tourism and re-crested ethnicity', pp. 343–352 in *Annals of Tourism Research* 11.

Van den Berghe, Pierre L. 1992 'Tourism and the ethnic divison of labor', pp. 234–249 in *Annals of Tourism Research* 19.

Wood, Robert E. 1984 'Ethnic tourism, the state, and cultural change in Southeast Asia', pp. 353–374 in *Annals of Tourism Research* 11 (3).

5

PEOPLES UNDER GLASS

A Tale of Two Museums[1]

Laurel Kendall

Public museums emerged with the development of national consciousness in Europe (Duncan 1991). Since then, museums have been
conspicuous monuments to emergent nationalisms throughout the
globe, telling the story of 'us' and 'Other' (Kaeppler 1994; Kaplan
1993, 1994; Morales-Moreno 1994). As the several contributors to
Flora Kaplan's (1994) volume make manifest, the judgements that
inform the spatial and visual construction of this telling may be as
varied as the national identities that museums of national and local
culture seek to make manifest. If national museums world-wide have
anything in common, it is their identity as a particular and inherently
contradictory kind of public space.

Museum buildings are often conceived as monumental. An imposing
bulk of contemporary construction gives nodding architectural allusion
to the past glories that the structure holds within its grasp by
incorporating a neo-classic façade, an imperial Chinese roof line, the
replica of a temple frieze. With government buildings, parks,
monuments, and grand boulevards, museums fill the urbanscape with
the presence of the state and its works, but museums are more overtly
didactic than any of these. The exhibits within a museum are intended
to *instruct* the public. *Education* is the high-minded purpose that
permits a dialogue among curators from all corners of the globe, causes
culture workers in distant Chinese towns to assemble and catalogue the
relics of revolutionary struggle, and brings crowds of Korean school
children to stand before glass cases and chant the otherwise forgotten
words for ritual equipment and antique household paraphernalia.

But museums are, along with public parks, also leisure spaces. With
the exception of the groups of school children that march through their
halls, attendance at a museum is not mandatory; museums must
compete for their public in an urban marketplace of leisure activities

(Ames 1992). If museum visits are conceived as a high-minded or self-improving means of spending time, this notion of moral purpose can be stultifying; if the museum's message is to be consumed, it cannot be force-fed. Acknowledging the entertainment value of museums in turn-of-the-century New York, anthropologist and curator Franz Boas opined that 'every attraction that counteracts the influence of the saloon and of the race track is of great social importance' (Boas 1907:222). Today, among curators within the United States, one hears constant discussion of the challenge posed by theme parks, debates over the degree to which a museum can reinvigorate a staid and musty image without compromising its own identity and purpose.[2] These concerns are echoed in the new museums of Asia such that one begins to find among curators a global conversation about the sorts of display techniques and entertainments that might yet bring a jaded public through the door, remarks commingled with local assessments of why this is often so difficult: the lack of any long-standing tradition of museum visiting, a more general lack of education, or the sheer exhaustion of a populace whose energies are directed to exploiting new capitalist niches.

This is a tale of two museums for the 1990s. The National Folklore Museum in Seoul, Republic of Korea, has recently moved to a new location and opened new exhibits. The Yunnan Museum of National-ities in south-west China was in its planning phase when I visited Kunming. Curators in each of these museums have attempted to provide something new, a response both to national moods and trends in Korea and China and to their own perceptions of the public they hope to lure inside. I have visited the Korean National Folklore Museum many times through its incarnations in three different locations over the past twenty years. My remarks on the museum in Kunming are based on discussions with curators and staff regarding the issues of display and representation that they considered critical to the execution of their mandates. I will be concerned with how these two very different museums choose to package for public consumption the story of a national 'us'.

The two museums coexist with other sorts of state-supported museum endeavors; most significantly, they may be contrasted with national museums of history. The history museums of East Asia have much in common with the fine arts museums of the West insofar as they set forth the choicest treasures of art and archeology for didactic and aesthetic contemplation. Their exhibits lay claim to a grand sweep of culture, from the earliest evidence of human habitation, through

112

bronze, to an art historian's periodization of sculptures, ceramics, and paintings. In China, the narrative often concludes with relics of resistance and revolution. Irrespective of whether the original inhabitants of an archeological site have only the most tenuous links to the nation's present-day inhabitants or whether only a small fraction of the population once enjoyed the objects of high culture on display, the exhibits in a history museum are offered as evidence of the depth of a people's roots in the land and the sophistication of their attainments.

The history museum differs from the fine arts museum in the expressly *national* sweep of its story (and in the somewhat more overt didacticism of its presentation). The early European museums used the looted treasures of the ancient world to further their own claims as the rightful heirs of Western civilization (Duncan 1991). The history museums of Korea, China, and Vietnam, even apart from the availability of loot, are concerned with distinctive national stories: China in the name of Chinese Civilization,[3] Korea and Vietnam because their nationalisms were constructed against perceptions of Chinese-derived Confucian culture's stifling conservatism (Robinson 1988; Marr 1981).[4]

Folk Museum/Museum of Ethnology

If the task of the history museum is to claim the full treasury of high culture in the name of a collective citizenry, the task of the folklore museum is to define the people in whose behalf national culture is claimed. Its subjects are the farmers, hunters, and artisans who inhabit a pre-industrial memory space, almost inevitably a rural space. In Europe (Linke 1990), China (Linke 1990; Hung 1985), Japan (Yanagita 1970 [1945]), and Korea (Choi 1987; Janelli 1986), scholars have gone to the countryside in pursuit of folklore, a project intertwined with emergent nationalisms in the construction of national identities. In Korea, the gleanings of this enterprise, reconstructed as museum exhibits, would obliterate the litany of historic ruptures that beset the nation in this century – colonization, national division, and the dizzy pace of social and economic transformation – would permit contemporary Koreans to find their own reflection in the faces of an authentic 'folk'. In the words of a Korean curator, 'the damage inflicted during the [Korean] war and the influx of foreign influences from abroad made it urgently necessary for Korea to collect and preserve the rapidly disappearing vestiges of folk culture' (Lee 1986:33). The 'urgency' of this statement stems from a perception that without the 'folk', Korea is unmoored and likely swamped by the cultural hegemony of Japan and the United States.

The cultures that will be portrayed in the Nationalities Museum in Kunming are also seen as fragile, in need of preservation, but as a part of whose story? The displays in this museum, like displays in ethnology museums world-wide, necessarily signify difference, not only between the peoples portrayed and the mainstream majority culture, but also between the several peoples portrayed in distinctive styles of embroidered garments with their inventories of unique tools and weapons and signature annual customs. In contrast to those projects whereby, in Curtis Hinsley's terms, an expansionist state affirms the reach of its interests by absorbing artifacts from the periphery into metropolitan displays (Hinsley 1991), the subjects of Chinese ethnographic displays are already internal Others. Like Native Americans, they are legally designated ethnicities – certified by ethnographic scrutiny – within the larger nation state. The museum's embrace is not a metaphor for the state's political or economic aspirations so much as it is a catalogue of a *fait accompli*. The task of the ethnology museum is to bring the peoples under glass within the national narrative, render their diversity part of a larger collective 'us'. This contradiction, simultaneously inside and Other, is a mirror image of that at the heart of the Korean Folk Museum where, if the manikins in glass cases are intended as an 'us' – one people, one race, one history – the necessity of casting them in pre-industrial time and rural space renders them simultaneously and emphatically 'not us'. How then do these two museums tell their stories and navigate their own contradictions?

The National Folk Museum, Korea

> The National Folk Museum is a main center for the collection of the folk art objects of Korea, a country which has a 5,000 year history. These objects are used for study, for display and for the education of people.
>
> *Guide to the National Folk Museum*, 1994, Seoul, Korea

Before it was moved to new quarters in 1993, the Korean National Folk Museum displayed a basic cultural inventory: handicrafts and technology, clothing, food, living quarters, folk beliefs, rituals of the life cycle, and performing arts and games. This same scheme could be found, more or less intact, in numerous other folk museums in many corners of the globe. It is reminiscent of the topics outlined in the English-speaking anthropologist's old field guide, *Notes and Queries on Anthropology*, the table of contents for *An Introduction to Korean Ethnology (Han'guk minsokhak kaesol*, Yi, Yi, and Chang 1974), published as a textbook for Korean college students, and numerous other projects that would record and represent a holistic vision of a people's 'customs and traditions'. The time frame is always pre-industrial, vaguely nineteenth century. In the Korean Folk Museum, a few contemporary photographs of farmers, fishermen, and weaver women in rural settings hint at the possibility of a durable folk culture outside the cities where, by the mid 1970s, a majority of the Korean population had come to reside.

The Korean folklorists' endeavor, like many scholarly pursuits, developed as a tension between specifics and generalities. Folklorists have been fascinated by regional variations in language and custom while at the same time, they have attempted to distil an essential 'Korean' substance from beneath a multiplicity of surface variations: 'the traditional Korean wedding', 'the basic structure of a Korean shaman ritual'. While this pull toward cultural holism may be found in other national folklores, it is particularly poignant in the Republic of Korea, half of a divided country and in recent decades, a polity scarred by political acrimony between the people of the Southeast and Southwest.[5] In its depictions of how a common Korean ancestry lived, worked, honored the gods and ancestors, and played, the Folk Museum presents a nearly homogenized national product. Regional variations are acknowledged in plastic replicas of local specialty foods and in the new Folk Museum, in models of regional house types.[6]

This basic ethnographic script – livelihood, material culture, life cycle, rituals, and games – is replicated in a private folk museum in the town of Onyang and in regional folk museums throughout Korea. In these different venues, the Korean master text is adapted to local styles as patterns and variations upon common Korean themes. Characteristic regional furniture is incorporated into portrayals of recognizably Korean life cycle events. Local rituals are absorbed into a Korean round of customary celebration. A habitat group in the Kwangju Folk Museum includes one of the famous yellow dogs of nearby Chin Island. The diving women of Cheju Island are part of the local presentation of fishing and farming.

In February of 1993, the Korean National Folk Museum reopened in new, expanded quarters in a building that had originally housed the National History Museum.[7] Although the Folk Museum retains its familiar ethnographic core, it has also expanded in entirely new directions even as the story of Korean identity is being retold. Between 1975, when the museum was last relocated and its exhibits reinstalled, and 1993, when the new museum opened, Korea's self-image had been profoundly transformed. In the 1970s, although material conditions were changing, seemingly at the blink of an eye, Korea was still considered a poor and underdeveloped country experiencing the trauma of rapid industrialization and urban dislocation. In the early 1980s, Korea entered the ranks of the Newly Industrialized Countries. In 1988, Korea hosted the summer Olympics, an event celebrated locally as a coming-of-age and stature in the global community. By the end of the 1980s, Korean companies were moving factories off shore to take advantage of a cheaper labor market while guest workers from Bangladesh, Pakistan, Burma, and Indochina became a visible presence, taking up such undesirable factory, construction, and domestic work as the members of a newly affluent society now disdained. Korean businesses were competing successfully for opportunities in the new markets of Eastern Europe, China, Russia, and Siberia. 'Globalization' (*segyehwa*) would become the watchword of the 1990s.

The nationalist subtext for the new museum suggests a shift in emphasis from a defensive struggle to preserve remnants of Korean culture against onslaughts of foreign influence (although this concern is still actively articulated in Korea) to a newfound pride in national accomplishment and a celebration of the national spirit that made it possible. In this, Korean nationalist discourses in the 1990s begin to resemble the cultural nationalism of late twentieth century Japan, a product of perceived strength and accomplishment rather than of perceived economic deprivation and threat (Yoshino 1992:86).

As a symbol of the new Korea, the first sight that greets the visitor's gaze in the foyer of the new Folk Museum is an architect's model of the Seoul Sports Complex designed for the 1988 Olympics. A label explains how various elements from a Korean cultural lexicon were incorporated into the stadium design, 'The stands surrounding the oval stadium field were built to resemble a Chosŏn white porcelain admired for its simplistic beauty and graceful curves. The baseball ground and the indoor pool were inspired by a *ching*, a traditional percussion instrument, and a turtle boat.[8] With its spectacular ability to function as a contemporary sports facility as well as represent Korean traditional architectural elements, the Seoul Sports Complex greatly contributed to the success of the 1988 Seoul Summer Olympics'. By implication,

116

Korean culture provided the inspiration that made the Seoul Olympics possible. By further implication, the cultural accomplishments of the past testify to the resources of the Korean people as they have emerged from war-time devastation to industrial accomplishment. The model in the foyer is a parable of the Museum's intentions.

No longer exclusively concerned with preserving the vanished pre-industrial past, the folk of folk memory and grandmother time, the museum has expended into the domain of the history museum. While the Folk Museum cannot match the quality of objects from ancient and dynastic times that are exhibited in the National History Museum, its own tradition of museology permits a great variety of didactic graphics, dioramas and habitat groups that provide an imagined context for familiar cultural relics usually displayed in the isolation of an exhibition case. An entire gallery is devoted to recreations of prehistoric communities and to the ancient Korean kingdoms of the bronze age. The folk now march through the long sweep of Korean history. One meets them on entering the first gallery and examining a large photographic mural of faces, the faces from a bronze age bell, an ancient roof tile, a Buddhist sculpture, tomb murals, genre paintings, and mortuary portraits, faces from the distant past and from more recent centuries, a composite of 'Korean faces' *(Han'guginǔi ǒlgul)*.

A slick illuminated diagram of early cultural influences on the Korean peninsula emphasizes paths of migration and cultural and linguistic transmission from northern peoples. Korean cultural historians have long found it necessary to counter a Japanese colonial historiography that saw the Japanese archipelago as the source of early cultural influences reaching Korea (Janelli 1986). The Korean people of the bronze age are described as descendants of the Tungus who reached Korea via northeastern China (Manchuria) and Mongolia, places of intense interest to Korean businessmen and tourists today. Significantly, a great deal of space is devoted to the Koguryŏ Kingdom whose archeological sites are in the North. By this emphasis, the Museum claims a common cultural history for all Koreans, North and South. Also noteworthy is a map detailing the swath of northern Korea and Manchuria that was once considered part of the Koguryŏ Kingdom. In the late 1980s, one heard a great deal about Korea's bronze age claims on Manchuria, even as Korean businessmen readied themselves for investment in the region and Korean journalists and tourists rediscovered Korean brethren who are citizens of China.

Exhibits on the prehistoric period and on the Three Kingdoms of the bronze age contain little archeological material since this is the domain of the history museum. Instead, museum artifice simulates the people of the past in active mode. Rather than simply replicating excavation sites, several dioramas suggest how the grave goods might have been used in recognizably Korean ways in the distant past. The blanks seem sometimes to have been filled in with comfortable assumptions about Korean 'tradition' as it was lived in more recent and historically accessible centuries. A bronze-age Paekche (before 663 a.d.) coastal site at Kyokp'o-ri, in Puan County, which yielded several earthenware vessels and bronze objects, is believed to have been a place where offerings were made to ensure good fishing and safe navigation. The imagined ritual, as portrayed in a diorama, suggests the form and solemnity of a Confucian rite as practiced centuries later in Chosŏn period Korea (1392–1910) although the bronze bells and replicas of armor found in the site might as easily have suggested shamanic practices. Following a Confucian prototype, the exhibit's creators also assume that all of the officiants at this Paekche ritual were necessarily male. The projection of Confucian gender assumptions is also evident in the manikins representing a Silla king and queen of the fifth to sixth century. The queen's subordination is reflected both in her short stature and in the small diadem she wears in contrast to the ornate gold crown that sits upon the king's head, although in the only Silla burial where gender can be definitively established, the gold crown is buried with the queen (Nelson 1993).

In the museum displays, manikins representing the royalty of fifteen centuries past have faces that conform to contemporary Korean standards of beauty with a suggestion of noses and eyelids that have been surgically altered.[9] With this modern look, the manikins in their freshly tailored costumes resemble the actors and actresses in Korean television dramas set during the Three Kingdoms period. By the familiarity of such embodiments and through the filter of better known 'traditions', the people of the murkiest distant past are claimed for a Korean 'us'.

Also new is a gallery that celebrates Korea's scientific and technological accomplishments. While celadon ceramic wares are exhibited for aesthetic appreciation in the History Museum (and in virtually any major installation of Korean art world wide), the Folk Museum explains the techniques of their manufacture. The viewer learns that eleventh and twelfth century Korean potters independently advanced celadon technologies introduced from ninth century China. Another case provides an overview of Korean achievements in astronomy, meteorology, geography, medicine, agriculture, printing, and the manufacturing of weapons during the Chosŏn period and particularly during the reign of King Sejong. Rain gauges, sundials, and water clocks, like those on display in the new Palace Museum, are represented in the Folk Museum by miniatures and drawings to make a comprehensive story.

The invention of the Korean *han'gul* alphabet is attributed to the 'deep national consciousness of King Sejong' (r.1418–1450) (The National Folk Museum 1994:24). In the section on printing, the second carving of the Koryŏ period Tripitaka Koreana is hailed as the 'greatest achievement in the history of world woodblock printing', and Korea's role in the development of moveable metal type is underscored. In sum, the contents of this gallery are a long way from the hand-looms, wooden plows, and millstones that filled the exhibits of the old Folk Museum. In 1990s Korea, the folk have become the legitimate ancestors of a technologically adept late twentieth century population.

Elsewhere in the museum, ethnographic exhibits have been refurbished but not significantly altered, save for one telling addition. A new section on 'Transportation and Communication' describes sophisticated commercial transactions and the extent of the market system in late dynastic times. This section has a subtext in the 'capitalist sprouts' theory favored by current Korean historiography. By this argument, the Korean economy was not so underdeveloped as its early modern detractors maintained. Had Korea been left to its own devices, the logic follows, it would have developed an indigenous modern capitalism without the trauma of colonial exploitation. The market becomes an important part of a reconstituted past, both here and in the Folk Village amusement park near the town of Suwŏn.[10] (In the amusement park, the 'traditional marketplace' provides a venue for vendors of food, drink, and souvenirs).

Korea's new global consciousness is evident in at least two display contexts within the museum. The *han'gul* display documents literacy in the Korean script in such places as North America, Central America, The (former) Soviet Union, and China, thus situating the diasporic community among the folk. A more striking departure may be found in the Special Exhibition Room, which displays 'Folk Arts of the World', Eskimo stone sculptures, Balinese wood carvings, 'folk objects from Asia, Africa, Europe, North America, South America and Oceania to represent all of mankind' (The National Folk Museum 1994:88). The museum catalogue describes this exhibition as an initial step in the creation of a new anthropological and ethnological museum. The folk have claimed their own metropole and are gathering to themselves the

119

new iconography of their expanded horizons of investment and consumption.

Yunnan Museum of Nationalities, Kunming, China

Establishing an ethnological museum is an integral component of our nationalities work as a whole. It is also a major task in the area of ethnological research. . . .Ours is a country of many nationalities united together, the country as a whole is composed of fifty-six national components. In particular, since Liberation and under the brilliant guidance of the party's nationalities policy, we have achieved tremendous results in every area of endeavor. In all the world, we stand alone as an example; this is a tremendous victory for our people of all nationalities, something of which we ought to be proud. And yet today we still do not have a formal public museum of ethnology.

Lin Yaohua, 'China's New Ethnology: Research' (1990:159)

When I visited Kunming in the spring of 1993, the Museum of Nationalities existed only as a level building site, an architect's drawing, and the plans and dreams of its future director and staff.[11] The museum is intended to represent the 25 officially recognized minority nationalities of Yunnan Province. China presents itself as a multi-ethnic society, 'a country of many nationalities united together' (ibid.). In today's China, minority nationality status carries such real privileges as permission to have more children (outside urban areas), pay fewer taxes, and have easier access to education than does the majority Han Chinese population (Gladney 1991, 1994:5). Louisa Schein suggests that by showcasing nationality cultures in museums and cultural performances, the Chinese state underscores its assertion that cultural and religious diversity within China is not only tolerated but also fostered (Schein 1989:210). Within China, nationality status is designated on the basis of a 'flexible' application of essentially Stalinist criterion – the possession of a common language, territory, and culture – all verified by scholars through fieldwork (Gladney 1991:66–67, Guldin 1994:104–8). Throughout China, ethnographic displays and cultural performances reify for popular consumption the fifty-six nationalities that have been defined and validated as such through the state's own criteria.

Ethnographic traditions within China regard nationality cultures as 'living fossils', representatives of one or another stage in the evolution of human society as defined by Lewis Henry Morgan and borrowed into Engels' *The Origin of the Family, Private Property, and the State* (Gladney 1991:72, Tong 1989). Ethnology is thus defined as 'the science that studies nationalities, including all human communities at various stages of social development' (Huang 1990 [1981]:165).[12] As in an older Western anthropology (with Marx, the product of nineteenth century evolutionary thinking), the premise that cultural development follows upon stages of technological advancement has a strong resonance within museums. The materialist enterprise is, after all, grounded in things. Curators of scholarly collections in China have happily sorted hunting equipment, loom types, fish hooks, and agricultural tools as signifiers of evolutionary phases.

These two intellectual threads – the conceptualization of nationalities as discrete cultural groups presented in great variety, and the notion of the minority nationalities as 'primitive peoples' – have taken an interesting spin within the popular imagination of post-Mao China. That the nationalities are 'primitive peoples' surviving in isolation permits the romantic envisioning of places far removed from the complexity and confusion of the contemporary moment, even as the new rich smugly mark their own distance from the hinterland (Schein 1994). That nationality cultures are portrayed as distinct, different, and unique each unto itself, invariably clothed in exotic costumes and possessed of unusual customs, provides a counter-image, an antidote of the imagination, to chase the gray-suited and monologic experience of the Maoist era (Gladney 1994:5).

China's minority nationalities, invariably described as 'colorful', are a tourist draw. Their costumed images are reproduced in postcards, travel brochures, paintings, batiks, and souvenir dolls. Their handicrafts (or mass produced facsimiles thereof) are sold in Friendship Stores and major tourist hotels. The work of photo-journalists who frequent minority areas is to be found in publications for both internal and external consumption. In a complex interplay of state sponsorship and local initiative, minority areas offer encounters with nationality cultures to both foreign and newly-prosperous domestic tourists (Schein 1989). Dru Gladney describes a contemporary Chinese scene in which 'one might even say it has become popular to be 'ethnic' in today's China. Mongolian hot pot, Muslim noodle, and Korean barbecue restaurants proliferate in every city, while minority clothing, artistic motifs, and cultural styles adorn Chinese bodies and private homes' (Gladney 1991:5). He describes a popular restaurant in Beijing, Thai Family Village, 'complete with beautiful waitresses in revealing Dai-style sarongs and short tops, sensually singing and dancing, while exotic foods such as snake's blood are enjoyed by the young Han nouveau riche' (Gladney 1991:5). In Guizhou Province, Schein encountered some enterprising young dancers who perform in ethnic costume in the clubs of distant Shanghai, Shenzen, and Beijing, replaying rituals on stage and dancing 'in unrecognizable ways that appear primitive' (Schein 1994:153).

Louisa Schein suggests that ethnic cultures have become a commodity for internal consumption (Schein 1994). The majority population would take unto itself their seemingly primitive vitality and sensuality. Han Chinese artists and musicians, and photo-journalists visit minority areas in search of inspiration for their own work (Schein 1989). In the 1980s, choreographers combed the hinterlands, seeking dances and movements to copy in 'a national search for a more earthy style' (*China Daily* 18 March 1992). A team of Chinese scholars is devoted to the study of Lunar New Year dances performed in nationality communities in central and southwest China which they see as embodying the cultural motifs of the bronze and jade masks unearthed from ancient Chinese tombs (*China Daily* 24 January 1992). In these examples, the cultural products of minority nationalities are valorized not merely as 'living fossils' but as 'living fossils from *China's* folk culture', a source of one's own primal vitality that can be reclaimed and ingested like an invigorating tonic.

The new Yunnan Museum of Nationalities is heir both to intellectual traditions in nationality studies and to the enthusiasms of the contemporary moment. As of 1993, the provincial government of Yunnan Province had authorized the construction of a museum with three major exhibition halls to exhibit nationality cultures, the natural history of Yunnan Province, and local history (formerly revolutionary history). The itinerary – from natural science, through history, to ethnicity – replicates the exhibition scheme of the Yunnan Provincial Museum and that of the proposed Kunming City Museum. The minority nationalities would seem to mediate between nature and the larger history of China in a manner consistent with a social evolutionary view of ethnology. The planning committee for the Nationalities Museum did not seem to be particularly enthused about nature and history; they see the exhibition of nationality cultures as the museum's central project and assume that a nod in other directions will be sufficient to satisfy the specifications of the Provincial Government.

The Nationalities Museum's expressed purpose is as a center for cultural preservation, research, and public education. Through a program of international travel and dialogue with museum specialists outside of China, organized by the Center for United States-China Arts Exchange and funded primarily by the Ford Foundation,[13] the museum now articulates a sense of mission that includes the performance and demonstration of nationality arts and handicrafts, education, outreach, and satellite programs that serve remote communities, including and most particularly nationality communities. That the land allocated for the Museum is across the road from a popular theme park in a developing lake-side area suggests that provincial-level planners might also see the museum as a source of tourist revenue.[14]

If the Museum stands to benefit from the 'ethnic boom', members of the planning committee see their own task as having been compromised by the opening of a 'Nationalities Village' (*Minzu Cun*) theme park, modeled on a successful venture in the southern industrial city of Shenzen and run by the Travel and Tourism Administration of Yunnan Province. The tension between education and popular entertainment could not be felt more acutely than in the case of the Yunnan Museum of Nationalities where the competing theme park is quite literally in their own backyard. Sections of the park are devoted to different nationalities, with 'typical' architecture, food, handicrafts, and costumed attendants who are almost invariably pretty young women. Famous sites, including the pagodas of Xishuangbanna and the decorated Bai houses of Dali, have been simulated and provide picturesque backdrops for many a souvenir photograph. A central performance area features music, dances, and feats of skill from the different nationalities. On the day that I visited the park, someone was climbing a ladder of knives in approximation of a Lisu ceremony. On a sunny Sunday afternoon, the Nationalities Village was filled with local crowds dressed in their best, mostly in family groups.

Scholars from the planning committee for the new Nationalities Museum, a group that includes members of Yunnan nationalities, grumbled that their own ideas for presenting ethnic music and dance performances and serving ethnic foods had been preempted by the theme park. The Museum's own plan had called for an auditorium for ethnic performances, but this had not been authorized by the provincial government, probably because it was seen as duplicating facilities available in the theme park. The planners were now forced to make a case to the provincial government that there was merit in the museum's hosting authentic cultural performances despite the entertainment offered across the way. The experts' more scathing critique of the Nationalities Village was that it was constructed as a money-making venture, not as an accurate portrayal of nationality cultures. In their view, the architectural representations, costumes, and performances are not always representative of the groups they are purported to portray and the costumed 'Bai', 'Dai', 'Yi', and 'Naxi' who greet guests, serve snacks, and perform are often just stand-ins, not authentic members of the ethnicities they claim to represent (echoes of a complaint that one hears often in the vicinity of Waikiki Beach). Even so, the theme park was drawing crowds, and drawing them some distance from the city. Its open-air expanse, filled with numerous sights and amusements, food vendors, and comfortable spots where one might simply sit and rest, holds the prospect of several pleasant hours. Could those attracted by the amusements of the Nationalities Village be lured across the way to the new museum?

At the time of our conversations, the Director placed great hope in the novelty of technology, envisioning a splashy video installation in the foyer as a comprehensive introduction to the museum and its exhibits. This would be a pleasant departure from the austerely cavernous foyers of so many Chinese museums. 'Authenticity' is another banner under which the new Museum might rally, tempting the theme park's visitors with a glimpse of the 'real thing'.

The planning committee is already very much concerned with the preservation of the nationalities' culture and arts. Where, in the past, nationality villages were considered sites for enlightenment and uplift, they are now seen as cultures at risk, in need of protection and preservation as the siren song of the market economy reaches even the most isolated communities. One hears how the booming tourist industry tempts the youth of nationality villages to abbreviate, improvise, or otherwise bastardize traditional performing arts for the benefit of tour groups 'who don't know any better'. Shoddily produced 'ethnic' bags and embroideries are sold on the streets of Kunming and in the theme park in crude approximation of local handicrafts.[15] This is a familiar story of global proportions, but this very fact gives a sense of urgency to the Museum's intention of recognizing exemplary performers and artisans and including their work as an integral part of its program.[16]

Whether as living fossils or as cultures at risk, the weight of the Chinese intellectual tradition and the romantic needs of the contemporary moment ensure that the Nationalities will be portrayed as in and of the past, of a piece with the older ethnology exhibits in the Korean National Folklore Museum. Several of the consultants sent to Kunming under auspices of the United States-China Arts Exchange, raised the critiques leveled by Native Americans that museums have long neglected to portray them as contemporary people possessed of a living and innovative culture.[17] When this issue was raised by a fellow curator during my visit, it proved to be a point of profound cross-cultural disagreement, at least as of 1993. One member of the planning committee, who had seen some of the new Native American installations in the United States, felt that the inclusion of works of non-traditional Native American art in museums alongside more traditional artifacts was a mistake. He felt that the celebration of unabashedly invented traditions such as the pow-wow were inappropriate and a potentially corrosive influence. When the Director was asked if he would collect the pair of factory-produced athletic shoes that might be worn with a traditional festival costume, he replied that he might photograph the whole costume, but he would not collect the shoes. When an American curator persisted in emphasizing the need to represent contrasts in the living of contemporary lives, the Director felt that in today's China, the contrasts are self-evident, 'When members of the Nationalities come into the Museum in Kunming, wearing their modern clothing, when they look into the glass cases, that is contrast enough'.

Summary and Conclusion

Far beyond the didactic intentions of their displays, museums tell us a great deal about those who constructed them (Clifford 1985, 1988; Haraway 1985; Jordanova 1991). The voluminous literature on museums and museum displays has most often posed its critique in terms of the West and the rest, defining the acquisition of objects from the periphery and the portrayal of peoples under glass as both sign and affirmation of the hegemony of the metropole (Clifford 1985; Corbey 1993; Hinsley 1991; Jones 1993; Marcus 1991; Rydell 1984; Stocking 1985). But museums are nearly ubiquitous within post-colonial nation states where they serve as handmaidens to the telling of new national stories. Even where the museum is a colonial legacy, as in Korea and Vietnam, it has been swiftly and seamlessly transformed into a repository for tangible symbols of the national imaginary (see Anderson 1993).[18] The very familiarity of museum forms – art museums, history museums, museums of folklore and ethnology – works against an appreciation of the subtleties of local variations that might also, in the manner of any cultural text, tell us a great deal about those who constructed them. The value of exploring the relationship between local histories of museum construction and display and specific national stories is suggested by several essays in the volume edited by Kaplan (1994), contributions to a special issue of *Museum Anthropology* (1995) on museums and the politics of nationalism, and recent work by Richard and Sally Price (1995). My own contribution to this discussion would be to underscore that 'nationalisms' contained within museums are infinitely variable. Familiar institutional forms and display techniques may be deployed to articulate profoundly different notions of 'nation' and 'citizen'. Even a single museological tradition can be colored by shifting perceptions of a national 'us'.

Displays of artifacts and costumed manikins set in 'folkloric time' vest folk and ethnology museums with a cozy air of familiarity wherever in the world one encounters them. Like many other museums in many other places worldwide, both the Korean national Folk Museum and the Yunnan Museum of Nationalities came into being at moments when the cultures they portrayed were seen as jeopardized, in post-war Korea by industrialization, demographic shifts, and foreign influences; in the mountains of Yunnan by the lure of towns, mass culture, and the new market economy that has ushered in a burgeoning tourist industry. Like most folk and ethnology museums, the museum in Seoul and the museum in Kunming would preserve the fragile essence of a preindustrial past, something witnessed by, but transcendent of, the artifacts and recorded customs portrayed in their exhibits. The Korean folk hold the key to a distinctive national identity. China's minority nationalities retain a vitality that has been lost to (but might yet be reappropriated by) the majority population.

So much for the similarities. The Korean National Folklore Museum constructs its folk as one unitary people,[19] reconciling regional differences into a cohesive body of Korean custom recognizable across space and through time. In the new museum, reflecting the more confident nationalism of late twentieth century Korea, the story has stretched pre-industrial memories backward through the ancient bronze age kingdoms to the neolithic. The exhibits are no longer restricted to homespun folkways; they now include the heirlooms that provide an ancestral pedigree for Korea's more recent accomplishments in technology, commerce, and industry. This is not just a story of 'the way we were', but of 'who we are and have always been'.

China, by contrast, defines itself as a multi-ethnic society and shores up this message with ethnographic displays that witness diversity. The new museum in Kunming takes shape at a moment when nationality cultures are being romanticized and their images, songs, dances, and handicrafts are being widely consumed by newly prosperous urban Chinese. This moment gives the new museum a vast potential audience but it also poses a new threat to the 'authenticity' of nationality cultures, the *raison d'être* of the museum. In Kunming, local arts and handicrafts are already streamlined for mass consumption, nowhere more immediately than in the amusement park that threatens the museum's flank. The incorporation of live performers and artisans into the museum's own program is one response to the challenge posed by commodified minority cultures, but the concluding chapters of this story are still being written.

Neither the Korean nor the Chinese museum resonated with the American curator's imperative to acknowledge ethnographic subjects 'as they are today'. The National Folklore Museum made one link between 'then' and 'now' with its model of the Olympic Stadium, a structure encrusted with symbolic representations of 'Korean culture' and constructed to mark an event often seen as a culmination of decades of national effort, a 'coming out party' for a developed country. Koreans define themselves as a people with a 5,000 year history; 'yesterday' and 'today' are self-evident. In historical exhibits constructed by Koreans for Koreans, a nod to the contemporary is as irrelevant as it would be to Americans visitors at 'Colonial Williamsburg;' present-day life intrudes all around, or to borrow the phrase of the Chinese director, the museum visitor in modern dress is 'contrast enough'. The distinction between past and present, between 'us' and the peoples under glass, is murkier in Kunming. The numerous urbanized members of minority nationalities who might visit the new museum may well regard the exhibits as history, but other visitors, heirs to an intellectual tradition that regards the nationalities as 'primitives' (albeit increasingly romantic and desirable primitives) and sees them as inhabiting distant communities deep in the mountains may be less inclined to assume a historic frame for the peoples under glass.

The Nationalities Museum chooses to tell a story about 'authenticity' for an audience that wants to believe in places where cultural integrity persists, where it might be encountered, consumed, ingested into the self. For urban Koreans, 'the countryside' has long provided an imaginary space, a repository of pure traditions in the face of profound and unsettling changes (Kendall 1996). It has become increasingly difficult to believe in the persistence of such a space outside of a few intentionally preserved or carefully simulated 'Folk Villages'. The Eskimo stone sculptures and Balinese wood carvings displayed in a special exhibition hall of the new Korean National Folklore Museum as a promise of things to come suggest a new imaginary that has begun to take shape, both in the popular imagination and under glass.

Notes

1 I traveled to Kunming under the auspices of the Center for United States-China Arts Exchange. I am grateful to the staff of the Center and to the scholars and museum personnel in Kunming who made this trip so memorable. I would acknowledge, in particular, the generous hospitality of Gao Zongyu, then First Deputy Director, Preparatory Committee, Yunnan Nationalities Museum, now Director of the Museum. In Kunming, Stephen A. Becker, then Director of the Museum of Indian Arts and Culture, now Executive Director of the Turtle Bay Park and Museum, posed many of the questions and offered many of the insights that made this effort possible. Young-kyu Park has enriched my knowledge of Korean museums. Chou Wen-chung, Molly Lee, Susan Rhodes, and Enid Schildkrout had many useful comments on an early draft of this paper. The opinions and interpretations contained in this paper are my own and I alone am responsible for its many shortcomings.

2 For example, in the recent *New Yorker* article, 'Shake Them Bones' (Traub 1995), American Museum of Natural History President Ellen Futter plays the negative image of a staid and musty museum against her own vision of AMNH's future.

3 Books of Chinese connoisseurship include mention of exotic tribute goods, but these are not a normal part of the contemporary historical display (Clunas 1991). One striking exception is the Palace Museum's collection of ornate Western clocks bestowed upon Emperors by Europeans seeking trade and other advantages in China. In this instance, China is metropole to a European periphery.

4 The distant fourth floor of the National History Museum of Korea housed a rare collection of artifacts from Japanese excavations on the Silk Road purchased in colonial times by the Japanese Governor-General of Korea for a nascent museum in Seoul (Hopkirk 1980:232–233). Until the late 1980s, when the Museum moved to enlarged quarters, the collection was kept in storage. See note 7 below.

5 Park Chung Hee, who seized power in 1961 through a military *coup d'état*, and his successors were military men who hailed from the Southeast. Kim Dae Jung, for many years the opposition leader, came from the Southwest, an impoverished region with a pedigree for oppositional politics that could be traced back to late dynastic times. In the Park years, it was widely perceived that persons from the southern provinces of North and South Kyŏngsang were favored in all manner of appointments, contracts, and disputes, while the government's ambitious development projects initially bypassed southwestern provinces of North and South Chŏlla. The massacre of protesting citizens by the military in the southwestern city of Kwangju in 1980 was similarly perceived in regional terms. Korea elected a civilian president in 1992 who was not strongly identified with east or west. Kim Dae Jung was elected in 1997.

6 Regional house types, in some cases assemblages of original structures, are prominent in the displays in the privately-owned Korean Folk Village amusement park near the town of Suwŏn.

7 After much debate, the National History Museum was relocated in the old capital building, leaving the structure that it had inhabited since the early 1970s to the Folk Museum. The History Museum's move to the capital building never sat well with those nationalist interests who saw the structure as a relic of the Japanese colonial presence. The old capital building, set in front of the Kyŏngbok Palace at the center of Seoul, spatially and symbolically superseded the royal structure and is widely believed to have been intentionally located so as to cut the flow of beneficent geomantic properties form the palace to the Korean nation. At the time of this writing, the National History Museum will be relocated to a new building. The old capital was destroyed in commemoration of the fiftieth anniversary of Korea's liberation from Japanese rule. The obliteration of Japanese colonial influences from the Seoul skyline and attempts to restore old royal structures to their pre-colonial splendor is, itself, an interesting tale in cultural politics.

8 Iron-clad boats in the broad shape of turtles were used by the hero Admiral Yi Sunsin in successful battles against Hideyoshi's invasion force in the late sixteenth century. The turtle boat is a potent national symbol, a frequent image for nick-knacks and children's toys, and a popular name for all manner of products.

9 I was sensitized to this observation by the museum's own temporary exhibition on 'the Korean face', on view in the summer of 1994, which did consider changing standards of masculine and feminine beauty over time. According to one survey reported in a weekly magazine in 1989, from twenty to thirty per cent of all unmarried Korean women in thier early twenties have cosmetic surgery performed on their eyes, noses, mouths, or breasts in approximation of 'Western' standards of beauty (cited in Hart 1991:256).

10 For a discussion and critique of this issue, see Eckert (1991:ch.1).

11 The museum has since opened, but my remarks are necessarily restricted to the time of my visit.

12 Until very recently, Chinese anthropology was conceptualized as 'the study of nationalities', the literal translation of *minzuxue*, the term commonly translated as 'ethnology' (Huang 1990 [1981]:165; Gulden 1994:104–8). Emerging from under the onus cast upon their discipline during the Cultural Revolution, Chinese anthropologists have begun since the 1980s to seek new directions, new sources of theoretical inspiration, and to define their discipline more broadly. For some sense of the dialogue that has taken place see Guldin (1994); Huang (1990 [1981]); and Zhou (1993).

13 The project was also funded by the Asian Cultural Council and the United Board for Christian Higher Education in Asia.

14 In China, museums and other public points of interest often charge a higher admission fee to obvious foreigners than they do to local visitors.

15 Between my first visit to Kunming in 1987 and my second in 1991, the street vendors had learned the English phrase 'small stitch, small stitch' in an appeal to the more discriminating buyer.

16 The implications of certifying 'authentic' folk performers, as in the case of the Human National Treasures systems of Japan, Korea, and Thailand deserves a more extended discussion than space allows here. Suffice it to say here that these questions were discussed in Kunming.

17 American, Asian, and Native American visitors were sensitive to this issue.
18 Even where the post-colonial museum may be burdened by a legacy that privileged colonial and military history over indigenous culture, its potential role in nation building is assumed. See Munjeri's (1991) description of the situation in Zimbabwe.
19 The term *minjok* in Korean signifies 'a people,' 'a race,' 'a nationality'. The phrase *Han minjok*, 'The Korean people' (*Hanminjok*, the people descended from the ancient *Han* tribes) carries the homophonous meaning 'one people' (*hanminjok*).

References

Ames, Michael M. 1992. *Cannibal Tours and Glass Boxes: the anthropology of museums*, Vancouver: UBC Press.

Anderson, Benedict 1983 *Imagined Communities: reflections on the origins and spread of nationalism*, London: Verso.

Boas, Franz 1907 'Some principles of museum administration', pp. 921–933 in *Science*, n. s. 25.

Bureau of Cultural Properties Preservation, Republic of Korea 1969 (1966) *Guide to Museum of Korean Folk-lore*, Seoul: Bureau of Cultural Properties Preservation, Republic of Korea.

Bureau of Cultural Properties 1978 *Guide to the National Folklore Museum*, Seoul: Ministry of Culture, Bureau of Cultural Properties Preservation.

Choi, In-Hak 1987 'Non-academic factors in the development of Korean and Japanese folklore scholarship,' paper presented to the Annual Meeting of the American Anthropological Association, Chicago, Illinois, November, 1987.

Clifford, James 1985 'Objects and selves' pp. 236–246 in G. W. Stocking, Jr. (ed.) *Objects and Others: Essays on Museums and Material Culture*, Madison: University of Wisconsin Press.

Clifford, James 1988 'On ethnographic surrealism', pp. 117–151 in J. Clifford *The Predicament of Culture: twentieth-century ethnography, literature, and art*, Cambridge (Massachusetts) and London: Harvard University Press.

Clunas, Craig 1991 *Superfluous Things: material culture and social status in early modern China*, Urbana and Chicago: University of Illinois Press.

Corbey, Raymond 1993 'Ethnographic showcases, 1870–1930', pp. 338–369 in *Cultural Anthropology* 8 (3).

Duncan, Carol 1991 'Art museums and the ritual of citizenship' pp. 88–103 in I. Karp and S. D. Levine (eds.) *Exhibiting Cultures: the poetics and politics of museum display*, Washington and London: Smithsonian Institution Press.

Eckert, Carter J. 1991 *Offspring of Empire: the Koch'ang Kims and the colonial origins of Korean capitalism*, Seattle: University of Washington Press.

Gladney, Dru C. 1991 *Muslim Chinese: ethnic nationalism in the People's Republic*, Cambridge (Massachusetts) and London: Harvard University Press.

Gladney, Dru C. 1985 'China's Ethnic Reawakening', pp. 1–8 in *Asia Pacific Issues* 18 (January),.

Gulden, Gregory Eliyu 1994 *The Saga of Anthropology in China: from Malinowski to Moscow to Mao*, Armonk, New York and London.

Haraway, Donna 1985 'Teddy bear patriarchy: taxidermy in the garden of Eden, New York City, 1908–1936', pp. 20–64 in *Social Text* 32.

Hart, Dennis Michael 1991 'From Tradition to consumption: the rise of a materialist culture in South Korea', Ph.D. dissertation, University of Washington.

Hinsley, Curtis M. 1991 'The world as marketplace: commodification of the exotic at the world's Columbian Exposition, Chicago, 1893', pp. 344–365 in I. Karp and S. D. Levine (eds.) 1991 *Exhibiting Cultures: the poetics and politics of museum display*, Washington and London: Smithsonian Institution Press.

Hopkirk, Peter 1980 *Foreign Devils on the Silk Road: the search for the lost cities and treasures of Chinese Central Asia*, Amherst, The University of Massachusetts Press.

Huang Shuping 1990 (1981) 'Developing ethnology in our country is what the construction of Socialism needs', pp. 162–173 in G. E. Gulden (ed.) 1990 *Anthropology in China: defining the discipline*, Armonk, New York and London: M.E. Sharpe, Inc.

Hung, Chang-tai 1985 *Going to the People: Chinese intellectuals and folk literature, 1918–1937*, Cambridge, Massachusetts: Council on East Asian Studies, Harvard University.

Janelli, Roger L. 1986 'The origins of Korean folklore scholarship', pp. 24–49 in *Journal of American Folklore* 99 (391).

Jones, Anna Laura 1993 'Exploding Canons: The Anthropology of Museums', pp. 201–219 in *Annual Review of Anthropology* 22.

Jordanova, Ludmilla 1991 'Objects of knowledge: a historical perspective on museums', pp. 22–40 in P. Vergo (ed.) *The New Museology*, London: Reaktion Books.

Kaeppler, Adrianne L. 1994 'Paradise Regained: The Role of Pacific Museums in Forging National Identity', pp. 19–44 in F. E. Kaplan (ed.) *Museums and the Making of Ourselves*, Leicester: Leicester University Press.

Kaplan, Flora E. S. 1993 'Mexican museums in the creation of a national image in world tourism', pp. 103–126 in J. Nash (ed.) *Crafts in the World Market: the impact of global exchange on Middle American artisans*, Albany: State University of New York Press.

Kaplan, Flora E. S. (ed.) 1994a *Museums and the Making of Ourselves*, Leicester: Leicester University Press.

Kaplan, Flora E. S. 1994b 'Nigerian museums: envisaging culture as national identity', pp. 45–78 in F. E. Kaplan (ed.) *Museums and the Making of Ourselves*, Leicester: Leicester University Press.

Kendall, Laurel 1996 *Getting Married in Korea: of gender, morality, and modernity*, Berkeley and Los Angeles: University of California Press.

Lee, Nan-young 1986 'Museums in the Republic of Korea', pp. 30–35 in *Museum* 149.

Lin, Yaohua 1990 'China's new ethnology: Research', pp. 141–161 in G. E. Gulden (ed.) *Anthropology in China: defining the discipline*, Armonk, New York and London: M.E. Sharpe, Inc.

Linke, Uli 1990 'Folklore, Anthropology, and the Government of Social Life', pp. 117–148 in *Comparative Studies in Society and History* 32 (1).

Marcus, Julie 1991 'Postmodernity and the museum', pp. 10–19 in *Postmodern Critical Thinking* 30 (December).

Marr, David G. 1981 *Vietnamese Tradition on Trial, 1920–1945*, Berkeley and Los Angeles: University of California Press.

Morales-Moreno, Luis Gerardo 1994 'History and patriotism in the national museum of Mexico', pp. 171–191 in F. E. Kaplan (ed.) *Museums and the Making of Ourselves*, Leicester: Leicester University Press.

Munjeri, Dawson 1991 'Refocusing or reorientation? the exhibit or the populace: Zimbabwe on the threshold', pp. 444–456 in I. Karp and S. D. Levine (eds.) *Exhibiting Cultures: the poetics and politics of museum display*, Washington and London: Smithsonian Institution Press.

Museum Anthropology 1995 19(2) = Special Issue on Museums and Nationalism.

The National Folk Museum 1994 *Guide to the National Folk Museum*, Seoul: The National Folk Museum.

Nelson, Sarah M. 1993 'Gender Hierarchy and the Queens of Silla', pp. 297–315 in B.D. Miller (ed.) *Sex and Gender Hierarchies*, Cambridge U. Press.

Price, Richard, and Sally Price 1995 'Executing culture: musée, museo, museum', pp. 97–109 in *American Anthropologist* 97 (1).

Robinson, Michael Edson 1988 *Cultural Nationalism in Colonial Korea, 1920–1925*, Seattle: University of Washington Press.

Rydell, Robert W. 1984 *All the World's a Fair*, Chicago: University of Chicago Press.

Schein, Louisa 1989 'The dynamics of cultural revival among the Miao in Guizhou', pp. 119–212 in *New Asia Academic Bulletin* 8.

Schein, Louisa 1994 'The consumption of color and the politics of white skin in post-Mao China', pp. 143–164 in *Social Text* 41.

Stocking, George W., Jr. 1985 'Essays on museums and material culture', pp. 3–14 in G. W. Stocking, Jr. (ed.) *Objects and Others: Essays on Museums and Material Culture*, Madison: University of Wisconsin Press.

Tong, Enzheng 1989 'Morgan's model and the study of ancient Chinese society', pp. 182–205 in *Social Sciences in China* (June).

Traub, James 1995 'Shake them bones', pp. 48–62 in *The New Yorker* 13 March 1995.

Yanagita, Kunio 1970 (1945) *About our Ancestors*, Tokyo: Ministry of Education.

Yi Kwanggyu, Yi Tuhyŏn, and Chang Chugun 1974 *Han'guk Minsokhak Kaesŏl (Introduction to Korean Folklore)*, Seoul: Minjung Sŏgwan.

Yoshino, Kosaku 1992 *Cultural Nationalism in Contemporary Japan*, London and New York: Routledge.

Zhou, Daming 1993 'Review of a decade of the re-establishment of anthropology in China', pp. 95–106 in *Social Sciences in China* (Summer).

6

CONSUMING ANTHROPOLOGY

The Social Sciences and
Nation-Formation in Malaysia

Shamsul A.B.

Introduction

Contemporary discourse on 'consumption and consumerism in Asia' is overwhelmed by discussions of the lifestyle and habits of the ever-expanding middle-class in various parts of the continent. This should be no surprise as Asia has been, at least until 1997–98, generally perceived, in economic growth terms, as the continent of the next millennium. Inevitably, this has led to the rapid growth of a research and publication industry on 'Asian middle class', at least in the last five years, both within and outside Asia (Robinson and David Goodman 1996; Kahn, 1996; Abdul Rahman, 1996; Tanter and Young 1990; Gomes 1994). Such a keen interest in the Asian middle class is a response both to the general market demand in Asia, because big consumer-product-oriented companies want to know what the Asian middle class like to spend their money on, as well as academic market demand, perhaps because it is easier to get research fund, to get one's work published and to get academic jobs if one researches and writes on the Asian middle class.

What has been neglected by observers and analysts of Asian socio-economic affairs is Asia's newfound political appetite, especially amongst the Asia-Pacific countries, for 'consuming' a different sort of 'consumer item', namely, the latest arms and weapons produced mainly in the Western advanced countries. In expenditure terms, these are equal to or may be much larger than what the middle class in each of the countries spends on consumer goods. More importantly, Asia has always been a big consumer of ideas and knowledge of all sorts, especially those originating from the West, long before the term 'information technology' was invented. For instance, for purposes of maintaining political stability and a semblance of democracy in its race to become industrialised as well in its attempt at 'nation-building', Asian countries have also become a big consumer of new methods of intelligence gathering and social control. Perhaps it is not really fashionable for 'post-modernists' to deal with 'meta-narratives' on consumerism of arms race and control involving 'countries' or 'regions' as units of analysis, preferring instead a more manageable 'the other', such as the 'individual' or smaller 'social collective'.

This modest chapter intends to redress this problem of an over-emphasis on the Asian middle class in the discourse on 'consumption and consumerism in Asia' by examining in some detail how knowledge, especially in the social sciences, has been produced and consumed by the colonial or postcolonial state for purposes of economic, bureaucratic and political control, and carried out under the guise of fulfilling the needs of economic growth or nation-formation. We have observed, both during the colonial and postcolonial era, how the state produced and consumed knowledge by defining and classifying space, making separations between public and private spheres, by recording transactions such as property sale, by counting and categorizing the populations, and by standardizing languages and scripts (Cohn 1996). The state recognised some activities as legal and suppressed others as illegal or immoral. The schools became the crucial 'civilizing' institutions, and nation-states came to be seen as the natural embodiments of history, territory and society. Thus, the establishment and maintenance of the state depended upon determining, codifying, controlling, and representing the past as well as re-inventing the past for contemporary political consumption purposes.

This chapter first focuses on the role and consumption of anthropological knowledge and, later, anthropology as an academic discipline in the process of state as well as nation-making in Malaysia during the colonial and post colonial era. It also offers a broader framework against which an explanation can be made as to why anthropology, or anthropology-related knowledge, has become an important 'consumer item' at the grassroot level in contemporary nation-formation process in Malaysia, leading in turn to the reconstitution, or 'Malaysianization', of anthropology in Malaysia. We shall now turn to a brief discussion of the dialectical relations between nation-formation and social scientific knowledge production and consumption before proceeding to take a closer look at the Malaysian case.

Consuming knowledge for nation-formation

In recent literature on nationalism and nation-formation, we rarely find any attempt being made to explore the relationship between nation-formation and the social sciences, except in the most oblique manner (see, e.g. Hutchinson and Smith [1994] and Guibenau [1996]). This is despite the widely acknowledged fact that the birth of the social sciences is closely related to the many-faceted circumstances that led to the birth of the nation. For instance, Giddens argued that the modern nation-state and social science, particularly sociology as a social scientific discipline, are intimately linked (Giddens 1990, 1996). This is not at all surprising because the self-understanding of a national community as a culturally homogenous and spatio-temporally delimited entity, or as 'the nation', especially in 18th century Europe, provided the model, under the conditions of modernity, for a distinct sphere of 'the social'. This new understanding of 'the social' as a theoretical category made social science possible.

We also observe that the close links which social science has with the nation-state were forged at a time when European nation-states were engaged in establishing a new global order. Colonialism, and later imperialism, required that the main Western powers reach an understanding for an efficient exploitation of their resources. The global economy then required the increasing co-ordination of transnational regions of production, exchange and consumption. This required a basis of consensus beyond the nation, which was provided by the transnational community of scholars, namely, the social scientists, who then provided the much needed ideals of a universal and empirical (social) science. In fact, 'orientalism' as a form of knowledge, says Edward Said, also emerged and came to be propagated and consolidated within such circumstances.

According to Cohn (1996:4), based on a detailed systematic study, over three decades, of British rule in India, knowledge which replaced indigenous knowledge through the introduction of 'officializing procedures' that finally conquered the 'epistemological space' of the native should be termed as 'colonial knowledge'. The colonial state took control of the epistemological space by defining and classifying physical and social space, making separations between public and private spheres, replacing religious institutions as the registrar of births, marriages and deaths, and by standardizing language and scripts. They also collected a massive amount of data which they analysed and documented and became the basis of their capacity to govern. These created data became 'facts'. Subsequently, colonial knowledge came to be perceived as the natural embodiments of history, territory and society of the post-colonial nation-state.

It is also important to recognise that both the nation-state and social science are modern inventions and an acknowledged feature of modernity is the crucial role of knowledge for the expression, maintenance and reproduction of power. While knowledge represents a form of power, certain modes of power, such as policing and crowd control, in the conditions of modernity can only be expressed through its relationship with knowledge, such as the activity of spying and surveillance. However, we are not suggesting that social science is the 'slave of the nation-state'. Even as social science requires the resources of the modern nation-states for its teaching and research needs, especially in the postcolonial context, it is equally dependent on a vigorous civil culture distinct from the state, lest the state conflates its interests (particularly in 'nationhood') with (civil) society at large. In other words, knowledge is not only a relationship of power. Rather power requires new forms of knowledge, such as social science, for its effectiveness in modern society. Hence, as many have argued, a critical social science is necessary to counterbalance modern society's functional goals because social science has emancipatory as well as instrumental goals (Syed Husin Ali 1995; Shamsul 1997).

Therefore, there has been an established relationship between nation-formation and social science, both in the past and at present. In spite of 'globalization' and the 'borderless world', the nation-state remains arguably the single most important political unit, both as a polity as well as an analytical category that frames global social conduct. This affects the way social sciences develops, the approach to social science research, and how it is taught as a corpus of knowledge. While one could claim its universality, for many reasons, social science and its practice remain trapped in its 'dividedness' and organized usually within a 'the nation-state'. For instance, in bureaucratic terms, the teaching of social science has always been divided along the disciplinary lines and rarely taught as a single knowledge entity. It could be divided up, in organizational terms, into departments, institutes, centres and faculties (faculty of economics, faculty of arts and so on).

Nonetheless, however fragmented the organization of the teaching, research and publication within the social science, the divided-up parts are often 'united' or 'grouped' under the umbrella of the 'nation-state', be it under or within an organization such as a 'national social science commission', 'social science research council', 'national liaison committee for social science' or 'social science academy'. It is in this context that social science and its practice becomes intricately linked with the interests of the nation-state; almost without exception nation-states in the world today are run and governed by social scientists, who, in turn, often have prominent local and foreign social scientists as their advisors.[1]

The academic social scientists often find this situation difficult to cope with especially if they are employed in state-sponsored universities and yet wanting to voice dissenting views on social issues that could be perceived as 'criticizing the government' or, worse still, as 'threatening national security and political stability' of the country. This also happened during the colonial era, where independence fighters and nationalists, most of whom are social scientists employed in various vocations and levels, were put behind bars for 'anti-establishment' activities. Draconian laws and regulations were often introduced to prevent these activists from 'poisoning' the mind of the people. In other words, there is, embedded within social science, a potentially 'explosive' political element, one that is viewed by the powers as having the capability to subvert the state. Therefore, it is inevitable that the nature of the relationship between nation-state and social science has always been a dialectical one.

It is against this backdrop that an examination of the contemporary relationship between nation-formation and social science becomes more useful and significant. In order to allow us to conduct such an examination in a more fruitful manner, it is useful to refer to a concrete experience. This chapter intends to present some of the experiences from the Malaysian case. To be more specific, this chapter wishes to investigate the central role of anthropology in the growth of social scientific knowledge on Malaysia, on simply known as 'Malaysian studies',[2] as well as in Malaysia's nation-formation process, especially as a dominant disciplinary approach within 'Malay studies', which has been the core of Malaysian studies. Therefore the main focus is on the historical and intellectual role of anthropology, both during the colonial and post-colonial period, as the 'midwife' of Malay studies. The chapter will also present a brief description and analysis of the 'Malaysianization' of anthropology in its curriculum and content, as it is being taught in contemporary Malaysia. In the subsequent section, 'the grass-roots' response to anthropology will be presented, both as an academic discipline as well as for career development in the public and private sector in Malaysia. Finally, an attempt will be made to project the future path of anthropology in Malaysia, especially within the context of its effort at nation-formation.

From 'Anthropological Studies' to 'Anthropology'

Within the social sciences and humanities, anthropology came into existence as a formally recognized academic discipline in the late nineteenth century. However in Malaysia it was only about eighty years later, in 1970, that anthropology was taught formally as a discipline and entered the faculty structure as a full-fledged academic department. This had more to do with state-level factors than with the state of anthropology itself.

Before 1970, and particularly during the colonial period (1819–1957), anthropology, as a medium of intellectual discourse and as a method of knowledge accumulation, was an integral part of the administrative science of the colonial state, instrumental in the construction of the colonial imagination and knowledge about the 'natives' of Malaysia, a process which was deeply rooted in 'British orientalism'. At that time, anthropological knowledge was perceived as critical in the implementation of the British policy of 'indirect rule', that is, the formal delegation of power to native authorities and native courts. This made knowledge of indigenous Malaya and Borneo political and legal institutions, particularly those of the Malays, an important pre-requisite for colonial administrators. However the British preferred to teach anthropology to their officers, rather than putting up with the idiosyncrasies of particular anthropologists whose interests were not always similar to those of the administration.[3]

Consequently, the anthropologically-conscious colonial officers took up the role of researchers also. They began to publish extensively on various aspects of Malay culture and history, mostly in the publications of the local branch of the London-based Royal Asiatic Society, such as in the *Journal of the Straits Settlement Branch of the Royal Asiatic Society* (JSSBRAS) which later became the *Journal of the Malayan Branch of the Royal Asiatic Society* (JMBRAS). The Society, too, published numerous monographs on the culture and history of the various native groups. The two most prolific colonial administrator-scholars were R.J. Wilkinson and R.O.W. Winstedt, whose works on Malay history, literature and customs are still cited today.

It was only after the Second World War, with the involvement of anthropologists such as Raymond Firth (*Malay Fisherman*, 1946, *Report on Social Science in Malaya*, 1948), Edmund Leach (*Social*

Science Research in Sarawak, 1950), Rodney Needham (on the Penan in Sarawak), Derek Freeman (*Iban Agriculture*, 1955), William Geddes (*The Land Dayaks of Sarawak*, 1954) and later their students, that 'professional' anthropology (research and teaching) began to take root in Malaysia, sponsored first by the colonial state and later, after the Independence in 1957, by the post-colonial state.

The influence of their style of anthropology, namely British social anthropology, found its way into the local tertiary institution, the University of Malaya, through courses taught and research conducted mainly in the 'oriental studies'-like Department of Malay Studies and, to a lesser extent in other departments within the Faculty of Arts and the Faculty of Economic and Administration. This university was established in 1949 and remained the only university in Malaysia before 1970. An interesting feature of the teaching of anthropology in the Department of Malay Studies was the way in which it was combined with sociology. The unwritten rationale was that if anthropology in the place of its origin, the West, examined non-Western societies, then anthropology in Malaysia was suited for the study of any local native groups, including the Malays. Since sociology in the modern industrial West was deemed to be the 'science of society', then it was also thought to be relevant for investigating Malay society which was in the process of modernization.

It was no surprise then that the preoccupation of foreign and local anthropologists in the 1950s and 1960s was to study the process of social change being experienced by Malay society, using approaches informed by both positivist and non-positivist theories and concepts, drawn from anthropology and from sociology. Even ethnographic studies conducted in Sarawak and Sabah during this period showed a similar orientation. Thus an impressive collection of anthropological studies on Malaysia was generated, some of which contributed to the advancement of anthropological theory, such as theory on the structure of cognatic societies. There was also a marked increase in the number of 'raw empirical' studies of the Malays in the form of undergraduate dissertations, some of which were of excellent quality and were eventually published.

The introduction of anthropology within the Department of Anthropology and Sociology in the University of Malaya in 1970 was not only related to the interest of the post-colonial state, then struggling with some urgency to restore the ruptured social order as a consequence of a bloody ethnic riot in 1969, but also to the global and regional interests of the USA then deeply involved in the Vietnam War.

Clutching at straws, the Malaysian state immediately adopted the recommendations of a report entitled *Social Science Research for National Unity* (29 April 1970), authored by four prominent US social scientists, whose brief 'research' for the report was funded by the Ford Foundation. Anthropology and sociology and other disciplines within the social sciences were introduced and taught at the local universities within this context. However, anthropology remained combined with sociology, as it had been in the Department of Malay Studies. In fact, many of the founding academic staff of the Departments of Anthropology and Sociology in the local universities in Malaysia in the 1970s were graduates or academics recruited from the Department of Malay Studies. They were joined by anthropology and sociology graduates from universities in the Commonwealth and the United States. A few expatriates and established anthropologists were also recruited, such as Shuichi and Judith Nagata both of whom are now professors of anthropology in Canada.

The new departments also embarked on aggressive training programmes, fully sponsored by the state. Each department sent graduates or prospective academic staff to universities in the Commonwealth or the USA for graduate studies, or recruited those who were already abroad completing their studies. Others were trained locally for their Masters degree and subsequently went abroad for their PhD. Almost all of them came back to Malaysia to conduct field research. Hence the project to train local staff resulted in a sudden increase in the number of in-depth anthropological studies, mostly in the form of unpublished MA and PhD thesis, not only on the Malays but also on other ethnic groups in Peninsular Malaysia, Sabah and Sarawak. These covered a number of themes, ranging from the burial rites of the Sarawak Iban to the career pattern of members of the Malaysian scientific community, and employed a variety of theoretical approaches in vogue in the 1970s and 1980s in the USA, the Commonwealth, Latin America and Continental Europe. A few were published and became classics of the genre.

These works, and the contributions of foreign researchers from that period, enriched anthropological studies about Malaysia and kept alive interest in Malaysian social studies abroad (see, e.g. Kessler [1969] and Rogers [1977]). One interesting feature of anthropological studies in Malaysia, which reflects the unresolved majority-minority discourse in this multiethnic society, is that it shows a tendency to be ethnicized: anthropology is used as an instrument to support the cause of one ethnic group or to launch a purportedly 'objective and scientific' critique of ethnic relations (Shamsul 1996). Some anthropologists seemed to adopt a 'prophet of doom' approach in their analyses of social life in Malaysia, giving the picture that the outbreak of another ethnic riot is imminent (Nash 1989: 21–60). In this sense, anthropological and sociological studies of Malaysia are rather politicized.[4]

However, the most encouraging development in the last decade has been the increased popularity of anthropology amongst Malaysian undergraduates. Being very sensitive to the demands of the job market, they enrolled in the hundreds in the various departments of anthropology in the local universities. For instance, taking the Department of Anthropology and Sociology at the National University of Malaysia alone, for the last decade there has been an average annual enrollment of nearly a thousand students. This would make many anthropology departments abroad envious, especially those struggling to survive. This situation has arisen because both the public and private sector in Malaysia prefer to employ anthropology graduates. They have the perception that anthropology graduates are excellent generalists, good at 'peddling cultural knowledge', and are thus best suited for Malaysia's multiethnic public, the market, or people employed as civil servants, business executives or development workers at the grassroots level.

Anthropology in Malaysia has a bright future. To what extent this is due to anthropology as a discipline, to the nature of contemporary Malaysian society or to the state sponsorship is yet to be examined seriously. It was once said that anthropology was 'the child of colonialism'. In light of the fact that increasing numbers of anthropologists now come from non-Western countries, many of which have been branded as 'authoritarian', could this then mean that anthropology will become the 'servant of the modern nation-state'? The Malaysian case is worth watching.[5]

For that reason it is perhaps useful to examine the so-called 'Malaysianization' process that anthropology in Malaysia has undergone in the last twenty five years. I have chosen to call that process a 'Malaysianization' instead of an 'indigenization' process is because of the fact that the latter is historically and politically a problematic term, indeed a highly contentious one.[6] This is particularly true in Malaysia for it has its specific domestic implications. In fact the English term 'indigenous' has a local Malay equivalent called *bumiputera*, or literally meaning the 'son of the soil.'

The 'Malaysianization' of Anthropology: The Tales of Two 'Experiments' in Malaysian Anthropology

I would argue that the 'Malaysianization' process began in the early 1970s with the setting up of, for the first time ever, three full-fledged teaching departments of anthropology and sociology at Universiti Sains Malaysia (USM), Universiti Malaya (UM) and Universiti Kebangsaan Malaysia (UKM). There are at least four main reasons why I call it a 'Malaysianization' process.

First, the establishment of the departments of anthropology signaled a critical departure in the development path of anthropological studies in Malaysia. Previously, anthropology was part and parcel of an area studies called 'Malay studies' introduced during the colonial era by colonial administrator-scholars informed by various forms of orientalism, perhaps to serve some aspects of the colonial state's needs. But, in the early 1970s it began to chart and embark on a new course rather consciously as a result of the academic-cum-bureaucratic demand imposed by its new form of existence as a 'teaching department'. It was inevitable then that careful and detailed planning of courses to be taught in these new anthropology departments had to be done, and in such a circumstance there was a conscious effort to ensure that a certain percentage of the courses contained 'Malaysian content'.

Second, following the above, an equally important reason was the need for trained academic staff in anthropology to teach in the new departments. Funded by the government, these departments went on an aggressive training programme, sending their newly-recruited staff to the USA, UK, Australia, New Zealand and even continental Europe. This itself enriched the content of the growing anthropology in Malaysia feeding into it numerous different traditions which when combined formed a unique 'Malaysianized version'.

Third, the ethnic riot in 1969 became a critical watershed to Malaysians not only in terms of its collective impact on the overall post-colonial modern Malaysian history but also in terms of its individual, personal impact on all Malaysians from various ethnic groups and classes. One could argue that after that tragic event there was a heightened ethnic consciousness informed by centrifugal concerns. The government of the day and the 'non-evil and friendly team' of the Cold War contingent, led by the USA, realised this, and they successfully worked together to 'solve the problem' fulfilling their different interests. The setting up of the Department of National Unity, for instance, was one of the many solutions thought to implement to bring together and unite all Malaysians after the tragic May 13 ethnic riot incidence. There was then a conscious, planned effort to create a united Malaysian nation. The emphasis here is on 'Malaysian'.

As a consequence, previously if 'Malay studies' informed the construction of anthropological knowledge in Malaysia, now the 'non-Malay studies' component, as it were, has to be seriously considered. This conscious effort to combine the Malay and non-Malay component, both within the public and private sector, gave rise, for the first time since after the war, to a genuine attempt to see Malaysia not only as a 'plural entity' in socio-political terms but also in analytical terms. This led to the sudden increase, for instance, in the study of inter-ethnic relations, as opposed to the study of a mono- and intra-ethnic relations. This pattern of change has been critical in shaping what we see as Malaysian studies today.

The fourth reason, following the second, perhaps is the most critical in the Malaysianization process of anthropology in Malaysia. The role of both the public and private sector is important here, especially in its attitude towards graduates of the new anthropology departments. We must also recognize the role, and enthusiasm, of the 'new graduates' of anthropology in the early 1970s particularly their tireless collective effort to impress upon the 'senior managers' of both of the public and private sector that they could become capable civil servant officers or company executives.

On the 'manager' side, there was a general awareness amongst them that as a result of the conscious effort by the government to foster 'national unity' amongst the various ethnically-mixed population they also had to reposition themselves to suit this new socio-political environment. In the public sector, there was an obvious need, for instance, for 'community development' officers to attend to the interests of each of the ethnic groups at the grass-roots. Anthropology graduates were then perceived as the most suitable and they began to be recruited into the civil service. The fact that they dominated the top twenty positions in the civil servant entrance examination in the early 1970s government exams enhanced the relevance of 'anthropology' in the eyes of the senior civil servants because, previously, these graduates were employed only in the department of museum and prehistory or in the department of aboriginal affairs. But after 1970, these graduates came to be accepted by the government as 'useful' in a variety of fields and departments including the psychological war unit, the drug rehabilitation centres, the social welfare departments, the immigration department, the labour department and even in the customs and police departments. (A more detailed examination of the reasons as to why the anthropology graduates have had good reception from both the private and public sector is presented in the next section of this chapter.)

Perhaps it is useful to examine briefly the 'Malaysianization' process of anthropology in Malaysia by viewing in some detail as to how anthropology and anthropology-related disciplines are organized and taught at the university-level to fulfil both academic and non-academic needs, particularly, local Malaysian needs. This is especially important in view of the fact that these universities are state-sponsored. Thus we can see the direct and indirect links between nation-state formation and social science, in this special context, involving anthropology as a social science discipline.

I wish to use the examples taken from the experiences of the two major departments of anthropology in Malaysia, one at the University of Malaya and the other at the National University of Malaysia (well-known for its Malay acronym UKM). I completed my BA and MA studies at the former and taught there too for some time and have been employed at the latter since 1975. Therefore, I think I qualify to give a 'participant observation' account on the experiences of both departments.

I would characterize, if arbitrarily, the University of Malaya's Department of Anthropology and Sociology, as heavily 'Malay Studies'-oriented, while the one at UKM is 'discipline'-oriented. These characterizations are strictly for analytical purposes. It is not a value judgement on the quality of the academic staff and their contributions or the courses they teach.[7]

The former became 'Malay Studies'-oriented because most of its academic staff were trained in Malay Studies and only recently new discipline-oriented lecturers were recruited into the department. In fact, the current senior staff members of the department were all Malay Studies graduates. However, because the structure of the courses and content shaped in the early years of the department has hardly changed, with the core courses still divided along the anthropology and sociology divide, similar to the ones found in the Malay Studies Department, the empirical focus remains, primarily, on Malay society. Any new course introduced in the 1980s, such as, on consumerism, social work, and sociology of education, has empirically been heavily Malay and Malaysian focused. There are no courses on Melanesian, South Asian, African or Latin American ethnography. There was no conscious effort made by the department to re-think the possibility of integrating fully the anthropology and sociology content of the courses. Thus 'social psychology' is seen as a totally unrelated to 'psychological anthropology', and the two courses are taught separately. In short, both the disciplines were hardly re-constituted.

On the other hand, the Department of Anthropology and Sociology at UKM, from the beginning, consciously recruited academic staff with a variety of academic backgrounds and training. Some were graduates of Malay Studies and many were those who graduated with anthropology degree or sociology degree from universities abroad and, later, locally. Therefore, the department had trained anthropologists, sociologists and Malay Studies specialists as lecturers or faculty members. In the original plan of UKM, the anthropology and sociology component were to separate and form their own departments, namely, a Department of Anthropology (which were supposed to be divided into two sections, social/cultural anthropology and physical anthropology) and a Department of Sociology. This was supposed to take place towards the end of the 1970s when enough qualified staff were available to operate these departments.

When the time came, there was a big debate amongst anthropologists and sociologists of the department whether to remain 'married' or be 'divorced', as it was called at that time. The overwhelming decision was to remain 'married' but with certain conditions. It was the implementation of these conditions which transformed not only the course contents but also the way anthropology and sociology was presented. This eventually led to a reconstitution of anthropology and sociology in the department even though the name of the department remains the Department of Anthropology and Sociology.

The first condition was to collapse the anthropology and sociology divide, as much as possible, both in name and content and to divide the courses into 'core' and 'specialist courses'. The 'core courses' were labeled as 'social thought and theory' courses, where both the contributions of the social philosophers, such as, Marx, Weber, Khaldun, and Durkheim, and those of Radcliffe-Brown, Parsons, Garfinkel, Goffman, Mead, and Malinowski were given equal treatment and considered as important to the development of anthropology and sociology in particular, and social scientific thinking in general. Besides, courses previously called 'political anthropology' and 'political sociology' were combined to become 'politics and society', theoretically addressing the contributions of social philosophers, such as Mosca, Montesquieu, Michels and Machiavelli, and the more recent ones such as, Gluckman, Bailey, Barrington-Moore and Skocpol, as well as drawing empirical examples from Africa, South Asia, Europe and East and Southeast Asia. In fact, a number of other 'overlapping' courses were combined in such a manner.

The 'specialist courses' refer to specific thematics or fields of interest in which each individual member of the department has developed and specialized in, especially in their PhD research and subsequent careers. We have, for instance, a specialist field labeled as 'peasantry and modernization', combining, from the sociology side, 'sociology of development' and 'rural sociology' with 'peasant studies' and 'applied anthropology', from the anthropology side. In fact, from this modest beginning, this particular 'package' of 'peasantry and modernization' in our department became the basis for the establishment of a full faculty-level institution in UKM, in the mid-1980s, called the Faculty of Development Science, necessarily expanded in content and form.

In the early 1990s the courses in my department were again reformed on the rationale that it has to respond to present and future demands and to keep pace, information and knowledge-wise, with the rapid change in Malaysian society. Our rural, 'agrarian societies' have become partly 'urbanized and industrialized', as a result of the big push for industrialization in Malaysia since the mid-1980s, and we believe that in no time part of the our urban-industrial society will become 'information societies' belonging to the 'borderless' world. That these three forms of 'societies' co-exist within one nation-state boundary, such as ours, demands that as teachers of anthropology we equip our undergraduates intellectually, conceptually and empirically with enough analytical tools and examples to enable them, firstly, to understand what is going around them, and, secondly, to effectively and comfortably participate within all the three 'societies' mentioned.

As a result, at the first-year level, we have introduced only two main courses, one named 'Humankind, Society and Culture' and the other 'The Growth of the Malaysian Social System'. The main aim of the former is to allow the students in the first year to grasp some basic analytical tools both in the general social scientific fields as much as in anthropology and sociology, drawing empirical cases from a broad spectrum of ethnographic studies and sociological surveys of societies in the North and South. In the latter, the students are encouraged to grasp the dynamics of Malaysian society, in the past and present, using the analytical tools introduced to the in the 'Humankind, society and culture' course.

These two courses, we imagine would give the student a general sense of the 'two-level social reality' they have to cope, namely, an 'everyday social reality', which is experienced, and an 'authority-defined social reality', which is derived from observation and interpretation, as defined by people who are part of the dominant power structure. It is within this general sociological context that we hope our student could gain some perspective of Malaysia as part of the world and, at the same time, view that world as a complex entity that they have to grasp competently because Malaysia cannot escape its influence. With this 'sociological imagination' in place, these students can decide on their own in which department they want to major in their second and third-year level, it could be with us or other departments. Our attitude is, if they were to major in another discipline, hence another department, they should be able to approach the subject matter of that discipline or department anthropologically and socio-logically and turn their intellectual engagement with that discipline (say, history, geography or linguistics) into an interesting academic and personal enterprise. We are yet to conduct a survey to evaluate the success and failure of our recent ambitious reform programme. But we have some ideas about the impact of our previous reforms based on surveys we conducted amongst our alumnis, the findings of which, at least the major ones, are presented below.

Anthropology Consumed: The Sweet and Sour of Private and Public Sector Response to Anthropology

The positive reaction that the anthropology graduates received from the private sector was a total surprise to many. Sensitive as usual to market demands, senior company executives from big and small-size companies began to realise that in a highly ethnically-conscientized society, especially after the May 13th 1969 incident, 'peddling stereotypes' became more important in everyday idiom-making as well in shaping the perception of people at the grassroots. This led to the public exercise of 'essentializing' ethnicities, such as 'Malayness', 'Chineseness', 'Indianness' and so on, be it in the print or electronic media or in political campaigns. From the market surveys conducted in the early 1970s, the senior company executives knew that there was a need for marketing officers with some 'cultural knowledge', as they put it. It was not a coincidence that a large number of anthropology graduates began to apply for jobs in the private sector around the same period. The combination of these two circumstances worked well for anthropology in Malaysia, as well as making it more Malaysian-oriented.

As a result, potential university students, who are always sensitive to job opportunities available in the public sphere and decide what they want to specialize at the university according to the job market demand, started to get interested in anthropology and they enrolled in the hundreds in the three departments of anthropology in Malaysia. Realising this positive trend, these departments, in their routine exercise of up-dating the courses, began to increase more Malaysian content in their courses. Here I wish to narrate the experience of my own department at Universiti Kebangsaan Malaysia (UKM).

I shall focus specifically on the result of a pilot survey I conducted in mid-1993 amongst ex-students of my department at UKM and their employers, both in the public and private sector, with a small sample of 150 students and 50 employers. The intention of the survey was to find out, or more specifically, to give me some ideas on two inter-related things. Firstly, I was interested in the 'intellectual impact' of our courses (a big word, and not easy to measure) upon our students, namely, whether they find them intellectually enlightened or interesting, and whether or not the courses have equipped them sufficiently to comprehend both general and specific contexts of their social environs and give them a certain measure of confidence in dealing with the immediate demands of their workplace. Secondly, I was interested in finding about the general job-market situation for our graduates. For example, the range of jobs they are holding and how they cope with or find a niche within the job; what other knowledge they need to make them more conceptually competent to handle their jobs; what opportunities there are for promotion; and what salaries they receive.

It was indeed an exciting research because I did not use any research assistant for I was intent on gathering the information personally and, at the same, meeting face-to-face with my former students and the employers. It took me, in between teaching, meetings and commitment abroad, about 10 months to complete the whole task. By the end, I had grown rounder and rounder as a result of the lavish lunches and dinners that my ex-students, some of whom were employers themselves, generously provided because to them it was a reunion meeting with a teacher and a chance to hear the latest gossip about 'their' department. 20 of these interviews (involving 40 persons), particularly with the ex-students, were conducted in twos and at least 6 were married couples. Here are some of my findings.

Only 10 per cent of the ex-students was interested in pursuing academic careers before they joined the university but decided otherwise when they learnt of the good job prospects with an undergraduate degree in anthropology. About 85 per cent knew exactly which department they wanted to enroll in based on job prospect after graduating and the relatively short waiting period of getting employment. All had prior knowledge about the department from ex-graduates and also from their own research. They also knew about the department through the contributions of the department's lecturers in local print media, such as, in newspapers and magazines. Many of these lecturers previously came to their schools to give talks on all kinds of issues during 'speech day' celebration or on other special occasions. (Of course, we did not realise that we have been doing some public relations exercise through our contribution to the public.)

Of the 150 ex-students, 50 worked in the public sector (in government departments and other semi-government bodies) and the rest in the private sector. Those who joined the public sector did not expect to get their jobs based on their special interest in anthropology because they needed only a good degree (first and second class honours). But, according to government officials and executives of the semi-government bodies in-charge of recruiting new officers and executives, they found anthropology graduates performed very well in the entrance exam and interviews compared to graduates in history, geography or Malay studies. The anthropology graduates seemed to have a good all-round knowledge about important government policies, the internal dynamics of Malaysian society, global issues besetting countries of the South, Malaysia's position relative to other countries in the world, and were able to handle competently national issues conceptually, such as, on the issue of 'national unity', 'ethnic politics', 'federal-state relations', 'absolute and relative poverty', and 'development planning and social change'. The employers' conclusion was that the anthropology graduates were excellent 'generalists' and well-suited to become good civil servants and executives of semi-government bodies who have to deal with the implementation of government policies.

Those who joined the private sector, all began as 'marketing officers' in companies involved in a wide-range of business activities from selling Coca-Cola to computers, banks to bakeries, soya sauce to sporting goods, detergents to dental equipment, and recreational clubs to real estate. The attraction, from the ex-students perspective, was that these jobs paid good starting salaries and perks, involved a lot of travelling, locally and abroad, and opportunities for quick promotion based on performance evaluation. They can also change their jobs or companies relatively easy should an opportunity to increase their income arise. Often, they were allowed to use company cars or given credit cards for their expenses. It seemed their dream to live a middle-class lifestyle became a reality as 'marketing officer'.

However, the employers seemed to have other reasons for employing them, which are interesting for us to take note of. Ignoring personality differences, they were of the opinion that our anthropology graduates, compared to economic or business school graduates whom they have employed, can understand their clients, habits, culture, and behaviour patterns much quicker and are thus able to clinch sales, big and small, faster. They were able to learn basic accounting quickly because they have a good grounding in statistics and were computer literate. They were able to understand the market better and willing to conduct, on their own initiative, their own market research. They were also good at entertaining their clients (in karaoke bars, perhaps), able to talk on all sorts of things relating to Malaysia and some other general issues and very aware of government policies affecting the businesses of their employers. Most importantly, they seemed to know each of the ethnic communities in Malaysia, their subcultures and stereotypes, much better and be able to understand and mingle with the prospective buyers and government officials without much difficulty. This enhanced the opportunity of the employers expanding their business networks and at the same time remain in the good books of the relevant local government officials.

At the beginning of the research, I was wondering why private financial institutions, such as banks, found anthropology students useful to be employed as executives. The explanation given by personnel officers from two banks which employed a number of anthropology graduates was that from experience they found that they make excellent credit officers, especially, in the rural areas, where the size of the Malay, Chinese and Indian communities are almost equal. They seemed to understand the borrowing habits of each of the communities better and quickly understand the cultural preference of each community as to the type of collateral each liked to offer when borrowing loans. For instance, the Malays prefer to use land, the Chinese real estate property (mainly house or apartments) and Indian gold. A good understanding and empathy regarding cultural issues such as these allowed a smoother negotiation for the amount loan to be given to the client, the choice of collateral, the method of payment, and in completing the paperwork itself. Often, problems related to loan defaulters were able to be resolved by the anthropology graduates amicably. One must also be reminded that banks as a money lending institution are relatively new in Malaysian rural society, most of whose inhabitants prefer private money lenders or the pawnshop as a source of credit or loan for reasons of expedience (no paper work) and privacy (going to the banks to borrow money is perceived as a public activity).

I do not wish to paint too rosy a picture about the 'marketability' of our graduates but nonetheless they seemed to be in demand for their supposed 'anthropological talent'. One must also take into account of the good economic conditions in Malaysia at present. For instance, between 1988 and 96, Malaysia has posted a phenomenal over 8 per cent annual economic growth, the highest in the world. The economy, technically speaking, is experiencing full employment. The jobless are jobless because of their own choice not because the lack of employment. Previously 'walk-in' interviews was a method of labour recruitment utilized by plantation companies to get part-time contract workers. But now the same method is being used by most companies in Malaysia, local and foreign, to recruit employees, be they engineers, computer programmers, nurses, lawyers or production workers in semi-conductor factories. In such an excellent economic situation, it is generally easier for graduates to obtain employment quite quickly after successfully completing their studies.

So, the privilege the anthropology graduates thus far enjoyed in terms of job-placement could simply disappear tomorrow if the economy continues to turn for the worse. But then again this would affect all graduates, not only anthropology graduates. The bottom line is every employer would only choose the best to work for them, whether the economy is good or not. In fact, they need the best when the economy is not at its best. The reality is, at present, the 'hot' choice seems to be anthropology graduates. They seemed to be very good at 'peddling cultures' which is all-important in a multi-ethnic Malaysia. Whether this would work in other multi-ethnic societies of the world, I am not quite sure. Even if it does work, anthropology departments may not exist there. Or, if they exist, the departments could be seen as producing too many radicals and critics of the state, for anthropology not only teaches its students to have in-depth knowledge about many things, to acquire a good range of analytical tools and to apply them well, but also trains its students in 'critical thinking', directly and indirectly, and to continuously seek alternative and comparative explanations on all social phenomena without fear or favour. This may not sit well with authoritarian or fascist states of the world.

151

Conclusion: Malaysia's 'anthropology pendulum'

We have witnessed worldwide how, first, 'anthropological studies' and, later, 'anthropology' became part and parcel of the investigative modality of the colonial state which, in turn, produced what is now known as 'colonial knowledge' (Cohn 1996). This approach was necessary for the colonialists in their entry to a new world which they could only begin to comprehend using their own forms of knowing and thinking. Through a massive and continuous exercise of data gathering, analysis and documentation over decades this material and information became 'normalized' and thus the basis of the colonialists' capacity to govern. These created data became 'facts', often taken for granted or as givens, that needed to be interpreted by trained bureaucrats with deep knowledge of indigenous culture.

In the Malaysian context, colonial knowledge not only elaborated and explained about but also sustained and justified the whole concept of plural society through the construction of essentialized ethnic categories which became the key to the success of the divide-and-rule policy of the British for more than a century. The concept of 'ethnic minority' emerged, historically, from this historical context. However, there is no direct evidence of anthropology or anthropologist's complicity in the making of ethnic minorities in Malaysia, as some would like to believe. In fact, the British preferred to teach anthropology to their officers, rather than putting up with the idiosyncrasies of particular anthropologists whose interests were not always similar to those of the colonial administration (Moore 1994). However, the nature of colonial knowledge was, of course, not only social scientific or humanities-based but also informed by the natural sciences built around European's social scientific and natural science theory and concepts as well as classificatory schema.

It is not surprising therefore that nation-states, as Cohn brilliantly argued (1996:3), have become the natural embodiments of history, territory and society built entirely on colonial knowledge. Thus the establishment and maintenance of the post-colonial nation-state depended upon determining, codifying, controlling and representing the past as well as the present by repeating the techniques of the construction of 'facts' and 'knowledge' already set in place by the colonial state. The setting up of tertiary educational institutions by the colonial state, such as a university and the 'ethnic-based' academic departments within it, shaped in the orientalist mould (e.g. the Department of Malay Studies, University of Malaya), necessarily became the logical extension of the colonial epistemological invasion which, surprisingly, the post-colonial state finds rather unproblematic.

In the Malaysian case, for instance, we witnessed how the anthropology-based Department of Malay Studies has been critical in the construction of 'Malay' and 'Malayness' for the Malay-dominated government and, subsequently, in its effort to create a homogenized 'national culture' with Malay culture as the core. The pro-Malay affirmative action policy implemented by the government (1971–1990) was also informed by such 'Malay anthropological understanding'. However, we also observed the contrasting case of anthropology taught as anthropology, not under the guise of Malay studies, in a rather different political period and scenario. Anthropology played an equally 'unifying', if utilitarian role, due to market or consumers' demand but, at the same time, created significant space for heterogeneous elements in the society be articulated openly. The high demand for anthropology graduates in the both the public and private sector demonstrates this healthy trend.

In the former, what we observed is that in its quest for homogeneity, expressed in idioms such as 'national unity', 'national culture' and 'national identity', authority-defined national narratives, informed by anthropological knowledge, often erase difference. But in the latter, local and ethnic interests found space to air both their differences as well as encourage the notion of 'difference' in Derrida's sense to flourish – an activity indeed corresponding to the emancipatory needs of civil society. Such being the case, it could be argued that anthropology in Malaysia occupies an interesting and indeed unique position. It is consumed by both the state and civil society for almost opposing rationales, one for the pursuit of the ever-elusive homogeneity and the other to maintain and enrich heterogeneity.

This is the 'anthropology pendulum' in Malaysia, serving both the state and civil society in its own creative ways. It could be argued that the direction of its swing in the future depends very much on the condition of state-civil society relations in Malaysia. But one thing is certain though: anthropology has proven to be the 'staple food' consumed comfortably by both the state and civil society in Malaysia in conducting its activities. As such, anthropology occupies an important niche in Malaysia. Perhaps what is most interesting to observe is how anthropology would reinvent itself or get reconstituted over time in respond to the speed and nature of the swing of the 'state-civil society pendulum'.

Acknowledgements

This chapter originated from an article entitled 'The superiority of indigenous scholars? Some fact and fallacies with special reference to Malay anthropologists and sociologists in fieldwork', published in *Manusia dan Masyarakat* in 1982, a journal of the Department of Anthropology and Sociology, University of Malaya, the university from which I received my BA and MA degrees. Some of the ideas from this publication were expanded and elaborated over the next decade or so, mainly in the various seminars and courses I taught at my university and abroad, and finally presented in the form of a working paper, entitled 'Anthropology at home: In search of an indigenous anthropology', to a group of students and scholars at the University of Melbourne in 1991. Subsequently, it was developed to become a basis for a full-fledged research on 'Intellectual life and institutions in Malaysia' that I began to conduct on my own in 1992. I wish to thank Universiti Kebangsaan Malaysia for giving me the necessary research fund and leave, also to my wife, Dr. Wendy Smith of the Department of Japanese Studies, Monash University, Australia for all her comments and criticisms, and finally to Dr. Kosaku Yoshino of Tokyo University, whose patience I greatly admire and without whose encouragement this chapter would not have been completed. To all of them a big *terima kasih*.

Notes

1 I have discussed these issues in some detail in Shamsul (1982, 1991, 1993, 1995a, 1995b, 1997).

2 Important historic contributions made by Malaysianists from the United States of America towards the creation of Malaysian studies are found in Lent 1979 and Lent & Mulliner 1986. Similar efforts have been made by those Malaysianists in Australia and the Great Britain. See the useful bibligraphy compiled by Tan Chee Beng (1992).

3 There has been much written on the role of anthropology in Western imperialism, the recent ones are by Dirk 1992, Moore 1994, Kuklick 1991, Thomas 1994, Goody 1995.

4 It is also politicized in the *realpolitik* terms. It is a common knowledge that social science disciplines, particularly anthropology and sociology, have been perceived by the ruling elites of many Third World states as having real and imagined highly 'subversive' or 'revolutionary' potentials. This has been the case in Malaysia, too. In fact, a prominent Malaysian anthropologist, Professor Syed Husin Ali, was detained without trial for a period of six years (1974–1980) for his political 'wrong-doing' of teaching Marxism and radical theories, see Syed Husin Ali 1995.

154

5 It is worth watching if viewed from the 'indigenization' perspective, especially to what extent it has been reconstituted to suit contemporary local demands. For further discussion on the indigenization of the social sciences in general, and anthropology in particular, see, Alatas 1993, Choong 1990, Jackson 1990, Loubser 1988, Marsden 1994, Wazir Karim Jahan 1993, 1994, 1995, 1996. As to the future of anthropology, see, Giddens 1995, 1996, Akber Ahmed & Shore 1995, Appadurai 1991, Fox 1991 and Vidyarthi 1979.

6 The term 'indigineous' is a highly politicised and contentious one in multi-ethnic Malaysia, especially amongst the Muslim Bumiputera (lt. sons of the soil) and the non-Muslim Bumiputera (eg. The Iban. Kadazan, Penan, Orang Asli and many more), and it has dominated, for the last four decades, the discourse on identity in Malaysia (see, Shamsul 1996a).

7 For a more informed discussion on the academic development of these two important departments please see, Abdul Rahman Embong 1995.

References

Abdul Rahman Embong (ed.) 1995 *Antropologi dan Sosiologi: menggaris arah baru*, Bangi: Penerbit Universiti Kebangsaan Malaysia.

Abdul Rahman Embong 1996 'Social transformation, the state and the middle classes in post-independence Malaysia', pp. 524–547 in *Southeast Asian Studies* (Kyoto), 34(3).

Akbar Ahmed & Chris Shore. (ed.) 1994 *The Future of Anthropology and its Relevance to the Contemporary World*, London: Athlone Press.

Alatas, Syed Farid 1993 'Some problems of indigenization', Working Paper No. 114, Department of Sociology, National University of Singapore.

Appadurai, Arjun 1991 'Global ethnoscapes: notes and queries for a transnational anthropology', pp. 191–210 in Richard G. Fox (ed.) *Recapturing Anthropology: working in the present*, Santa Fe, New Mexico: School of American Press.

Choong, Soon Kim 1990 'The role of the non-Western anthropologist reconsidered: illusion versus reality', pp. 197–200 in *Current Anthropology*, 31(2).

Cohn, Bernard S. 1996 *Colonialism and its Form of Knowledge: the British in India*, Princeton, N.J.: Princeton University Press.

Dirks, Nicholas (ed.) 1992 *Colonialism and Culture*, Ann Arbor: University of Michigan Press.

Fox, Richard G. 1991 'Introduction', pp. 1–16 in Richard G. Fox (ed.) *Recapturing Anthropology: working in the present*, Santa Fe, New Mexico: School of American Press.

Jackson, Anthony (ed.) 1990 *Anthropology at Home*, ASA Monograph 25, London: Tavistock.

Giddens, Anthony 1990 *The Consequences of Modernity*, Stanford: Stanford University Press.

Giddens, Anthony 1995 'Epilogue: notes on the future of anthropology', pp. 272–277 in Akber Ahmed and Chris Shore (ed.) *The Future of Anthropology and it Relevance to the Contemporary World*, London: Athlone.

Giddens, Anthony 1996 'In defence of sociology', pp. 1–7 in Anthony Giddens, *In Defence of Sociology: essays, interpretations and rejoinders*, Oxford: Polity Press.

Glazer, Nathan, Samuel Huntington, Manning Nash and Myron Weiner 1970 *Social Science Research for National Unity: a confidential report to the Government of Malaysia*, 29 April, New York: Ford Foundation.

Gomes, Alberto (eds.) 1994 *Modernity and Identity: Asian Illustration*, Bundoora, Vic. Australia: La Trobe University Press.

Goody, Jack 1995 *The Expansive Moment: anthropology in Britain and Africa*, Cambridge: Cambridge University Press.

Guibenau, Monteseraat 1996 *Nationalisms: the nation-state and nationalism in the twentieth century*, Oxford: Polity .

Hutchinson, John and Anthony D. Smith (eds.) 1994 *Nationalism: Oxford reader*, Oxford: Oxford University Press.

Kahn, Joel Kahn 1996 'Middle class as a field of ethnological study', pp. 12–33 in Muhammad Ikmal Said and Zahid Emby (eds.) *Malaysia: critical Perspectives* (Essays in Honour of Syed Husin Ali), Kuala Lumpur: Malaysian Social Science Association.

Kessler, Clive 1969 *Islam and Politics in a Malay State: Kelantan 1939–1946*, Ithaca, NY: Cornell University Press.

Kuklick, Henrika 1991 *The Savage Within: the social history of British anthropology, 1885–1945*, Cambridge: Cambridge University Press.

Lent, John (ed.) 1979 *Malaysian Studies: present knowledge and research trends*, Occasional Paper No. 7, Dekalb, Illinois: Center for Southeast Asian Studies, Northern Illiniois University.

Lent, John and K. Mulliner (eds.) 1986 *Malaysian Studies: archaeology, historiography, geography and bibliography*, Occasional Paper No. 11, DeKalb, Illinois: Center for Southeast Asian Studies, Northern Illinois University.

Loubser, Jan J. 1988 'The need for the indigenization of the social sciences', pp. 179–187 in *International Sociology* 33(2).

Marsden, David 1994 'Indigenous management and the management of indigenous knowledge', pp. 41–55 in Susan Wright (ed.) *Anthropology of Organizations*, London: Routledge.

Moore, Sally Falk 1994 *Anthropology and Africa: changing perspectives on a changing scene*, Charlottesville and London: The University Press of Virginia.

Nash, Manning 1989 *The Cauldron of Ethnicity in the Modern World*, Chicago: Chicago University Press.

Robinson, Richard and David Goodman (eds.) 1996 *The New Rich In Asia: mobile phones, McDonalds and the middle-class revolutions*, London and New York: Routledge.

Rogers, Marvin 1977 *Sungai Raya: a socio-political study of a Malay rural community*, Center for South and Southeast Asian Studies, Research Monograph, no. 15, Berkeley: University of California.

Shamsul A.B. 1982 'The superiority of indigenous scholars?: some facts and fallacies with special reference to Malay anthropologists and sociologists in fieldwork', pp. 23–33 in *Manusia dan Masyarakat* (New Series) 3.

—— 1991 'Anthropology at home: in search of an indigenous anthropology'.

Paper read at the Departmental Seminar, Department of Anthropology, University of Melbourne, Australia, 22 May.

—— 1993. *Antropologi dan Modenisasi: mengungkapkan pengalaman Malaysia*, Syarahan Perdana, Bangi: Penerbit UKM.

—— 1995a 'Malaysia: the Kratonization of social science', pp. 87–109 in Nico S. Nordholt and Leontine Visser (ed.) *Social Science in Southeast Asia: from particularism to universalism*, Amsterdam: VU University Press.

—— 1995b 'The state of anthropology and anthropology and the state in Malaysia', pp. 5–6 in *Minpaku Anthropological Newsletter* 1(1).

—— 1996 'Nations-of-intent in Malaysia', pp. 323–347 in Stein Tønnesson and Hans Antlöv (eds.) *Asian Forms of the Nation*, London: Curzon and Nordic Institute of Asian Studies.

—— 1996a 'Debating about identity in Malaysia: a discourse analysis', pp. 566–600 in *Southeast Asian Studies* 34(3).

—— 1997 'Social sciences in Malaysia observed, 1970–1995: a personal reflection', Paper for a conference on 'Social Science and Humanities in the Era of Industrialization', organized by the Faculty of Social Sciences and Humanities, Universiti Kebangsaan Malaysia. 2–3 January.

Syed Husin Ali 1995 *Two Faces*, Kuala Lumpur: Forum.

Tan Chee Beng 1992 *Bibliography on Ethnicity and Race Relations in Malaysia*, Kuala Lumpur: Institut Pengajian Tinggi, Universiti Malaya.

Tanter, Richard and Kenneth, Young (eds.) 1990 *The Politics of Middle Class in Indonesia*, Clayton, Vic. Australia: Centre for Southeast Asian Studies, Monash University.

Tham Seong Chee 1981 *Social Science Research in Malaysia*, Singapore: Graham Brash.

Thomas, Nicholas 1994 *Colonialism's Culture: anthropology, travel and government*, Princeton, NJ.: Princeton University Press.

Vidyarthi, L.P. 1979 *Trends in World Anthropology*, Delhi: Concept Publishing.

Wazir Karim Jahan 1993 'Epilogue: the "nativised" self and the "native"', pp. 249–251 in Diane Bell, Pat Caplan and Wazir Karim Jahan (eds), *Gendered Fields: women, men, ethnography*, London: Routledge.

—— 1994 '*Do Not Forget Us'*: *the intellectual in indigenous anthropology*, Public Lecture, Universiti Sains Malaysia, 22 January.

—— 1995 'Introduction: genderising anthropology in Southeast Asia', pp. 11–74 Wazir Karim Jahanin (ed.), *Male & Female in Developing Southeast Asia*, Oxford: Berg.

—— 1996 'Anthropology without tears: how a "local" sees the "local" and the "global"', pp. 115–138 in Henrietta Moore (ed.) *The Future of Anthropological Knowledge*, London: Routledge.

7

DISTANT HOMELANDS

Nation as Place in
Japanese Popular Song[1]

Christine R. Yano

In this chapter I use the concept of 'homeland' to unpack some of the
meanings of place to which the Japanese nation ascribes in a popular
song genre known as *enka*. Nostrand and Estaville, Jr. define homelands
as 'places that people identify with and have strong feelings about',
citing five basic factors in their conceptualization: first, people who
define themselves as a group; second, a natural environment to which
this group of people have adjusted; third, sense of place, developed
through emotional feelings of attachment, desire to possess, and
compulsion to defend that territory; fourth, control of place, that is
demographic and political power within that place; and fifth, time for
the sense of place to develop (1993:2–3). This chapter focuses on the
third of these factors – sense of place – as reified in popular song.

The concept of homeland ties intimately to the concept of the nation,
defined by Boyarin as 'a sharply bounded, continuously occupied space
controlled by a single sovereign state, comprising a set of autonomous
yet essentially identical individuals' (1994:2). Both conceptualizations
share a foundation in place, people, history, and power. Conceiving of
the nation in terms of homeland lends an affective immediacy and
intimacy which the larger political sphere often lacks.

As Lefebvre points out, space is not a neutral, natural, value-free
empty area, but 'a projection onto a (spatial) field of all aspects,
elements and moments of social practice' (1991:8; see Keith and Pile
1993). This 'space of social practice' adheres meanings, actions, and
emotions in its very production. I argue that the meanings given to
space in modern Japan have transformed the local into the national.
These identities, once regionally bound and fiercely protected, have
been co-opted as part of a national project of internal homogeneity (see
Weiner 1997). In producing meaning of these spaces, provincial regions
have been both generalized as center(s) of a true national identity, as

well as particularized as idiosyncratic margins peripheral to the nation-culture. They are at once core and periphery, internal and exotic, whole and apart (see Ivy 1995). These and other manipulations of place have been critical to Japan's modern imagining (Anderson 1983).

One effective style by which nations may be imagined is through collective memory. Maurice Halbwachs' pioneering work theorizes that human memory functions primarily as collective memory – that is, within the context of groups, evoked by constant reminders such as memorials, holidays, and songs (Coser 1992). Collective memory becomes a fundamental tool in creating a past, 'selectively organizing events . . . [as an] act of self-definition' (Friedman 1992:837). Memory and identity intertwine and overlap as conjoined practices (Boyarin 1994). Collective remembering (including inventing) and its obverse, collective forgetting, then, are central to the project of creating national culture (Fujitani 1993). One of the most powerful and effective ideological apparatuses is popular music. This is music industrially produced, ubiquitously overheard, and with the potential to be emotionally compelling.

Inventing *Enka* as National Culture

The significance of the melodramatic ballads of *enka* in this project of collective memory lies in its reputation as '*nihon no uta*' (song of Japan), expression of '*nihonjin no kokoro*' (heart/soul of Japanese) (IASPM-Japan 1991:12). The word '*enka*' (lit., performed song) has its historical roots in the *jiyū minken undō* (People's Freedom and Rights Movement) of the late 19th century, when songs were used to express political thoughts banned from public speech. This *enka* was more speech than song, performed by *enkashi* (*enka* singer/speaker) initially unaccompanied, and later with violin. When the movement died down, the song form remained, singing of far less political topics. These early *enka*, however, bear little resemblance to today's *enka*.[2]

These songs of romance and hometowns find closer musical ancestry in what was generally called *ryūkōka* (popular song), a generalized umbrella to include mass-mediated musics disseminated electronically throughout the nation by way of radio, film, recordings, and eventually television. Beginning with 'Katiusha no Uta' (Kachusha's Song) in 1915, and continuing to 'Sendō Kouta' (Boat-man's Song) in 1921, these *ryūkōka* swept the nation in wave after wave of consumer frenzy, first as sheet music, then as records. *Enkashi*, street entertainers, sang some of these *ryūkōka* in order to sell the sheet music. Later, with the rise of the record industry, *enkashi* gradually died out as both performers and salespersons. So did the term '*enka*'.

The term re-emerged decades later, but in a different guise with reconfigured significance. In the late 1960s and 1970s, the rise of cultural nationalism brought about not only a body of pseudo-intellectual discourse known as *nihonjinron* (theories of being Japanese), which formulated national identity upon claims of racial, geographical, and cultural uniqueness, but also a body of popular music continuing from the past which addressed some of these same issues. This music was labelled *enka* by the media and record companies, to distinguish popular music which 'sounded Japanese'.[3] I view *enka* as a part of the 'introspection boom' of the late 1960s and 1970s, addressing the question of 'Who are we Japanese?' (see Kelly 1993:93). Part of 'who the Japanese people are' was constructed through music as an affective community. *Enka* became a boundary marker of national taste, as one of two broad categories of popular music. The category against which *enka* has been defined is *poppusu* ('pops'), popular music overtly derivative of that from the United States and Europe. *Enka* became a label attached to distinguish 'our' (Japan's) music from 'theirs' (Euro-America's).

In a process I call genrification, *enka* both built upon, as well as created, difference. 'Sounding Japanese' entailed traditional scales, vocalisms, and textual themes of longing and sadness reminiscent of earlier literary forms such as *waka* (thirty-one syllable Japanese poetic form popular from sixth through sixteenth centuries). *Enka* differs from *ryūkōka* in sounding more Japanese than ever, emphasizing vocalisms of 'traditional' genres. Its singers typically sing within the genre rather than experimenting within a wider range of styles. This 'song of Japan' asserts its reputation not so much for an international world, but for a domestic one, as national expression, as 'tradition' whose making has been collectively forgotten.

Although sales of *enka* lag far behind that of other genres in 1990s Japan (4 per cent of recording sales in 1992, Oricon 1993), its place within national culture remains consistent. This is not to say that *enka* is entirely unchanging or unchallenged, either in its content or reception. There are many – in particular youths and some intellectuals – who actively dislike it. These detractors claim that *enka*, not only as an older genre, but also as a reputedly blue-collar and 'rural' genre, retains loathsome, outdated values and conceptualizations. Japan, they say, has moved well beyond this feudalistic world to gain a strong foothold in the international world of the late twentieth century. These people dismiss *enka* as an anachronism whose place within present-day Japanese society should not be central, but peripheral. On the other hand, *enka*'s adherents claim that those loci of popularity – working class and rural – also become the loci of what is considered 'truer', fundamental, indigenous Japanese culture. This reputation links *enka* with tradition, identity, and the nation. Much of this reputation has been fused through nostalgia. I argue here that nostalgia for times past has been incorporated into, and sometimes reconfigured as, nostalgia for places distant in *enka*.

Enka's status as national music is far from unquestioned. For one, *enka*'s market includes not only Japan, but also other East and Southeast Asian countries, many of whom have found a receptive ear to the sounds of the genre. Part of this exists as remnant of Japan's twentieth-century colonial legacy which officially ended in 1945, but continues in popular culture through the 1990s, in particular among a generation for whom the colonizer's music became theirs. Part of this continues to be reinforced and/or spread through Japan-originated media, such as magazines, films, television, and *karaoke* (singing to pre-recorded music), whose cultural inroads throughout Asia (and much of the industrial world) increase yearly (e.g. Ching 1996).[4] Part of this has been theorized as the appeal of indigenous music by those who question *enka*'s origins as Korean, not Japanese, dating from the 1920s when Japanese colonists in Korea included composer Koga Masao (1904–78), who was to codify the music and lyrics in its present darkly melodramatic image. The logical question arises, should *enka* be more appropriately called 'the heart/soul of Asia'? The answer to that depends upon how and when the music industry decides to address issues of boundaries and difference, becoming 'Asian' in one instance, and 'Japanese' the next. This deliberate invoking of the nation/culture in apparent disregard of transnational capitalistic enterprises is, according to Treat, 'at best nostalgic, at worse ideologically complicit' (1996:2).

Furusato as Homeland

In spite of these contigencies, *enka* retains its hold in Japan as national music, built upon nostalgia. The focal point of that nostalgia is *furusato* (hometown), literally meaning 'old village', but generalized since the late 1960s and 1970s as a national space (Robertson 1991:5,14).[5] Within this '*furusato* boom', *furusato* became homeland of the nation, with an originary, emotive, homogenizing sense of place. In *furusato*, history becomes spatialized so that Then becomes There. Moreover, *furusato* provides a point of imaginary distance, an internal exotic – at once removed from many people's lives while remaining central to this version of nationhood (Ivy 1995). *Enka* provides iterations of distant *furusato*/homeland heard over radio, television, karaoke, and cable broadcasting. Although its main audience is primarily older adults, *enka* forms part of the national soundscape. Because of its promotion as national culture through governmentally controlled media networks such as NHK (Nihon Hōsō Kyōkai, or Japan Broadcasting Corporation) and others, within a country of high population density and relatively few other media options, *enka* becomes at the very least, 'music overheard', even for its younger and/or elitist detractors.

NHK may be considered part of 'the apparatus of discourses, technologies, and institutions (print capitalism, education, mass media, and so forth) which *produces* what is generally recognized as 'the national culture' (Donald 1993:167). Donald makes the important point that the nation – by which he means a sense of the nation, or the imagined community which is the nation – is an effect of these cultural technologies, not their origin (cf. Anderson 1983). This nation is in a constantly emergent state of production and re-production as a 'system of cultural signification' (Bhabha 1990:1). *Enka* sets itself up as widely disseminated musical discourse which reproduces a set of 'hierarchically organized values, dispositions, and differences' reified as the nation (Donald 1993:167). My aim here is to examine ways in which those values, dispositions, and differences inform the concept of *furusato*/homeland. These homelands in song fuse the local to the national, thereby giving the imaginary its spatial substance through a sense of place.

One of the most effective ways in which various regional localities have been nationalized is through a process of incorporation. By this, various urban-rural divides become less relevant than a single center-periphery divide. The symbolic split in twentieth-century Japan is not city versus country, so much as Tokyo versus not-Tokyo, labelled variously *chihō* (provinces), *inaka* (rustic countryside), or *kokyō/furusato*[6] (hometown). Each of these gives different nuances to the sense of place. *Chihō* is most neutral in defining lands which are outside Tokyo. *Inaka* imparts a sense of cultural backwaters, as well as physical distancing. *Furusato* is the most affectively binding of the three. Areas labelled by these 'not-Tokyo' terms include cities with populations well over one million, such as Sapporo, Hiroshima, and Fukuoka (Ueda 1992:36).

Urbanization is not a new phenomenon in Japan. Although the nation's urban population did not exceed the rural one until the late 1950s, cities have shaped the nation's socio-cultural life and ethos for centuries. Pre-modern cities, in fact, scattered throughout the country as castle towns are part of what gave regional identities their force. Establishing Tokyo as a political, economic, and cultural center within Japan was part of the Meiji era (1868–1912) project of building a 'sense of nation' (Gluck 1985:21). Tokyo's subsequent domination of the nation's culture-scape attests to the success of the project. In postwar Japan, the domination continues in spite of efforts to decentralize. Moreover, with the incorporation of rural areas into what has been constructed as a Tokyo-centric national urban culture in part through assimilation, the urban-rural split carries less and less meaning (Ivy 1993; Kelly 1993).

This process of incorporation does not imply thoroughgoing homogenization. Regional differences, some meticulously derived and zealously upheld, are in fact part of the construction of *furusato*, in song and other forms of public discourse. These differences become part of the texture of a generalized *furusato*. Various regions of Japan are characterized not only by language, food, folklore, music, and scenery, but also by the look and personality types of people that live there. But it is more than texture that is at work here. Through regional and sub-regional differences, residents become locals, bound to spatial identities. When these differences become the very construction of the *furusato* umbrella, then being a local means being a national citizen. The doublespeak discourse accepts difference as the threads – separate, distinct, and representative – of the national fabric. As Ivy points out, 'Representative value becomes a mobile sign, detachable from locale but dependent on perpetually evoking it' (1995:13). It is this simultaneous detachability, as well as constant invoking of difference which is the crux of the subject here. Furthermore, separate does not mean equal; the distribution of power and control over national culture is by no means shared evenly by center and peripheries, by 'urban' and 'rural', or by various regions within peripheries.

Mass-mediated *Furusato*

The close link between *enka* and *furusato* is epitomized in television broadcasts, such as the daytime song show, '*Enka no Furusato*' ('The Hometown of *Enka*').[7] Each weekly show features one 'rural' region of Japan, two regular hosts (male and female), representatives of that region, and several *enka* singers. The regional representatives typically include a member from the local tourist board, who displays the *meibutsu* (well-known products of the area) and offers regional food for tasting. At the end of the show, the hosts explain how to get there from Tokyo and show a map of the area. *Enka*, *furusato*, and tourism all become discursively linked through shows such as this.

The opening sequence of shots which begin each show give some of the iconography of *furusato* (cf. Cosgrove and Daniels 1988).[8] The title of the show is superimposed over a background shot of a castle, linking the present to not only a pre-modern past when those inhabiting castles held power, but more specifically to the seventeenth- and eighteenth-centuries when various regional castle towns (*jōka machi*) dominated the country economically and politically. The next shot gives a blur of green color, which gradually comes into focus as a close-up of maple leaves. Green – as signifier of nature, freshness, youth – becomes one of the most common visual evocations of *furusato*. The final shot of the introduction is of a train crossing a bridge over a ravine into a tunnel. Upon closer inspection, a viewer can see that the train is no ordinary electric train, but a steam-powered locomotive with open-air cars transporting tourists deep into the recesses of the mountainous countryside.[9]

Although each week's show purports to be about one specific area of Japan, in fact the discussion is not restricted to that area. The songs sung have no relationship to the region being featured. The *enka* singers talk about their own *furusato*, which is more likely than not different from that of the featured region. However, what is said may apply to any of a number of *furusato*. What results is a generalized discussion of *furusato* tied together with *enka*.

The comments made about *furusato* during the program tend to focus on the following: first, it is peaceful and quiet; second, it has many beautiful natural features; third, it is a place where one can hear, see, and smell nature (e.g. the sound of cicadas, the color green, the fragrance of the flowers); fourth, the food is especially good, with specific references to the freshness of the harvest; fifth, there are *onsen* (hot springs); sixth, there are *matsuri* (festivals); seventh, there are rice paddies, evocative of Japan's agrarian rice-based past; eighth, one's childhood there was blissful; ninth, one's parents are there, especially one's mother.

Furusato here is sanitized. There is no talk of long hours of labor, poverty, lack of modern amenities, social restrictions, or gossip prevalent in small towns. *Furusato* here is sensualized. Guests are asked to taste the products of the region. There is invariably at least one comment on smell – whether it is the smell of the food they are trying, or of a new perfume that has been made from the regional flowers. Guests recall the pleasure of steeping in the hot waters at the onsen, with its smells and sensations. *Furusato* here is commodified. You can buy yourself a taste of it. You can buy a part of it as a souvenir. *Furusato* here is also exoticized. This is *furusato* as seen from afar, not as lived. It is a Tokyoite's version of *furusato* as a tourist destination. Nobody claims they want to live there; they only want to visit 'exotic', romantic *furusato*.

Even television shows on *enka* that do not attempt so overt a link to *furusato*, make that link an assumption. The main *enka* television program broadcast in the 1990s is TV Tokyo's prime time weekly '*Enka* no Hanamichi'. In a special interview marking the fifteenth anniversary of the show, producer Hashiyama Atsushi explains the purpose of the show as follows:[10]

> I want to create a *furusato* of emotions. Everyone probably has a *furusato*, a place to which he or she wants to return. Probably people who have left their rural hometown, as well as those who have no such rural hometown, have a nostalgic desire to return. However in reality, there are few people who have the luxury of actually visiting these places. Therefore, the purpose of this program is to give the sense of a temporary return, through music and images.
>
> (*'Enka no Hanamichi' no Miryoku* 1993:14).

The fuzziness of the explanation demonstrates how *furusato* has become not a place, but a concept, an abstraction, a kind of atmosphere (see Field 1989). The vaguer the concept, the more effective the metonymic shorthand. The music and visual images which effect this return are *enka*, typically set amidst scenes of a dimly-lit inn in the country or a forlorn bar on a wharf.[11] These referents become more symbolically evocative than concretely manifest for many viewers/ listeners whose own life experiences do not necessarily include such places. These homelands are not actual, but theatricalized settings for emotions which define this version of the nation.

Every program begins with the same voice-over spoken by an older husky-voiced female narrator:[12] 'If the stage of the floating world has a surface [*omote*], it also has an underside [*ura*]'. The ponderous music (not *enka*), somber visual effects, and general tone set by the introduction are not unlike that of American soap operas in their immediate identification as a stylized melodrama. The contrast set up between the public surface [*omote*] and private underside [*ura*] suggest that what the viewer is about to partake exists behind the screen, spatialized as a '*furusato* of emotions'. Moreover, references to the 'stage of the floating world' evoke pre-modern Japanese art, literature, and drama.[13] This *furusato*, then, exists as a dream, a memory, a return to a floating world.

The rest of the introduction from a January 1993 broadcast is as follows:

> I have nothing but unforgettable memories of that trip to the snowy north country. I think over and over of that person. The awakening of love [*koi-gokoro*] in me. When I look at the sky which flows onward to the north, it touches my heart [*mi ni shimu*]. These are songs of the heart [*kokoro uta*].

These images define *enka*'s imagining: snowy north country, past love recast and remembered, and most importantly, songs of the heart. It is heart that becomes the link between the two main themes in *enka*, failed romance and yearning for home. *Furusato*/home becomes where the heart is, both in romance, in family, and in the nation.

Performing *Furusato*

Showing one's original and continuing links to *furusato* is one of the most important conditions for success as an *enka* singer. The majority of singers come from 'rural' regions, are trained in the city (Tokyo or Osaka), and then go back to their hometowns to garner support. Building upon the recognition and/or construction of minute regional differences, some singers embed their place of birth within their image, projecting themselves as typical persons of a particular region. These may be physicalized as in the case of singer Fuji Ayako, known as a 'typical Akita beauty'. Other singers emphasize their continuing connectedness to *furusato* by incorporating their place of birth into their stage name. One example is Kitajima Saburō, whose name means 'northern island', referring to his birthplace of Hokkaido.

If a singer happens to be born in Tokyo, promoters regularly emphasize the singer's roots in *shitamachi* (downtown), reputedly the most 'traditional', *furusato*-like areas within the city. This designation of particular areas of Tokyo considered repositories of pre-industrial (therefore, *furusato*-like) life, customs, and values, harbors communities constructed as 'friendly, openhearted, unpretentious, generous, and neighborly' (Bestor 1989:7). These qualities, more than any others, make shitamachi into urban oases of *furusato*-derived human virtues. Singers of shitamachi, then, become personifications of this urban-based *furusato* ethos.

Professional *enka* singers regularly perform at regional matsuri, which have themselves become emblematic of Japan's past (see Robertson 1991:38–71). Most singers wage their promotional campaigns in provincial areas first, before appearing in large cities. In concert, a singer from the provinces may speak in the regional dialect of his/her origins. Some singers also sing with a regional accent, which the music industry inteprets as part of their charm. Certain *enka* songs include brief quotations of regional folk songs, within the song itself or as an interlude between verses. Regional differences are not minimized, but emphasized as part of the very exotica of *furusato*. What is important here, however, is that *furusato*, including its many local differences, becomes nationalized as homeland(s) of the nation.

In the following song, regional matsuri provides the rhetoric for the local, as it extends to the national.

> Men bearing the festival palanquin
> On their shoulders were living life to the fullest.
> God of the mountains, god of the seas,
> We truly thank you for this past year.
> The snow swirls atop the young men
> In white loincloth.
> Festival! Festival! Festival! It's a festival for the year of abundance.
> These young men who have become permeated with the smell of
>   the earth –
> Their hands which till the soil are treasures.
> At the festival men
> Honed themselves as men.
> God of the mountains, god of the seas,
> We truly thank you for life.
> . . .
> The life of a man is one of sweat and tears.
> I am living to the fullest.
> This is a festival of Japan!

'Matsuri' (1984)

In fact, there is no one festival that may be called a 'festival of Japan'. Here, however, the particular becomes generalized; one local festival becomes a generic festival, representative of the nation as much as of the region (Ivy 1995:12–13).

This song was performed in 1993 as the finale of NHK's 44th annual Kōhaku Uta Gassen (Red and White Song Festival), a prime time example of national culture, televised as a New Year's Eve media ritual. Although the song contest includes various genres of popular music, *enka* typically dominates the latter, more prestigious half of the 2–1/2 hour program. In 1993 the theme of the show was '*kawaranu Nippon*' (unchanging Japan). Through song, and particularly through *enka*, the program presented the nation to itself as one which has not, and hereby stubbornly refuses to be, changed. In the song contest, the last number and its singer occupy the most prestigious position, and singer Kitajima Saburō's 1993 performance of 'Matsuri' was no exception. His performance included a panoply of the symbols of *furusato cum* Japan – cherry blossoms, festival, fans, rice, traditional costuming, and *enka* – amidst a testament to the public virility of this version of nationhood.[14]

The flash and glitter of a Las Vegas presentation which characterizes this and so many other *enka* performances is meant to dazzle with the understanding that the glitter is mere surface; beneath lies the country boy or girl at heart. The awe lies in the glittery display that this is how far 'our' hometown boy or girl has come. In contrast to singers and other show business personalities in the West, *enka* singers in Japan do not polish their looks by removing moles or warts, or straightening crooked teeth. Instead, these become kinds of badges of pre-modern ordinariness, emblems of their rural earthiness.[15] Television specials on these singers focus not on their present-day luxurious lifestyles, but on their humble, often poverty-stricken roots in their *furusato*.

Musically, as well, the exoticism of vocal production thrusts *enka* into enclaves of the *furusato* imaginary. Here I use the word exoticism to highlight the fact that these various vocal techniques do not find common usage in the popular music world, except within the specific boundaries of *enka*. The range of vocal techniques finds precedent in Japanese narrative genres, such as *gidayu* (narrative song accompanying puppet theater) and *naniwa-bushi* (narrative song originally from Osaka). Moreover, the very aesthetic of the genre as narrative, more than melody, links it to premodern vocal genres. According to this aesthetic, what is important is not so much a 'beautiful voice', but an ability to effectively tell a story or draw out a tear.

The intertwining of distant space and time is further defined in terms of the clothes singers wear and the images they cultivate. Typically, female singers reference the past by wearing kimono; male singers wear Western suits. This kind of dichotomization parallels the gender lag in Japan's early period of modernization, when men, but not women, were exhorted to become forerunners of public modernity by adopting Western hair and clothes. A singer's image as being rooted in the past is further enhanced by appearing in dramatic, non-singing roles in television *jidai-geki* (period dramas) set most often in the Tokugawa Era (1600–1867) and/or in month-long runs of period plays performed in combination with concerts. These performances make the past not remote, but compartmentalized as an option within daily life.

The concept of *furusato* as internal exotic becomes a deliberate part of song texts. Many *enka* songs are set outside big cities; in particular in the harsh countryside of northern Japan. Among titles of popular songs are 'Kita-guni no Haru' (Spring in the North Country), 'Kita no Daichi' (The Land of the North), and 'Kita no Yado Kara' (From an Inn in the North Country). The north becomes a site of otherness, defined not only for its remoteness, but also for its inherent physical hardship. And, as one composer has found, the more remote, the better. He wrote one of his most famous songs with Niigata (prefecture in the northwest of Honshu) as the location. However, he felt that Niigata had become too familiar in the public mind, especially with high-speed trains linking it to Tokyo, so he substituted a lesser known place. The song subsequently became one of his biggest hits (Nippon Hōsō Kyōkai 1992). The physical remoteness of *furusato* becomes part of its desiring. A common refrain heard in *enka* is: '*Kaeritai kaerenai*' (I want to go home, but I cannot.) This entire discourse of longing for homeland hinges upon the juxtaposition of desire (*-tai*) and failure (*-enai*).

Furusato has its highly gendered dimensions, too. *Enka* songs construct men and women of *furusato* following 'traditional' stereotypes of active men and passive women, of public men's worlds and private women's worlds. Romance becomes a melodrama of heartache and sorrow for both sexes, but in particular for women who have no recourse of action. Specifically, women of *furusato* are those who have been left behind. These include not only lovers, but also mothers.

Mother as Embodiment of *Furusato*

The connection between *furusato* and mother is not only logical – mother as a person's biologicaly *furusato* – but also highly emotional. Mother herself rarely appears in *enka* songs; rather, she surfaces as mother remembered, especially by sons/men. Mothers are remembered most primally through the senses. Several *enka* songs sing nostalgically of mother's breast, of sleeping with mother, of listening to her lullabies.

169

Lying on my mother's gentle arm like a pillow,
I listened to her lullabies until I fell asleep.
I dreamt and dreamt, and upon awakening,
I always searched for my mother's breast.

'Haha-goyomi' (1988)

Even now, I yearn to smell of my mother's milk.
I long to see her face, her tears. . . .
Even now, if I were to follow the path of my memories,
I would feel the tender warmth of the palm of her hand.
If I could only return to that distant time and place.
If I could only return . . .

'Haha-kage' (1992)

The sensuality with which mother and child co-sleep, co-bathe, and co-exist becomes a model of national knowing, based in infancy and early childhood.

In *enka* songs, as the child grows older, he/she comes to know and appreciate another aspect of mother – her wisdom.

Mother dear, mother dear,
I look up to the sky and find memories of you.
On rainy days, you are my umbrella;
You taught me to become an umbrella
For others in this world.
I will never forget
The truth of your words.
Mother dear, mother dear,
I gaze at the flowers and find memories of you.
You taught me that the purity of
A flower's spirit lives on with strength.
I will never forget
The truth of your words.
Mother dear, mother dear,
I look up to the mountains and find memories of you.
On snowy days, you are my warmth.
My dear, you taught me to give my love
To others in this world.
I will never forget
The truth of your words.

'Ofukurosan' (1971)

This, sung by male singer Mori Shin'ichi, typically brings tears to the eyes of his audience made up primarily of women in their 50s and 60s. Homeland here becomes the site of natal origins, moral standard bearer, and spiritual teachings encoded in the figure of mother remembered.

Mothers are also remembered as keepers of households which create Japanese citizens. She is the keeper of national tradition. In the following song, mother's miso soup, a simple, humble, and ubiquitous soup served equally at breakfast, lunch, and/or dinner, becomes the focus of Japaneseness.

It's freezing, isn't it!
Winter is so cold, making miso soup delicious.
Delicious miso soup, hot miso soup,
This is the flavor of my mother, isn't it? . . .
When people become adults,
They put on fancy airs like big shots . . . .
But when they drink hot miso soup,
They think of their mothers
And cannot forget her – such is the male spirit . . .
We should sleep on *futon* [mattress], and our underwear should
be *fundoshi* [loincloth],
And don't call *gohan* [rice] 'ra-i-su'!
Yes, people these days forget the important things in life.
Can we still call them Japanese?
If people are Japanese,
They shouldn't forget their *furusato*
Where they were born, and miso soup.
It's been sixteen years now since I left my *furusato*,
And I always see my mother's breast in my dreams. When I recall
thus, my heart aches terribly. Without realizing it, tears well up in
my eyes. . . .
I want to taste my mother's miso soup again.
Mama!!

'*Miso Shiru no Uta*' (1980)

Mother – as maker of soup, keeper of a house where people still sleep on futon, wise in her moral teachings, working hard without complaint – becomes the repository of *furusato*, and therefore all things Japanese.

Within a nation-as-family ideology, mother becomes the source not only of personal identity, but national one as well. In reifying the most physically intimate of relationships – that of mother and child – *enka* songs establish a sensual link between all Japanese national citizens as children of their mothers. Moreover, as the primary caregiver in a Japanese family, mother becomes the primary socializer, the primary nationalizer.

It is through her efforts that a child learns what it means to be Japanese – whether physically imbibed through the foods that she cooks or spiritually ingested through her example of humility, diligence, and suffering. Through mother, these *enka* songs create a biological definition of national identity. This makes that identity powerfully irrevocable. As a person will always be the child of his/her mother, so will Japanese theoretically always be Japanese. National identity accordingly courses in the blood. Through mother, these *enka* songs also create an emotional definition of national identity. This gives that identity a different, but no less important, kind of potency. As a person will always (especially in these songs) love and yearn for his/her mother, so will Japanese theoretically always love and yearn for being Japanese. In this way, national identity becomes rooted in the heart.

The relationship between child and mother, between Japanese and their identity as Japanese, however, becomes ambiguous. Separated, the child forever seeks the mother. Likewise in this construction of song, Japanese, internally separated from their homeland, now exoticized, seek their own Japaneseness. Japan's internal monologue, as expressed in *enka*, seems to say: 'We long for our past Japanese selves'. Nostalgia becomes a means through which this imaginary of homeland takes hold, keeping desire in place.

Conclusions

Homeland as a space of social practice constructs no less than the nation. As the local narrows down to specificities of individual mothers, distinctive hometowns, and regional minutiae of food, language, and topography, so does locale become a vital link to the larger spheres of racial blood, 'virtual' *furusato*, and national 'tradition'. *Enka* and its transmission via mass media become part of this social practice. One may 'do' *enka* – buying tapes, requesting songs, tuning in to programs, listening to and watching performances, attending concerts, joining fan clubs, singing at karaoke. And in doing, one takes part in a form of commercially-based national culture. This is not to say that *enka*'s doers adhere equally to all ideological aspects of the cultural product, or even agree on its meaning. Rather, doing keeps *enka* afloat in whatever guise, with whatever meaning that individual doers seek and find for themselves.

Yet, this is a nation circumscribed by its extremities, whose homelands, pluralized by differences, become Homeland, singularized by national need. *Furusato* in *enka* brings the hearth to the center stage of cultural nationalism, drawing the space of the nation in tight with fluids of intimacy – mother's milk, tears of longing, sweat of exertion. The collective memory jogged by *enka* reminds its listeners of their connections to past people, places, and emotions. Furthermore, it shapes listeners in the very act of listening, creating a nation in tears. More and less than a Durkheimian collective, however, this nation struggles within its own success as one still unsure of its international place, its reconstructed past, and its own people. Drawn by introspection, *enka* was re-created to ameliorate some of these dilemmas. With the faces of the homeland on television, with the sounds of *furusato* overheard, *enka* makes visible and audible the nation as place. This place may be drawn from the peripheries, yet it serves as center, obscuring the hinterlands while it lauds them.

Notes

1 I gratefully acknowledge the following sources of funding during fieldwork conducted in Tokyo/Yokohama 1991–93 and after: Japan Foundation Dissertation Fellowship, Crown Prince Akihito Scholarship Fund, Center for Japanese Studies (University of Hawaii), Edwin O. Reischauer Institute of Japanese Studies Postdoctoral Fellowship (Harvard University). Earlier partial versions of this article were presented at the International House of Japan (Tokyo), Conference on Changing Representations of Women and Feminisms, East and West (Honolulu), and the Reischauer Institute of Japanese Studies at Harvard University (Cambridge). Parts of this were previously published in *Proceedings of the Fifth Annual Ph.D. Kenkyukai Conference on Japanese Studies* (1994) and *Constructions and Confrontations: Changing Representations of Women and Feminisms, East and West* (1996), edited by Cristina Bacchilega and Cornelia N. Moore, Honolulu: College of Languages, Linguistics and Literature, University of Hawai'i. My thanks go to Takie Lebra and Judith Herd for their continuing support and guidance.

2 In 1993 when I asked Sakurai Toshio (b. 1910), the last remaining *enkashi*, whether or not there was any relation between what he used to sing and what is today *enkashi* called *enka*, he replied '*Zenzen*' (Not at all).

3 For example, a survey of older records at a Japanese music store in Hawai'i indicates that until about 1973, the major *enka*-producing company, Nippon Columbia, categorized what are now considered *enka* as *ryūkōka* as indicated on their labels.

4 Ching raises the important point that the documented spread of Japanese popular culture in Taiwan does not address the issue of the meanings or understandings of those cultural products for Taiwanese consumers (1996:186–87).

173

5 Robertson notes that the concept *furusato* invokes both time and space, with the first half of the word, *furu(i)* (old), signifying pastness, and the second half, *sato*, signifying natal, rural place (1991:4).

6 These two terms share their first character, meaning old, discussed previously. Kokyō gives a Chinese reading; the second character means village or native place. *Furusato* gives a Japanese reading, often interpreted as having a more native feel and conceptualization.

7 This show, a product of TV Tokyo, has been discontinued as of March 1993.

8 Daniels and Cosgrove draw parallels between Erwin Panofsky's notions of iconography as 'the identification of conventional, consciously inscribed symbols' and Clifford Geertz's definition of culture as a text of symbols (1988:2–4).

9 One such scenic railway line takes passengers from Kanaya (Shizuoka prefecture), about 200 kilometers southwest of Tokyo, into the mountains to Senzu and Ikawa over Sessokyō Gorge.

10 All text and song translations are those of the author.

11 Tansman lists *enka*'s 'mythic places' as the *roji* (alleyway), harbor, train station, and rural town (1996:116).

12 One viewer that I spoke with said that the female narrator is meant to sound like the female proprietress at a bar who listens to men's troubles and has had a few herself. In reality she is professional voice actress Kinomiya Ryōko, who has narrated the show since its inception. According to a producer of the show, before a recording session for the show, Kinomiya purposely goes to bars where she drinks and sings to get the characteristic huskiness in her voice (Wilson 1993:19–20).

13 The term *ukiyo* (floating world) refers to the Buddhist concept of a transitory world of pain and misery. However amidst the rise of merchant/ townspeople culture in the seventeenth-century, *ukiyo* increasingly came to refer to the transitory world of illusion and sensuality associated with the pleasure quarters, including that of popular theater (Lane 1978:11).

14 Moeran and Skov make the important point that many of these natural symbols of Japaneseness invoked in Japan are also those taken internationally as symbolic of the country (1997). Orientalism has helped shape stereotypes both from within and without.

15 The characterization of people from the countryside can be found, of course, in other forms of popular culture. In celebrated animator Hayao Miyazaki's 1993 feature-length film 'Tonari no Totoro' (My Neighbor Totoro), for example, rural people are depicted as being sincere, close to nature, and in touch with the spiritual world. These qualities become physicalized in a wise old rural woman, who has missing teeth, weathered brown skin, and a wart in the middle of her forehead.

References

Anderson, Benedict 1983 *Imagined Communities*, London: Verso.

Bhabha, Homi 1990 'Introduction', pp. 1–7, in Homi Bhabha (ed.), *Nation and Narration*, London: Routledge.

Boyarin, Jonathan (ed.) 1994 *Remapping Memory: the politics of timespace*, Minneapolis: University of Minnesota Press.

Ching, Leo 1996 'Imaginings in the Empires of the Sun', pp. 169–94 in John Treat (ed.), *Contemporary Japan and Popular Culture*, Honolulu: University of Hawaii Press.

Coser, Lewis A. (ed.) 1992 *Maurice Halbwachs on Collective Memory*, Chicago: The University of Chicago Press.

Cosgrove, Denis and Stephen Daniels 1988 *The Iconography of Landscape*, Cambridge: Cambridge University Press.

Daniels, Stephen and Denis Cosgrove 1988 'Introduction: iconography and landscape', pp. 1–10 in Denis Cosgrove and Stephen Daniels (ed.) *The Iconography of Landscape*, Cambridge: Cambridge University Press.

Donald, James 1993 'How English is it? popular literature and national culture', pp. 165–186 in Erica Carter, James Donald, and Judith Squires (eds.), *Space and Place: theories of identity and location*, London: Lawrence and Wishart.

'"Enka no Hanamichi" no miryoku' [The appeal of "Enka no Hanamichi"] 1993, pp. 14–17 in *Karaoke Taishō* 13 (4).

Field, Norma 1989 '*Somehow*: the postmodern as atmosphere', pp. 169–188 in Masao Miyoshi and H.D. Harootunian (ed.), *Postmodernism and Japan*, Durham: Duke University Press.

Friedman, Jonathan 1992 'The past in the future: history and the politics of identity', pp. 837–859 in *American Anthropologist* 94 (4).

Fujitani, Takashi 1993 'Inventing, forgetting, remembering: toward a historical ethnography of the nation-state', pp. 77–106 in H. Befu (ed.), *Cultural Nationalism in East Asia; representation and identity*, Berkeley: Institute of East Asian Studies, University of California, Berkeley.

Gluck, Carol 1985 *Japan's Modern Myths; ideology in the late Meiji period*, Princeton: Princeton University Press.

IASPM-Japan (Japan Branch of the International Association for the Study of Popular Music) 1991 *A Guide to Popular Music in Japan*, Japan: IASPM-Japan.

Ivy, Marilyn 1993 'Formations of mass culture', pp. 239–258 in Andrew Gordon (ed.), *Postwar Japan as History*, Berkeley: University of California Press.

Ivy, Marilyn 1995 *Discourses of the Vanishing: modernity, phantasm, Japan*, Chicago: University of Chicago Press.

Keith, Michael and Steve Pile 1993 'Introduction Part 1: The politics of place; Introduction Part 2: The place of politics', pp. 1–40 in Michael Keith and Steve Pile (eds.), *Place and the Politics of Identity*, London: Routledge.

Kelly, William 1993 'Finding a place in metropolitan Japan; ideologies, institutions and everyday life', pp. 189–216 in Andrew Gordon (ed.), *Postwar Japan as History*, Berkeley: University of California Press.

Lane, Richard 1978 *Images from the Floating World: the Japanese print*, Fribourg: Konecky & Konecky.

Lefebvre, Henri 1991 *The Production of Space*, trans. Donald Nicholson-Smith, Oxford: Basil Blackwell.

Moeran, Brian and Lise Skov 1997 'Mount Fuji and the cherry blossoms: a view from afar', pp. 181–205 in P. Asquith and A.Kalland (eds.) 1997 *Japanese Images of Nature; cultural perspectives*, Surrey: Curzon Press.

Nihon Hōsō Kyōkai 1992 *Nihonjin to Kayōkyoku: iku tabi kaeru tabi sasurau tabi* (Japanese People and Popular Song: travels going forth, travels returning home, wandering travels), Television program broadcast 2/11/92.

'Nihonjin ni wa enka ga niau' (*Enka* is well-suited to Japanese people) 1987, pp. 14–15 in *Nihon Keizai Shimbun*, Jan. 18.

Nostrand, Richard L. and Lawrence E. Estaville, Jr. 1993 'Introduction: the homeland concept', pp. 1–4 in *Journal of Cultural Geography* 13 (2).

Oricon Co., Ltd. 1993 *Orikon Nenkan 1993 Nenban* (1993 Oricon Yearbook), Tokyo: Oricon Co., Ltd.

Robertson, Jennifer 1991 *Native and Newcomer: making and remaking a Japanese city*, Berkeley: University of California Press.

Soja, Edward W. 1989 *Postmodern Geographies*, London: Verso.

Tansman, Alan M. 1996 'Mournful tears and *sake*: the postwar myth of Misora Hibari', pp. 103–33 in John Treat (ed.), *Contemporary Japan and Popular Culture*, Honolulu: University of Hawaii Press.

Treat, John Whittier 1996 'Introduction: Japanese studies into cultural studies', pp. 1–14 in John Treat (ed.), *Contemporary Japan and Popular Culture*, Honolulu: University of Hawaii Press.

Ueda Jinichiro (ed.) 1992 *Asahi Shimbun Japan Almanac*, Tokyo: Asahi Shimbun Publishing Co.

Weiner, Michael (ed.) 1997 *Japan's Minorities: the illusion of homogeneity*, London: Routledge.

Wilson, Jean 1993 'Enka no Hanamichi', pp. 18–21 in *Eye-Ai* 17 (196).

8

RETURN TO ASIA?

Japan in Asian Audiovisual Markets[1]

Koichi Iwabuchi

Introduction

Japan's modern history can be described in a simplifying manner as a dynamic cultural hybridization through 'westernization', 'Japanization' and 'de-Asianization'. The two famous slogans of late-nineteenth century Japan, '*Datsua Nyūō*' (escape from Asia, enter the West) and '*Wakon Yōsai*' (Japanese spirit, western technology) illustrate these dynamics. Since the mid-nineteenth century when Japan faced the threat of western imperial power, Japanese leaders have been keen to indigenize western culture, knowledge and technologies to enrich and strengthen the country. An extreme example of this was a proposal by the first Education Minister in 1873 to abolish Japanese language and to adopt English as the national language. Unlike some other Asian countries such as China which resisted western influences, Japanese leaders were willing to accept the notions of western 'progress' and of 'Asiatic backwardness'. Thus Japan had to escape from Asia.

However, Japan's de-Asianization has paradoxically coexisted with an Asianism which emphasized solidarity with fellow Asians against western imperialism, and Japan's role as the leader in Asia. In the prewar period, this ideological Asianism was not only distrusted by the Western powers but also strongly resisted by Asian nations who feared Japan's territorial ambitions. After all, Japan was the only non-western imperial country with a strong military force. Indeed, a discourse of Asianism was often advocated to justify Japan's expansion to Asia as well as to express its contestation of Western powers. Consequently, as Banno (1981) argues, although some Japanese leaders saw Japan's mission as the unifier of two global civilizations – Eastern and Western – they ultimately could not identify thoroughly with either. The failure of this Asianist agenda is especially stark in light of Japan's geographical and cultural proximity to other Asian – especially East Asian – countries.

In the early 1990s, a 'new Asianism' emerged in Japan. How to be a part of Asia became an important economic question for Japan. The United States warned that Japan should attach importance to APEC (the Asia Pacific Economic Cooperation Forum), which includes western countries such as the United States, Australia and New Zealand, rather than EAEC (the East Asia Economic Caucus), which excludes these 'white' economies. Although obeying the U.S. prompting not to join EAEC, Japan nonetheless cannot neglect Asia as a vital market for its products. Thus, Japan slowly 'returns to Asia'. In this move, economic motives are often disguised by nostalgic racial/cultural justifications. As the president of Fuji Xerox claims: '[J]ust as Gorbachov once declared that Russia's home was in Europe, so it is only natural for us to say that Japan's home is in Asia, not in the United States or Europe' (quoted in Saito 1992:17).

Though Japan's 'New Asianism' is principally economy-oriented, its impact is much wider. This chapter looks at this phenomenon by exploring what might be called 'Japan's postmodern return to Asia'. By this I mean the attempts on the part of the Japanese cultural industries to penetrate the fast-growing Asian audiovisual market. These attempts are especially relevant in the context of the production of images and signs, which are crucial for economic activities in the age of disorganized, postmodern capitalism (Lash and Urry, 1994). What the Japanese cultural industries are currently involved with is the construction of cultural affinities with the rest of Asia through popular culture and urban consumption.

It is often suggested that the enigma of Japanese economic superpowerdom lies in its astonishingly disproportionate lack of cultural influence upon the world. On the one hand, this of course has something to do with the overwhelming global cultural hegemony of 'the West'. On the other hand, however, the Japanese themselves are said to be reluctant to diffuse their culture to non-Japanese. As Hannerz (1989:67–8) argues, '[T]he Japanese . . . find it a strange notion that anyone can "become Japanese", and they put Japanese culture on exhibit, in the framework of organized international contacts, as a way of displaying irreducible distinctiveness rather than in order to make it spread'. The Japanese obsession with seeing their own culture as unique cannot be denied. Furthermore, what is put on exhibit as 'Japanese culture' in international forums is mostly officially sanctioned 'traditional' culture, which has little to do with contemporary Japanese urban society. It is a culture purposively constructed to be displayed as exhibit.

Contemporary Japanese popular culture did not cross the Japanese border very much until recently. While the Japanese cultural industries are quite powerful and well-organized, they did not actively export their cultural products (software), with the well-known exception of animation films. Japanese cultural exports tended to be limited to 'culturally odourless' items such as consumer technologies or, for that matter, animation. The scarce transnational circulation of Japanese cultural software reinforced the mysterious image of Japan, which is mainly represented by giant companies without human faces, economy without culture. This not only mystified people outside Japan but also frustrated the Japanese themselves. As the Japanese novelist Ōe Kenzaburō once lamented: 'You know why Honda is great. But we don't care about Honda. We care that our cultural life is unknown to you' (quoted in Bartu 1992:189).

Japan's postmodern return to Asia promotes the unprecedented circulation of Japanese popular culture in Asia. Nonetheless many Japanese cultural industries are still less concerned with the direct export of Japanese cultural products than with ridding cultural products of 'Japanese smell' and camouflaging themselves as being of 'local' origins. The practice is based upon the strategic necessity of what Sony calls 'global localization' – or 'glocalization' to use a business buzz word (see Robertson 1995; Iwabuchi 1996)– meaning that global companies should be sensitive to local preferences if they are to disseminate standardized commodities throughout the globe. In this context, it is interesting to note that what the Japanese cultural industries try to export to Asia are not products per se, but items of urban middle class culture constructed through an indigenization of 'the West'. As Ohmae (1990), a representative of Japanese globalism, argues, there is no nationality or national boundary for the desire and the right for people to consume commodities all over the globe. Thus, it is exactly this consumer culture that Japan can diffuse to a rapidly modernizing Asia, based on a claim of cultural proximity.

The implications of global localization as deployed by the Japanese cultural industries are contradictory. On the one hand, it should be considered as a form of Japanese neo-imperialism, as it conceals the one-way flow of capital under the guise of fostering Asian localities and the slogan of 'new Asianism'. This ugly face of Japan's return to Asia can also be discerned politically in that it enables Japanese leaders to use the assertion of Japan's sameness with Asia to facilitate a smooth penetration of Asian markets. This is a view which neglects the specificities of various local cultures throughout Asia and obliterates the history of Japanese imperialism.

On the other hand, global localization also presents another, more positive and forward-looking possibility. It precipitates a dialogue between peoples in Asia not through reified notions of 'tradition' or 'authentic culture', but through people's skilful negotiation with the symbols and powers of global capitalism. This is a contradiction which should not be reduced to a view of either optimism or pessimism, but which we should recognize as a constitutive component of the contemporary relationship between Japan and Asia.

In the following, I will first discuss Japan's peculiar position in the global audio-visual market. Then I will refer to the recent strategy of Japanese culture industries to target the profitable Asian markets. In particular, I will discuss the music industry, which provides an interesting case for analyzing the relationship between Japan and Asia in the age of globalization. Finally, I will evaluate 'Japan's postmodern return to Asia' in the context of a wider discourse of the 'Asianization of Asia', which has gained force in Japan in the 1990s.

Japan in the Global Cultural Flow

One of the most remarkable features of the Japanese audio-visual market is its near self-sufficiency in TV programming. Japan is the only country, apart from the United States, where more than 95 per cent of TV programmes are produced domestically. Japan's history of TV began in 1953 when two Japanese TV stations were established, one public, one private. In the 1950s and early 60s, Japan relied enormously upon imports from Hollywood for TV programming, but since the mid 1960s, this imbalance has drastically diminished. In 1980–1981, there were five commercial networks and two public channels, and just 5 per cent of the programmes were imported (Stronach 1989:142) and the same pattern was discerned in 1993 (Kawatake and Hara 1994).

There were several reasons for this quick change. First, two national events around 1960 contributed to the ascendancy of TV's popularity. One was the crown prince's wedding in 1959, and the other was the Tokyo Olympics in 1964. These two events created a nationwide boom in television sales. Second, the maturity of feature film production lent itself to the quick ascendancy of the TV industry, at the cost of its own decline. The popularity of TV decreased Japanese movie attendance, which declined drastically from 1.1 billion in 1958 to 373 million in 1965 (Stronach 1989:136). Accordingly, capable film makers turned to television and this led to the maturity of the TV industry. The number of feature films produced fell from more than 500 in 1960 to 58 in 1990 (Buck 1992:126). Finally, Japan's economic miracle and the size of the market made this quick development possible. The Japanese population of more than 120 million and its economic wealth make the Japanese audiovisual market, along with those of the United States, one of the two self-sufficient markets in the world.

This does not mean, however, that foreign TV programmes, information, music or films are not consumed and enjoyed in Japan. In fact, American popular culture has continued to influence Japan strongly. The Japanese have been saturated with American popular culture. Japan is one of the most important buyers of Hollywood movies, although Japanese movies still comprise around 50per cent of the domestic box office (O'Regan 1992:330). Many TV formats and concepts are also deeply influenced by and borrowed from American programmes, and information about the American way of life appears in the mass media frequently. But directly imported TV programmes have hardly become truly popular. In Japan, people can watch many popular American TV series such as *Dallas*, *Beverly Hills 90210*, or *The Simpsons*, but these programmes never get high ratings. Popularity does not depend upon whether the product is originally Japanese or not, but on how the Japanese product localizes the original. Who knows and cares, for example, whether the Japanese version of *The Price is Right* is of American origin or not. What Japanese audiences care about is whether the programme contains 'Japanese smell'. And as I will elaborate later, this indigenization is the key strategy adopted by Japanese culture industries entering Asian markets.

Despite the relative maturity of its cultural industries, Japan has not until recently actively exported TV programmes and films to other parts of the world except animation, although some products did become successful outside Japan, like *Tampopo* or *Oshin*. The unexportability of Japanese media products can be explained by the term 'cultural discount', which Colin Hoskins and Rolf Mirus describe as occurring when:

> A particular programme rooted in one culture and thus attractive in that environment will have a diminished appeal elsewhere as viewers find it difficult to identify with the style, values, beliefs,

institutions and behavioural patterns of the material in question. Included in the cultural discount are reductions in appreciation due to dubbing or subtitling.

(1988:500)

Cultural prestige, western hegemony, the universal appeal of American popular culture, and the prevalence of the English language are no doubt advantageous to Hollywood. Similar considerations can also explain why, compared to the popularity of Hong Kong films in Asian countries, the impact of Japanese popular film has been disproportionally low; a great number of overseas Chinese throughout Asia favours Hong Kong films. By contrast, Japanese is not spoken outside Japan, and Japan is supposedly obsessed with its own cultural uniqueness (see Iwabuchi 1994). It is an open question to what extent Asians consider Japanese cultural products 'culturally friendly', but it should be remembered that the perception of cultural proximity does not necessarily lead to cultural preference by consumers of other societies. Hollywood products, for example, are sometimes less a threat to the local ways precisely because they are conceived as 'foreign', while those originating from culturally proximate countries are perceived as more threatening (O'Regan 1992:343–344).

In this respect, the export of Japanese cultural products faces a major historical obstacle, namely Japan's brutal colonization of Asian countries earlier this century. The former colonies Taiwan and Korea have both banned Japanese films and music (although Taiwan overturned this policy around the end of 1993, while South Korea partly abolished its restriction policies in late 1998). The legacy of Japanese imperialism prevents Japan from actively exporting its 'culture' to Asian countries. The South Korean and Taiwanese governments might prefer American products to Japanese ones, because they are thought to be less culturally damaging and dangerous than the more culturally proximate products of 'the Japanese Empire'.

Thus, Japanese cultural exports have tended to be confined mainly to so-called 'culturally neutral' commodities. For such a product, country of origin has nothing to do with 'the way it works and the satisfaction he [sic] obtains from usage' (Hoskins and Mirus 1988:503). In other words, Japanese exports have to overcome their high cultural discount and the history of Japanese imperialism. The Japanese version of the export of meanings, 'cultural imperialism' if you like, requires the erasure of 'Japanese smell'. The major audiovisual products Japan exports overseas are what I call three C's of non-melly products:

comics/cartoons (animations), consumer technologies and computer games. Japan routinely exports animation films, in which racial or ethnic differences are erased or subdued. Animated films occupied 56 per cent of TV exports from Japan in 1980–1981 (Stronach, 1989) and 58 per cent in 1992–1993 (Kawatake and Hara, 1994). While other genres are mostly exported in the original Japanese language, only one per cent of animated exports were in Japanese. This means that animation is routinely intended for export (Stronach 1989:144).

However, there is no doubt that consumer technologies are Japan's biggest cultural exports. From VCRs, computer games, karaoke, the Walkman, video cameras to, more recently, digital TV and High Definition TV, the domination of Japanese consumer electronics in the global market place is so overwhelming that this success is now attributed to Japan's 'creative and original refinement', if not 'pure originality', rather than to its cunning ability to copy or imitate 'the West' (Forester 1993; Lardner 1987). For example, VCRs were originally invented by an American company, but it was Sony, Matsushita and JVC who refined and made them suitable for the consumer market with the input of many original ideas (Lardner 1987). This development is not totally contingent, but based upon a solid belief, 'First for consumers', to use the words of Ibuka Masaru, a founder of Sony (quoted in Lardner 1987:38). Freed from the obligation to devote its R&D energy for military purposes after the Second World War and with the help of the Japanese government, the Japanese electronics industry has successfully inverted the idea of 'scientific or military research first', to the extent that technological development in Japan is now pushed by consumer electronics (Forester 1993:4).

Japanese consumer technologies certainly have more universal appeal than Japanese films or TV programmes. The influence of new consumer technologies on everyday life is not culturally neutral and is, in a sense, more profound than that of Hollywood films. To use Jody Berland's term, they are 'cultural technologies' which mediate between 'producing texts, producing spaces, producing listeners' (1992:39). New technologies produce new spaces in which media texts are consumed by audiences. In turn, the cultural industries produce new media texts in order to create new audiences who inhabit the new technological space. A significant feature of the new media space is the market-driven privatization of consumer needs and desires. New cultural technologies open up new ways for capital to accommodate itself to the global flow of cultural products under the name of the sovereignty of the individual consumer. For example, VCRs have facilitated the transnational flow of VTR-recorded programmes through both legal channels and illegal piracy. This gave people, especially those in the developing countries whose appetites for information and entertainment have not been satisfied, access to diverse programmes which had been officially banned. In response, governments are changing their policies from rigid restriction of the flow of information and entertainment to more market-oriented control of the flow through, for example, the privatization of TV channels (Ganley and Ganley 1987; Boyd et al. 1989; O'Regan 1991).

On an individual level, Japanese electronic technologies have promoted strongly what Raymond Williams called 'mobile privatization' (1990:26). These consumer technologies give people greater choice and thus mobility through technologies in their media consumption activities in domestic, private spaces. It is an interesting question why such individualistic, private technologies have been developed and flourished in an apparently group-oriented society such as Japan. Kogawa (1984; 1988) coined the term 'electronic individualism' to characterize Japanese social relations, arguing that Japanese collectivity is increasingly based upon electronic communication and therefore becoming more precarious. Although Kogawa views the contemporary Japanese situation somewhat pessimistically, he points out that there are dual possibilities for the emancipation of individuals and the sophisticated control of individuals through technologies. Indeed, as Chambers argues, the Walkman is an ambivalent 'cultural activity' swaying between 'autonomy and autism' (1990:2). Such an activity can be seen as a form of escapism which makes individuals feel a sense of atomized freedom from the constraints of a rigidly controlled society, but it also has a possibility of substituting a privatized 'micro-narrative' for collective 'grand-narratives' (p. 3). Speaking about the Chinese context, Chow argues that listening to a Walkman is 'a "silent" sabotage of the technology of collectivization' (1993:398) (for a more thorough analysis of Walkman, see du Gay et al., 1997)

The development of cultural technologies and the audio-visual market has encouraged the global centralization of distribution and production of software, and lends itself to the further spread of American software. Despite the fear of profits being creamed off by piracy, VCRs have helped Hollywood to open up new markets and find ways of exploiting new technologies through video rental and export of TV programmes to newly privatized channels (see O'Regan 1992; Gomery,1988). Sony's purchase of Columbia in 1989 and Matsushita's purchase of MCA (Universal) in 1990, which dramatized the merger of hardware and software companies, should be seen as the logical extension of the centralization of distribution. Although there was considerable reaction from the United States against these buy-outs, claiming that 'the Japanese are buying our American soul', this has to be considered in the light of the broader logic of globalization. After all, the reason Sony and Matsushita bought Hollywood is not to dominate American minds, but to construct a total entertainment conglomerate through the acquisition of control over both audio-visual hardware and software. It was based upon a sober judgement that 'it is cultural distribution, not cultural production, that is the key locus of power and profit' (Garnham 1990:161–2). It was a confirmation of the supremacy of American software creation and therefore of Japan's second-rate ability as a software producer. Seen this way, the Japanese takeover is not to kill the American soul but, on the contrary, to make Hollywood omnipresent. Japanese ingenuity of hardware production and American genius of software go hand in hand, because (Japanese) consumer technologies work as 'distribution systems' for (American) entertainment products (Berland 1992: 46).

But this is not the total story. In the film, *Black Rain*, Japanese co-star Takakura Ken replied to Michael Douglas's antagonistic remark about Japanese economic expansion into the United States, 'Music and movies are all your culture is good for . . . We make the machines' (quoted in Morley and Robins 1992:145). The comment is perhaps an expression of America's perception of its supremacy in the making of popular culture and a certain disdain for Japanese fascination with pure technology. Apart from the take-over of Hollywood by Japanese companies, there may be good reasons to speculate the end of the era of 'American media supremacy'. Japanese consumer technologies have become so sophisticated that we can talk about a 'technoculture' in which 'cultural information and the technical artifact seem to merge' (Wark 1991:45). For example, computer game culture which becomes so popular even in the United States is an embodiment of a new aesthetic which emanates, if not completely, from Japanese cultural imagery and captures the new popular imagination (Wark 1994), even if it still does not have 'Japanese smell' for its consumers.

Global Localization and Asian Markets

Crucially, the development of the audio-visual market has also made the Japanese cultural industries aware of the need for cultural products

185

which are more sensitive to the diversity and tastes of local markets. Sony's strategy of 'global localization' most eloquently tells the beginning of the demise of U.S. domination of the media. In order to penetrate different local markets at once, global companies try to 'transcend vestigial national differences and to create standardized global markets, whilst remaining sensitive to the peculiarities of local markets and differentiated consumer segments' (Aksoy and Robins 1992:18). American cultural products are indeed powerful but not powerful enough to prevent other global cultural industries from making a profit. While capital still operates on the instrumentalist logic of transmission and dissemination of messages, global cultural industries exploit such a logic by emphasizing the sharing of symbols and aesthetic experiences among consumers in a particular niche market (see Carey 1989). Marketing localities/ethnicities is becoming the key emphasis.

This realization of the significance of local specificity by the cultural industries corresponds with the critique of the 'cultural imperialism thesis'. The thesis has been criticized for its implication of a 'more or less straightforward and deliberate imposition of dominant culture and ideology' and is therefore firmly based upon 'the transmission view of communication' (Ang 1994:196). Others have pointed to its reliance on the 'the center-periphery model' (see, for example, Sinclair 1991; Tomlinson 1991; Hannerz 1989), thus connoting a one-way flow of cultural products and meanings from the dominant to the dominated. However, in the 'real' world, foreign products are often domesticated by local consumers in terms of their meanings as well as their forms and content (Appadurai 1990). Moreover, regional centres such as Brazil, Hong Kong and India produce a significant amount of 'local' products for the regional and global markets (cf. Straubhaar 1991; McNeely and Soysal 1989). 'Global localization' tries to create local zones by gauging the practices of local media centres and the dynamic processes of indigenization. It is a strategy that incorporates the viewpoint of 'the dominated' who have long learned to negotiate with 'Western culture' in the local consumption of media products.

However, the question remains: which localities are to be exploited? Should a 'local market' be a small community, a national region, a nation-state or a broader region? How should such localities be represented in the mass media? These are vital questions for global cultural industries. It is in Asian markets that answers to these questions have been most eagerly pursued in the 1990s, though how the recent economic crisis will influence Asian media markets is still an uncertain issue. About 3 billion people live in the region, some parts of which have achieved high economic growth and where the states are increasingly privatizing their media and communication industries. However, the problem is that Asia consists of a considerable diversity of cultures, ethnicities and languages. Moreover, some countries such as Hong Kong and India have long established powerful cultural industries whose products have won the hearts of their people. It is precisely the irreducible cultural difference and people's preference for 'local' programmes in Asia as well as each government's control that STAR TV (Satellite Television Asian Region) is struggling with. STAR TV mistook centralization of distribution for that of transmission and neglected the existence of multiple 'locals'. The lesson STAR TV has learned is that exporting English-language programmes produced in Hollywood is no longer enough; as Rupert Murdoch said, 'we've committed ourselves to learning the nuance of the region's diverse cultures' (Asian Business Review May 1994). Rather than pursuing the old-fashioned 'communication as transmission view' of broadcasting pan-Asian programmes in one language, the strategy of STAR TV is changing into localizing programmes by finding local partners which assure them of local programmes. (*Far Eastern Economic Review*, 27 January 1994). Coupled with highly political reasons, STAR TV replaced BBC World News and the American MTV with more Chinese-sensitive programmes and a more localized music channel, Channel V (*The Australian*, 11 May 1994). And MTV Asia is striking back with much more localized programming.

In contrast, the 'local' industries in Asia are exploiting local specificities more subtly. For example, Hong Kong's leading television station, TVB, is actively cutting into Asian markets with its capacity for five thousand hours of programming a year (*Far Eastern Economic Review*, 27 January 1994). TVB not only exports its programmes but also co-produces locally tailor-made programmes. This co-production strategy has succeeded in the Mandarin language market of Taiwan and has now been extended to the Malay-language market with a Chinese-Indonesian partner (*Mainichi Shinbun*, 21 April 1994). Apart from production ability, the strength of TVB lies in its 'Chineseness' which may be more or less shared by a vast number of ethnic Chinese people in Asian region. What then about Japan whose 'unique' culture is supposed to have never been shared with any non-Japanese?

Japan in Asia

As mentioned earlier, the Japanese cultural industries have been largely domestic-oriented. This is partly because the industry was profitable enough within the affluent Japanese market itself. The desire to avoid accusations of 'cultural imperialism' by other Asian countries is another reason. Satellite TV was introduced in Japan as early as 1984, but its capacity has been used almost entirely to reach Japanese audiences, either in Japan itself or overseas. Even in Australia, one can watch Japanese-pay TV via satellite. TV has been thought to be a tool for national integration and the Japanese government has concentrated its policy on domestic TV stations.

But this domestic orientation is gradually changing. In 1994 the Japanese Ministry of Posts and Telecommunications decided to shift its rigid stance against satellite transmission from outside to an 'open skies' policy. The expansion of Asian markets has made Japanese corporations keen to do business in the global audio-visual market. With the proliferation of TV channels in Asia, Japanese programmes are increasingly being exported to fill the space. The television and film industry has begun to seriously explore the potential to export Japanese software. Since 1992 a Tokyo film market has been held each year to promote the sale of Japanese programmes. (This was replaced by Mip-Asia which has been held annually in Hong Kong since 1994). In 1997, Sumitomo Trading Co.Ltd. launched the first transnational Japanese channel, JET (Japan Entertainment Television) with TBS, a commercial TV station whose profits from selling programmes overseas are the highest in Japan. JET supplies seven Asian countries (Taiwan, Hong Kong, Thailand, Singapore, Malaysia, Indonesia and Philippines) with a channel exclusively of Japanese TV programmes by satellite up-link from Singapore. The service will be extended to China, Australia and New Zealand.

Recently, the Japanese TV industry has begun to promote 'concept trade' (*Asahi Shinbun*, 10 September 1993). This implies the sale of programme concepts rather than the programmes themselves, including video materials which do not contain 'Japanese smell'. In Asia, 'concept trade' is now promoted by the biggest advertising company in Japan, Dentsu. Like Hong Kong's TVB, Dentsu sells programme concepts of chat shows and game shows which have been well received in Japan, together with the video material, the supervision of production and Japanese sponsors to Asian TV stations (*Far Eastern Economic Review*, 16 June 1994). All local TV stations have to do is to provide local celebrities and audiences, and to learn the know-how of TV production from Japanese producers.

However, the most active exploitation of 'global localization' can be found in the music industry. In the past, some Japanese musicians have been popular in Asian countries such as Hong Kong or Singapore. More recently, a more systematic attempt to produce Asian stars has been launched by Sony under the name of 'Asia Major'. Music is attractive to the Japanese industries, not only because of its low cultural discount, but also because of its potential to promote associated consumer commodities such as CDs and CD players. The market of 'Asia Major' are those countries in East and Southeast Asia whose economic growth enables their populations to enjoy the consumption of cultural products, both of hardware and software. These include South Korea, Taiwan, Hong Kong, China, the Philippines, Thailand, Singapore, Malaysia and Indonesia.

Sony and Sony music entertainment began music auditions called 'Voice of Asia' in eight Southeast Asian countries for 'Asia Major' in 1992. About 4000 groups and singers competed against one another in 1992, and the winner was a Filipino female singer, Maribeth. The purpose of this audition was to promote sales not only for CDs but also CD players. In just four months, Maribeth's first album has sold more than 350,000 CDs and cassette tapes in Indonesia, which is close to Michael Jackson's best-selling figure, 400,000 (*Asahi Shinbun*, 1994 February 11).

The most powerful Japanese commercial TV station, Fuji Television whose media conglomerate group has a recording company, Pony Canyon, is also entering Asian music market. Fuji Television has been co-producing a TV programme with Singapore, Malaysia, Indonesia, and Taiwan. (Taiwan joined in 1994 after the Taiwanese government abolished its policy of banning the broadcasting of Japanese language programmes but left the programme in 1997 due to its overly Southeast Asian flavour.) The title of the programme is *Asia Bagus!*, which means 'Good Asia' in Malay/Indonesian. Each week, four amateur singers from five countries compete with one another. The grand champion is assured to make his/her/their debut as a professional act. The programme has three presenters, a Japanese woman, two Singaporean men. All presenters speak English and in addition each speaks respectively, Japanese, Malay/Indonesian and Mandarin Chinese.

This programme has been broadcast in each of the five countries since April 1992; in Singapore, on TCS 5 (former SBC), in Malaysia, on TV3 (NTV9 from 1997), and in Indonesia, on TVRI (since 1996 on

RCTI), and since 1994 in Taiwan, on TTV (since 1995 on a cable channel, TVBS). While it is scheduled at midnight in Japan, most of the other countries broadcast *Asia Bagus!* on prime time – Singapore and Malaysia – for example, broadcast it at 7:30 on Sunday night which is a most significant time for TV programming – and it is quite popular. Although *Asia Bagus* is directed and produced mainly by Japanese staff, the programme is made in close cooperation with the local TV industries and filmed in Singapore. Fuji Television and Pony Canyon work together with local TV stations and music industries rather than doing everything themselves. This is mainly because they are not a global corporation like Sony, but it is also based upon a policy to become an Asian industry rather than a Japanese one (*Nikkei Entertainment*, 9 September 1992). In this way, they try to transcend the irreducible cultural difference and the legacy of imperialism.

The talent agencies are also actively trying to find Asian pop stars. A major agency, Hori Production, has established branches in Hong Kong and Beijing. Chiba Mika, a Japanese female singer, made her recording debut in Taiwan in 1990 and became a star there. What makes her different from other Japanese singers who are also popular in Asia is that she sings in Mandarin-Chinese and is not popular in Japan. Hori Production's target is mainly the Mandarin-speaking market. Last year, Hori Production held auditions all over China to find Chinese pop stars. Five winners were selected from more than 400,000 contestants and made their debuts in 1994.

The assumption of the Japanese cultural industries about Asian audiences is their affluence and their willingness to be consumers, as the Japanese people have been since the late 1950s. With the development and diffusion of TV in Japan, the American middle class way of life represented in some American drama serials had a tremendous influence upon the Japanese. It was a life abundant with electric appliances. The Japanese electronic industry subtly exploited the desires of the people by using slogans advocating 'three treasures', associating the acquisition of electronic appliances with happy middle class life (see e.g. Kelly 1993; Ivy 1993): in the late 1950s, these three treasures were the three S's of *senpūki*, *sentakuki*, *suihanki* (electric fan, washing machines, electric rice cooker); in the 1960s they were the three C's of car, cooler (air conditioner), colour television. The strategy of the audition-based star system, combined with the promotion of consumer technologies, was also the vehicle for promoting consumerism in Japan, especially in the 1970s and early 80s. In the 1990s, the same strategies are being deployed in Asian markets. What the industries are trying to exploit and produce is the desire of the people to be a member of the middle class in modern capitalist society.

In these ventures, the Japanese music industries seek to find 'indigenous' pop stars for diverse local markets rather than exporting 'Japanese' products directly. While these stars are not necessarily 'indigenous' in the strict sense of the word – as we have seen, Filipino singer Maribeth is popular in Indonesia – what makes them popular is that they articulate experiences and aspirations common to several locales, dreams of affluent, commodity-saturated life styles. Highly 'westernized' Asian celebrities' fashions, hair styles, and attitudes are arguably much more stimulating to Asian viewers than American stars, because Asian stars are more 'realistic' and thus easier to identify with. It is this intimate proximity between stars and audiences that distinguishes the Japanese 'aidoru (idol) system' from the 'Hollywood Star System' (see Inamasu 1989; Ogawa, 1988; Ching, 1996). The frequent appearance of idols in commercial films and other TV programmes make him/her look like someone living next door or studying in the same classroom. Thus Sony made an advertisement for a CD player featuring Maribeth singing a song from her album, which contributed both to selling the CD players and to CDs. And Panasonic has appointed a winner of the auditions held by Hori Production as its imēji (image) girl for the Chinese market.

Moreover, auditions give audiences the feeling that anyone in Asia can become a star tomorrow. Here consumer technologies such as karaoke, the Walkman and CDs find new ways of revenue. People practise by themselves, sing together and listen to their own favourite songs to be a star, a fan and a consumer. Pioneer, a Japanese producer of audiovisual appliances, has been holding amateur karaoke contests in seven Asian countries since 1991 in order to promote sales of laser-disc players and discs. In 1993, more than 10,000 people joined the contests and Pioneer shipped 600,000 laserdisc players to the Asian region, which is more than double the figures of 1992 (*Asahi Shinbun*, 11 February 1994).

Asianization and Asianness

'Asia' is an ambiguous concept which includes too much and explains too little. Countries situated in the region called 'Asia' have very little in common in terms of language, religion and ethnicity. Nevertheless, these different countries are taxonomized under the category of 'Asia' – a legacy of European or western Orientalism. Against this historical background, the term has acquired mostly negative connotations: 'Asia' makes sense only as the Other of 'the West'. But the rapid economic growth of several countries in the region we now commonly call Asia is gradually turning this inherited negativity into a cultural positivity. Japan said 'No' to the United States with trade friction, Singapore with the caning of an American teenager convicted of vandalism, and Malaysia with the boycott of APEC, which prompted then Australian Prime Minister, Paul Keating's remark about Prime Minister Mahathir as 'recalcitrant'. In all these instances Asian countries have begun defining 'Asia' in a positive way. Funabashi (1993) has argued that what we witness today is less a case of 're-Asianization' than an 'Asianization' of 'Asia', because the contemporary search for 'Asian' identity is 'predominantly affirmative and forward-thinking, not reactionary or nostalgic' (p.77). Such 'Asianness' is more a 'workaday pragmatism, the social awakening of a flourishing middle class' (p. 75). Notably, the 'Asianness' expressed here is primarily articulated through a shared pursuit of urban consumption, of Americanized (westernized) popular culture. This 'nouveau riche Asianness' is to be taken positively because it signifies 'the birth of real Asia' (Ogura 1993) or 'the first commonness in the history between Japan and Asia' (Aoki 1993).

The emerging urban middle class culture in Asia is thus seen as a proof that Japan now has something in common with Asia. However, some intellectuals are using this emerging Asian consumer culture as a reactionary alibi for the search of shared Asian values, such as Confucianism, work ethics, and collectivism, all of which are quite opposite to hedonistic consumerism. For example, Ogura (1993) argues that in order to make 'the real Asia' more substantial, Asian people should search for features of the 'Asian spirit' to be offered to the rest of the world as universal values, some of which may be diligence, discipline and group harmony. This search should be done through a re-examination of traditional values and the education of the westernized youth who are deemed ignorant of these values.

Moreover, the 'Asia-becoming-as-Japan' idea is often utilized to confirm the shift of power from the United States to Japan (for example, Morita and Ishihara 1989). This view reflects a belief that Asian people are now yearning for Japanese affluence, technologies and popular culture in exactly the same way that the Japanese people used to yearn for American ways of life in the postwar era. In other words, the discourse of 'new Asianism' confers Japan with a cultural hegemony over Asia, while claiming a sameness between the Japanese and Asian peoples. Such cultural 'Japanization' is not totally illusory in the minds of Asian people. An Indonesian journalist called Japan the 'America of Asia' in that 'with its growing influences, Japan has become increasingly condescending towards others' (Choi 1994:148). Such criticism against Japan is strongly shared by many Asians who have never forgotten the legacy of Japanese brutal invasion.

Compared to the intellectuals, Japanese producers of popular culture seem to coolly see an 'Asian mimicry of Japan'. Isshiki Nobuyuki, a popular screen writer whose works include a comedy dealing with the gap between Japanese reality and the image Asian people have of affluent Japan, said that he found the exaggerated images of Japan held by Asians quite embarrassing, since they reminded him of a similar illusionary yearning for the United States he had in the early 1980s, an illusion that everyone in California must be a stylish surfer! (*Asahi Shinbun*, 22 September 1993). Although his remark also embraces the arrogance and confidence of the Japanese cultural industries, he seems to suggests that there exists an irreducible discrepancy between the 'real Japan' and the 'yearned-for Japan', and that such a yearning for Japan may work less as the colonization of Asians' minds than as a driving force for them to indigenize 'Japanese culture' for their own purposes. 'Japanization' may not necessarily lead to domination by Japanese culture but may problematize its authority and originality through mimicry (Bhabha 1994). But if mimicry of 'the West' is a significant determinant of contemporary 'Japanese culture' itself, is there any authentic 'Japaneseness' left to be indigenized by other Asian people?

If there is anything about Japan which attracts Asian people, Japanese cultural industries seem to assume, it would be precisely its hyperactive indigenization and domestication of 'the West', which makes modern Japanese culture scandalous to and subversive of 'the West'. In other words, behind the localizing strategy of Japanese music industries in Asian markets is there a firm conviction that it is the process of indigenization rather than the product per se that would capture the attention of Asian people. After all, the Japanese cultural industries do not try to offer, much less to impose, anything 'authentically Japanese' through TV concepts or pop stars. In a similar vein, Asian pop stars (including Japanese) are presenting neither a 'traditional national culture' nor an 'authentic Asianness', but various newly invented 'Asiannesses', put together through intense and skillful indigenizations of Western or American cultural forms. Western culture is appropriated in such a way by Asian pop stars, for example, that there is no longer a hierarchy between the original and its imitation, at least for their Asian audiences. What 'Asia Major' embodies is thus neither 'American' nor 'traditional Asian', but something new and hybrid. To put it differently, what Asian audiences are consuming is no longer 'the West' or 'a westernized Asia' but an 'indigenized (Asianized) West'; they are fascinated neither by 'originality' nor by 'tradition', but are actively constructing their own images and meanings at the receiving end. It is in this sense that the specificities or 'authenticity', if you like, of local cultures are to be found 'a posteriori not a priori, according to local consequences not local origins' (Miller 1992:181).

Yet this active construction of new, consumerist meanings takes place under the ever expanding system of global capitalism, in which Japan has a major role. The flow of cultural products and of profits is decisively one-sided and asymmetrical. People's freedom of negotiation at the receiving end of the global cultural flow coexists with an unambiguously centralized control of the system of distribution. No matter how localized the production process, financial power resides ultimately with the giant corporations. It is this contradiction between the localized negotiation of meanings and the highly centralized control of production which not only characterizes but also reinforces the strategy of 'global localization'. In other words, the strength of 'global localization' lies in the simultaneous mustering of 'local consequences' and of global structural control, which are intimately interconnected. While most people do not personally 'feel' the global forces that structure their everyday lives, these forces are nonetheless structurally and analytically 'real'.

It is also naive to generalize about the extent and reach of urban middle class culture in Asia. It still excludes too many peoples and regions across Asia. As Sreberny-Mohammadi (1991) argues, 'global players' are still confined to 'the affluent few' and the 'local' still tends to be equated officially with the 'national', neglecting various unprofitable 'locals' based upon subcultural, gender and ethnic identifications within each nation. Perhaps the new Asian consumer culture reflects more how the Japanese cultural industries imagine Asian audiences than how actual people live their everyday lives in their local realities.

Nevertheless, precisely because of such distortions, 'Asia' as imagined by the Japanese cultural industries seems to offer some direction for our analysis of the changing relationships between Japan and 'Asia' in the context of globalized capitalism. 'What was marked as foreign and exotic yesterday can become familiar today and traditionally Japanese tomorrow' (Tobin 1992:26). Indeed, this dynamic is exactly what the Japanese cultural industries are trying to produce in Asian markets and perhaps what other Asians have in common with the Japanese. In this forward-looking but contradictory process of the constant production of something new in multiple locales, the Japanese cultural industries attempt to become interpreters between 'Asia' and the 'West'. A most eloquent cultural producer of a Japanese production company told me that 'Americanization' of Asia cannot be avoided and the strength of Japan is its fifty-year-long experience and accumulated know-how of 'American education'. He proposed a term, USA, namely 'the United States of Asia': 'Like the United States of America where many different cultures are fused, our USA should fuse (*yūgō suru*) different cultures so something new emerges from Asia'. Japan can and should play an important role in this new USA.

Behind the confidence of Japanese music industries in terms of the know-how of indigenizing the 'West', however, there is a fear that Japan is being left behind in the expanding Asian audiovisual markets. A caution about Japan's capability as an interpreter was often expressed within Japanese cultural industries. The managing director of the Taiwan office of a Japanese recording company, for example, told me that Japanese companies wrongly assume that Japanese know-how and experience can be completely applicable to other Asian markets, but they do not understand how media environments are different and the system works differently outside Japan. According to him, the Japanese system is too self-contained (*jikokanketsu shiteiru*) to extend its power overseas. Unless Japanese cultural industries try seriously to learn the system of the local market and to cooperate with the local industry, Japanese know-how could not be effectively applied overseas. What is happening is that other Asian countries by-pass Japan and indigenize the West directly. Japan must be fused with other parts of Asia, particularly the Greater China cultural bloc, because Japanese cultural industries suspect that this is the only way for Japan not to be left out of transnational popular culture in Asia.

In addition to the difficulty Japanese cultural industries face in transferring their know-how to Asian markets, it should be noted that the strategy of global localization is mainly for relatively immature markets like China. Mature markets such as Taiwan and Hong Kong have long imitated and indigenized Japanese popular culture as well as Western (American) popular culture. Japanese cultural industries do not have much to tell them in terms of how to indigenize the foreign. Moreover, although its impact on Asian audiovisual markets is yet to be seen, recent economic and financial crisis in many parts of Asia and prolonged economic recession in Japan have also put a damper on an Asianism craze in Japan. Under these circumstances of the late 1990s, Japanese cultural industries have deployed global localisation strategies in Asian markets less vigorously than the early 1990s. This does not mean, however, that Japanese cultural industries and popular culture no longer have influence in Asia. On the contrary, while the export of the Japanese idol system is receding, the circulation of Japanese TV programmes and popular music in East Asia is becoming constant and conspicuous. This is particularly true with Taiwan where there are five cable television channels that broadcast exclusively Japanese programmes and where Japanese TV dramas have become an indispensable part of everyday gossip among teenagers. In Taiwan, Japanese cultural presence is not simply 'non-smelly' but associated more with the 'sweet scent' of being culturally modern in (East) Asia (Iwabuchi 1997, forthcoming). Whereas 'the West' elucidated its irreducible difference from Japan in its appreciation of Japanese traditional culture, modernized 'Asia' finds resonant meaning in Japanese popular culture, which, though highly commercialized, reminds Japan and 'Asia' alike of cultural proximity, coevalness and a common experience of non-western modernity – experiences which Western (American) popular culture cannot represent. An economic slump in Asia might temporarily discourage intra-regional cultural flow, but Japan's newly articulated connections with other parts of Asia through pop cultural flows show no sings of weakening.

Notes

1 'Return to Asia?': Japan in the global audiovisual market' by Koichi Iwabuchi first appeared in *Sojourn: Journal of Social Issues in Southeast Asia*, vol. 9, no. 2 (October 1994), pp. 226–245. Reproduced here with the kind permission of the publisher, Institute of Southeast Asian Studies. This chapter is a much revised and expanded version from the original article.

References

Aksoy, Asu and Kevin Robins 1992 'Hollywood for the 21st century: global competition for critical mass in image markets', pp. 1–22 in *Cambridge Journal of Economics* 16.

Ang, Ien 1994 'In the realm of uncertainty: the global village and capitalist postmodernity', pp. 192–213 in D. Crowley and D. Mitchell (eds.) *Communication Theory Today*, Cambridge: Polity Press.

Aoki, Tamotsu 1993 '*Ajia jirenma* (Asia dilemma)', pp. 16–43 in *Asution* 27.

Appadurai, Arjun 1990 'Disjuncture and difference in the global cultural economy', pp. 1–24 in *Public Culture* 2 (2).

Asahi Shinbun 1993a ''Bangumi urimasu', bei shinshutsu nerau minpou' ('TV programmes for sale', commercial tv stations advance to the American market), 10 September.

—— 1993b 'Ajia to nihon no zure egaku' (Representation of gaps between Asia and Japan), 22 September.

—— 1994 'Kyūseichō ajia nerau ongakusangyō' (The music industry targets the rapidly developing Asian market), 11 February.

The Australian 1994 'Star drops MTV to help it capture China', 11 May.

Asian Business Review 1994 'Satellite TV is way of off beam' by Hawke Ben. May 1994, pp. 24–25.

Banno, Junji 1981 'Japan's foreign policy and attitudes to the outside world, 1868–1945', pp. 11–31 in P. Drysdale and H. Kitaoji (eds.) *Japan and Australia*, Canberra: Australian National University Press.

Bartu, Friedmann 1992 *The Ugly Japanese: Nippon's economic empire in Asia*, Singapore: Longman.

Berland, Jody 1992 'Angels dancing: cultural technologies and the production of space', pp. 38–55 in L. Grossberg et al. (eds.) *Cultural Studies*, New York: Routledge.

Bhabha, Homi 1984 'Of mimicry and man: the ambivalence of colonial discourse', pp. 85–92 in Bhabha, *The Location of Culture*, London and New York: Routledge, 1994.

Boyd, Douglas A., Joseph D. Straubhaar and John A. Lent 1989 *Videocassette Recorders in the Third World*, New York: Longman.

Buck, Elizabeth B. 1992 'Asia and the global film industry', pp. 116–133 in *East-West Film Journal*, 6(2).

Carey, James W. 1989 *Communication as Culture: essays on media and society*, Boston: Unwin Hyman.

Chambers, Iain 1990 'A miniature history of the Walkman', pp. 1–4 in *New Formations* 11.

Ching, Leo 1996 'Imaginings in the empire of the sun: Japanese mass culture in Asia', pp. 169–194 in John. W. Treat (ed.) *Contemporary Japan and Popular Culture*, London: Curzon Press.

Choi, Il-nam 1994 'Japan: America of Asia', pp. 146–8 in *Korea Focus* 2 (2).

Chow Rey 1993 'Listening otherwise, music miniaturized: a different type of question about revolution', pp. 382–399 in S. During (ed.) *The Cultural Studies Reader*, London: Routledge.

du Gay, Paul, Stuart Hall, Linda Janes, Hugh Mackay, Keith Negu 1997 *Doing Cultural Studies: the story of the Sony Walkman*, London: Sage.

Far Eastern Economic Review 1994a 'Cast of thousands' by Jonathan Karp, 27 January.

—— 1994b 'Thought of in Japan', by Jonathan Friedland, 16 June

Forester, Tom 1993 'Consuming electronics: Japan's strategy for control', pp. 4–16 in *Media Information Australia* (67).

Funabashi, Yoichi 1993 'The Asianization of Asia', pp. 75–65 in *Foreign Affairs* 72 (5).

Ganley, Gladys D. and Ganley, Oswald H. 1987 *Global Political Fallout: the*

VCR's first decade. Program on information resources policy, Harvard University, Norwood, NJ: Ablex.

Garnham, Nicholas 1990 *Capitalism and Communication: global culture and the economics of information*, London: Sage.

Gomery, Douglas 1988 'Hollywood's hold on the new television technologies', pp. 82–8 in *Screen* 29 (2).

Hannerz, Ulf 1989 'Notes on the global Ecumene', pp. 66–75 in *Public Culture* 1 (2).

Hoskins, Colin and Mirus, Rolf 1988 'Reasons for the US dominance of the international trade in television programmes', pp. 499–515 in *Media, Culture and Society* 10.

Inamasu, Tatsuo 1989 *Aidoru kougaku* (Idol engineering), Tokyo: Chikuma Shobo.

Ivy, Marilyn 1993 'Formations of mass culture', pp. 239–258 in A. Gordon (ed.) *Postwar Japan as History*, Berkeley: University of California Press.

Iwabuchi, Koichi 1994 'Complicit exoticism: Japan and its other', pp. 49–82 in *Continuum* 8 (2).

—— 1996 'Idealess Japanization or purposeless globalization? Japanese cultural industries in Asia', pp. 33–42 in *Culture and Policy* 7(2).

—— 1997 'Genius for "glocalisation" or the sweet scent of Asian modernity: Japanese cultural export to Asia', paper presented at the 5th International Symposium on Film, Television and Video, 'Media Globalisation in Asia-Pacific Region', Taipei, Taiwan, May 1997.

—— forthcoming 'Becoming culturally proximate: a/scent of Japanese idol dramas in Taiwan', in Brian Moeran (ed.) *Asian Media Worlds*, London: Curzon Press.

Kawatake, Kazuo and Hara Yumiko 1994 'Nihon o chūshin to suru terebi bangumi no ryūtsū jōkyō' (The intenational flow of TV programmes from and into Japan), *Hōsō Kenkyū to Chōsa*, November.

Kelly, William W. 1993 'Finding a place in metropolitan Japan: ideologies, institutions, and everyday life', pp. 189–216 in A. Gordon (ed.) *Postwar Japan as History*, Berkeley: University of California Press.

Kogawa, Tetsuo 1984 'Beyond electronic individualism', pp. 15–19 in *Canadian Journal of Political and Social Theory*, 8 (3): 15–19.

—— 1988 'New trends in japanese popular culture', pp. 54–66 in G. McCormack and Y. Sugimoto (eds.), *Modernization and Beyond: the Japanese trajectory*, Cambridge: Cambridge University Press.

Lardner, James 1987 *Fast Forward: Hollywood, the Japanese, and the onslaught of the VCR*, New York: W. W. Norton & Company.

Lash, Scott and Urry, John 1994 *Economies of Signs and Space*, London: Sage.

Mainichi Shinbun 1994a 'Honkon TVB no chosen' (The challenge of Hong Kong's TVB), 21 April.

—— 1994b 'TV hōsō kokkyō o koe' (TV broadcasting cross the national border), 3 June.

McNeely, Connie and Yasemin Nuhoglu Soysal 1989 'International flows of television programming: a revisionist research orientation', pp. 136–144 in *Public Culture* 2 (1).

Miller, Daniel 1992 'The young and restless in Trinidad: a case of the local and global in mass consumption', pp. 163–182 in R. Silverstone and E. Hirsch (eds.), *Consuming Technologies: media and information in domestic spaces*, London: Routledge.

Morita, Akio and Ishihara Shintarō 1989 '*No' to ieru Nihon* (The Japan that can say NO), Tokyo: Kōbunsha.

Morley, David and Robins, Kevin 1992 'Techno-Orientalism: futures, foreigners and phobias', *New Formations* (16), Spring.

Nikkei Entertainment 1992 'Ongaku sangyo wa Ajia mejā o mezasu' (The music industry aims at producing Asian major', by Ikuko Hidaka, 9 September.

O'Regan, Tom 1991 'From piracy to sovereignty: international video cassette recorders trends', pp.112–135 in Continuum 4(2).

—— 1992 'Too popular by far: on Hollywood's international popularity', pp. 302–351 in *Continuum* 5 (2).

Ogawa, Hiroshi 1988 *Ongaku suru shakai* (Music playing society), Tokyo: Chikuma Shobo.

Ogura, Kazuo 1993 'A call for a new concept of Asia', pp. 37–44 in *Japan Echo* 20 (3).

Ohmae, Kenichi 1990 *The Borderless World*, London: Collins.

Robertson, Roland 1995 'Glocalization: time-space and hemogeneity-heterogeneity', pp. 25–44 in M. Fetherstone, S. Lash and R. Robertson (eds.) *Global Modernities*, London: Sage.

Saito, Seiichiro 1992 'The pitfalls of the new Asianism', pp. 14–19 in *Japan Echo* 19 (Special Issue, Japan and Asia).

Shimizu, Shinichi 1993 'The implication of transborder television for national cultures and broadcasting: a Japanese perspective', pp. 187–193 in *Media Asia* 20 (4).

Sinclair, John 1991 'Television in the postcolonial world', pp.127–134 in *Arena* 96.

Sreberny-Mohammadi, Annabelle 1991 'The global and the local in international communications', pp. 118–138 in J. Curran and M. Gurevitch (eds.) *Mass Media and Society*, London: Edward Arnold.

Straubhaar, Joseph 1991 'Beyond media imperialism: asymmetrical interdependence and cultural proximity', pp. 39–59 in *Critical Studies in Mass Communication* 8 (1).

Stronach, Bruce 1989 'Japanese television' in pp. 127–165 in R. Powers and H. Kato (eds.) *Handbook of Japanese Popular Culture*, Westport: Greenwood Press.

Tobin, Joseph J. 1992 'Introduction: domesticating the West', pp. 1–41 in J. Tobin (ed.) *Re-Made in Japan: everyday life and consumer taste in a changing society*, New Haven: Yale University Press.

Tomlinson, John 1991 *Cultural Imperialism: a critical introduction*, London: Pinter Publishers.

Wark, Mackenzie 1991 'From Fordism to Sonyism: perverse reading of the new world order', pp. 43–54 in *New Formations* (15).

—— 1994 'The video game as an emergent media form', pp. 21–30 in *Media Information Australia* (71).

Williams, Raymond 1990 *Television: technology and cultural form*, London: Routledge.

INDEX